KARL MARX
AND
PROPHETIC POLITICS

Neal Riemer

PRAEGER

New York
Westport, Connecticut
London

Library of Congress Cataloging in Publication Data

Riemer, Neal, 1922 –
  Karl Marx and prophetic politics.

  Bibliography: p.
  Includes index.
  1. Marx, Karl, 1818–1883. 2. Communism and
society. I. Title.
HX39.5.R49   1987   335.4'1   86-30242
ISBN 0-275-92543-9 (alk. paper)
ISBN 0-275-92635-4 (pbk.: alk. paper)

Library of Congress Catalog Card Number: 86-30242
ISBN: 0-275-92543-9
ISBN: 0-275-92635-4 **paper**

First published in 1987

Praeger Publishers, 521 Fifth Avenue, New York, NY 10175
A division of Greenwood Press, Inc.

Printed in the United States of America

The paper used in this book complies with the Permanent
Paper Standard issued by the National Information Standards
Organization (Z39.48-1984).

10 9 8 7 6 5 4 3 2 1

To my Grandson, Calmen Eliahu Riemer

Preface

Does Karl Marx illustrate the prophetic mode and challenge? Can we place him within the tradition of prophetic politics? Is he a true or false prophet? I ask these questions in order to explore the thought of Karl Marx in what is, I believe, a unique and fruitful way.

In this book the object of my analysis is the thought of Karl Marx. The mode of my analysis is a model of prophetic politics. In my examination of the thought of Marx I endeavor to present—as fairly and as objectively as I can—Marx's guiding values, his social scientific analysis and criticism of the existing order, his theory of revolutionary communist action, and his views of the future of economics, politics, society, and culture. I utilize the model of prophetic politics in order to present, analyze, and criticize Marx's thought.

Consequently, in Chapter 1, "Marx and the Tradition of Prophetic Politics," I set forth my understanding of prophetic politics, review briefly how some see Marx as prophetic, and indicate why I think it is profitable to explore Marx's thought within the framework of a model of prophetic politics. This chapter should set the stage for my inquiry.

In Chapters 2–5 I then attempt to present, analyze, and criticize Marx's thought. In Chapter 2, "Marx's Guiding Values and the Superior Universal Order," I explore Marx's own guiding ethical values, values that constitute his own standard of a superior order, values very much concerned with the "least free." I seek a fuller and deeper understanding of Marx's own preferred communist and human values.

In Chapter 3, "Marx and the Radical Social Scientific Analysis and 'Criticism of Everything Existing'," I investigate the character and substance of Marx's own critique of the existing nineteenth century bourgeois capitalist order. Here I treat, particularly, Marx's answer to the why and how of the exploitation and oppression of the proletariat. I focus especially on (what we today call) Marx's social science and his understanding of the critical mission of such a social science. This chapter thus explores Marx's concept of criticism, his still hotly debated materialist conception of history (and its sensitivity to technological and economic analysis, and to class struggle), his analysis of capitalist economics and the mechanism of exploitation, and his critique of the bourgeois superstructure of state, politics, religion, education, and so on. In my critique of Marx's social science, I note Marx's attention to, or neglect of, other powerful noneconomic forces in his own day—nationalism, racism, sexism, anti-semitism—forces exerting great influence on life before and during the nineteenth century; forces, moreover, destined also to influence significantly twentieth century history.

In Chapter 4, "Marx's Theory of Revolutionary Communist Action," I review Marx's judgments in four stages of revolutionary action—preparing for revolution, making the revolution, consolidating the revolution, and achieving mature communism. I then appraise Marx's theory of revolutionary action in the light of the prophetic model of the just revolution. This permits me to evaluate Marx's success or failure in addressing the difficult problem of the calculus of costs and benefits, the troubling problem that every theory of action must address.

In Chapter 5, "Marx and the Future of Economics, Politics, Society, and Culture," I examine Marx's vision of principles, practices, and problems of the future communist society and probe the extent to which he built into his thinking a theory of continual prophetic scrutiny and futuristic projection. Here I note what light Marx throws—or doesn't throw—on problems of communism and democracy in both the twentieth and the twenty-first centuries. I attempt to probe, in this regard, the often neglected problem of the political theorist's intellectual responsibility.

Finally, after examining Marx's thought in the light of the model of prophetic politics, I return, in Chapter 6, "Conclusion," to my original questions, summarize my answers, and share with the reader my concluding reflections about "Karl Marx and Prophetic Politics."

My approach and analysis, I appreciate, run the risk of fueling the controversy that surrounds the continuing conversation about Marx and his place in modern thought. Critics on the left will probably fault my presentation as incomplete and distorted, and my standard for appraisal as much too exacting and much too favorable to the status quo. Critics on the right will probably find me much too generous to Marx and not sufficiently appreciative of capitalism and liberal democracy. I join the conversation not in the expectation of satisfying all critics, but in the hope of illuminating Marx's salient ideas within the framework of a model of prophetic politics.

Acknowledgments

Several colleagues kindly read the penultimate draft of this book and shared with me their critical responses: Fred Curtis, Edward LeRoy Long, William Bruce Messmer, Thomas C. Oden, all of Drew University; and Glenn Tinder, University of Massachusetts—Boston. I have benefited from their constructive criticisms—of both substance and style—even when I could not entirely subscribe to them.

I also want to thank the members over the years of my seminar on Marx. They generously shared with me their reactions to my approach to Marx, and helped me to clarify my thinking on a number of points. In particular I want to acknowledge the careful reading of an earlier draft of this manuscript by Kenneth Daniel Ward, then a Drew student, now at Yale Law School.

It is a pleasure, too, to acknowledge the encouragement and help I have received from several editors at Praeger: Dorothy A. Breitbart, formerly a political science editor at Praeger; Catherine Woods-Cunningham, currently political science editor; Dan Eades, project editor, and David Good, copy editor. Good editors are worth their weight in gold!

Finally, I express my thanks to my wife, Ruby, She has helped to sustain and to enrich my ongoing conversation with and about Marx.

Contents

Preface   vii
Acknowledgments   ix

1   **MARX AND THE TRADITION OF PROPHETIC POLITICS**
    INTRODUCTION   1
    PROPHETIC POLITICS AS A MODEL   3
    THE CHARACTERISTICS/COMMITMENTS OF
      PROPHETIC POLITICS   3
    THE RELIGIOUS AND SECULAR ROOTS AND
      FLOWERING OF THE TRADITION OF
      PROPHETIC POLITICS   6
    MARX AND THE PROPHETIC: THE CONTINUING
      CONTROVERSY ABOUT LINKAGE   12
    CONCLUSION   18
    NOTES   20

2   **MARX'S GUIDING VALUES AND THE SUPERIOR**
    UNIVERSAL ORDER
    INTRODUCTION   25
    MARX'S VALUES AND VISION FOR HUMANITY   25
      Universal Human Freedom   26
      Integration, Harmony, and Peace   29
      The Truly Human Being and Community   30
      Rich Human Individual and Social Development   31
      Other Interrelated Values in Marx's Vision:
       Truth and Happiness   32
    CRITIQUE   33
    CONCLUSION   39
    NOTES   40

3   **MARX AND THE RADICAL SOCIAL SCIENTIFIC**
    ANALYSIS AND
    "CRITICISM OF EVERYTHING EXISTING"
    INTRODUCTION   43
    MARX'S CRITICISM OF THE BOURGEOIS
      CAPITALIST ORDER   44
      Marx's Concept of Criticism   44
      Marx's Materialistic Conception of History   46
      Marx's Substantive Criticism of the Bourgeois
       Capitalist Order   52

MARX'S CRITICISM OF THE ECONOMIC
   FOUNDATION OF BOURGEOIS CAPITALISM   53
   The Condition of the Working Class   53
   The Why and How of Capitalist Exploitation   56
   Why and How Capitalism Would Be Overcome   60
MARX'S CRITICISM OF THE BOURGEOIS
   SUPERSTRUCTURE   63
   Critique of Bourgeois Ideas   64
   Critique of the Bourgeois State   65
   Critique of Non-Communist Alternatives
      and Reformers   66
CRITIQUE   70
CONCLUSION   73
NOTES   74

4   **MARX'S THEORY OF REVOLUTIONARY COMMUNIST ACTION**
INTRODUCTION   79
MARX'S THEORY OF REVOLUTIONARY
   COMMUNIST ACTION   81
   Stage 1: Preparing for the Revolution   81
   MARX'S JUDGMENT ON COMMUNISM AS
      AN END   81
   MARX'S JUDGMENT ON PREPARATORY
      MEANS   82
   Stage 2: Making the Revolution   85
   PROLETARIAN MAJORITY REVOLUTION   86
   ALLIANCE OF WORKERS, PEASANTS, AND
      PROGRESSIVE BOURGEOISIE   88
   LEGAL, CONSTITUTIONAL, PEACEFUL
      REVOLUTION   91
   COMMUNISM VIA AN AGRARIAN REVOLUTION   95
   Stage 3: Consolidating the Revolution   97
   GENERAL JUDGMENTS ABOUT CONSOLIDATING
      THE REVOLUTION   97
   THE DICTATORSHIP OF THE PROLETARIAT   98
   Stage 4: Achieving Mature Communism   105
CRITIQUE   109
CONCLUSION   118
NOTES   121

5   **MARX AND THE FUTURE OF ECONOMICS, POLITICS, SOCIETY, AND CULTURE**
INTRODUCTION   127
COMMUNISM AS HUMANKIND'S FUTURE   128

Communism and Economic Life   128
Communism and the Life of the Polity   130
Communism and Social Life   132
Communism and Cultural Life   133
  CRITIQUE   133
  CONCLUSION   143
  NOTES   144
6 **CONCLUSION**
  INTRODUCTION   147
  THE STRENGTHS AND WEAKNESSES OF MARX'S
    THOUGHT   147
  CONCLUSION   151

Select Bibliography   153
Index   159
About the Author   164

1
Marx and the Tradition of Prophetic Politics

INTRODUCTION

In this chapter I should like to define and explicate my understanding of the tradition of prophetic politics, to review briefly how some observers see Marx's place within that tradition, and to suggest a model of prophetic politics as a framework for analyzing Marx's thought. To set the stage for those tasks it is important in this introduction to underscore the distinction between the prophetic and predicting, between the prophetic and the apocalyptic, and between the prophetic and the utopian. In making these distinctions I am beginning the task of clarifying my understanding of prophetic politics, an understanding that builds on the Hebraic prophets but incorporates secular ingredients of the constitutional and democratic traditions of Western thought.

After this introduction, I explain in the second section what I mean by a "model," and specifically, the model of prophetic politics, and how I propose to use my model as a heuristic tool in exploring Marx's thought. Next, I identify a little more fully my understanding of the characteristics or commitments of prophetic politics: The characteristics are commitments; the commitments are characteristics. Then, I call attention to the religious and secular roots and flowering of the tradition of prophetic politics. My model, although in part my own construction, does have historical roots and, I believe, a partly discernible historical flowering.[1]

In the fifth section of this chapter, I selectively explore the controversy about the linkage between Karl Marx and the prophetic.

My attempt to locate Marx in a tradition of prophetic politics is not new, but my sustained use of a model of prophetic politics to organize a presentation, analysis, and criticism of Marx is, I believe, novel. As Julius Carlebach in his *Karl Marx and the Radical Critique of Judaism* (1978) has noted, a number of scholars and observers compare Marx to the biblical prophets—and call Marx a prophet or prophetic. But, Carlebach observes—citing and agreeing with the argument of Albert Massiczek—these scholars do "not examine the concept of prophecy, or explain in any detail why they described Marx in this way."[2] Finally, in my conclusion, I return to the question of the value of my model, in general, and about its value, in particular, as a framework for analyzing and criticizing Marx's thought.

Let me now briefly distinguish (1) between the prophetic and the predictive, (2) between the prophetic and the apocalyptic, and (3) between the prophetic and the utopian. When I speak of the prophetic I am *not* necessarily talking about accurately predicting or forecasting the future. According to the biblical tradition, the prophet is one who speaks God's word, speaks the truth about the gap between ideal and reality, and enjoins people to fulfill the *mitzvot*—God's commandments. Similarly, secular prophets endorse a higher set of values, criticize the failure to abide by these values, and demand action to remedy the failure. Predicting the future enters in only as prophets warn of the dangers or the bright promise of the future if God's word, or a higher set of values, is or is not honored.[3]

I also distinguish between the prophetic and the apocalyptic. Prophets—religious or secular—function in this world within the framework of a covenant or constitution. They call for action, in this world, by human beings to transform the world. They do not give up on human efforts, within the convenantal or constitutional framework, to change the world. They do not rely only on God or inevitable destiny to transform the world miraculously. Those in the apocalyptic tradition tend to give up on human action and to rely only on God or destiny to transform the world, usually after a dreadful catastrophic event. After the apocalyptic event, human nature—as well as the world—will be transformed, and the need for covenant or constitution will no longer exist. Although some may argue that ingredients of the apocalyptic may be found in the biblical prophets, I shall here maintain the distinction I have drawn for my model of prophetic politics.[4]

Finally, I distinguish between the prophetic and the utopian. There are similarities between the genuinely prophetic and the soundly utopian: a common concern to overcome the ills of war, injustice, tyranny, inequality, enmity, disease, poverty, retardation, inferiority, misery, disintegration, sterility. But the foolishly utopian believes that these ills can be completely achieved in a feat—apparently premised on earthly salvation, harmony, and perfection—that will transform both human nature and the world through the creation of a new person in a new society. Those in the genuinely prophetic tradition may strive for but do not assume the possibility of universal earthly salvation, harmony, perfection. Those in the prophetic tradition maintain a belief in the divine/human (or higher law/lower law) contrast, in the eternal need for covenant or constitution to inspire, instruct, and restrain limited, fallible, finite, mortal human beings.[5] In the section following the next section below, in which I contrast prophetic and utopian politics, I develop my distinction more fully.

PROPHETIC POLITICS AS A MODEL

By prophetic politics as a "model" I mean a pattern and standard of politics. This pattern is an ethical standard, a standard of how politics ought to be conducted. Hence any other pattern of politics can be compared with it and found ethically in accord or at variance with the model of prophetic politics. In addition, this pattern has certain empirical characteristics that one can identify. Hence any other pattern of politics can be compared with it, and empirical concordance or divergence can be ascertained. Finally, this model or pattern provides one with a prudential standard, against which the political judgments and actions (wise or foolish) of political actors can be measured and evaluated. The model of prophetic politics thus highlights the ethical, empirical, and prudential components of politics.[6]

My model, like an ideal-type, selects and emphasizes what is central, important, crucial about the human experience that it seeks to understand as a pattern. The model thus highlights certain highly revealing characteristics. The model has a basis in historical reality, but it does not pretend to describe all aspects of the human experience it seeks to understand. I emphasize again that my model—the model of prophetic politics—unlike the concept of an ideal type, is designed not simply to understand empirical phenomena, but to provide an ethical, empirical, and prudential standard by which to judge agreement with, or deviation from, the model.

Now let me address the characteristics (and commitments) of the model of prophetic politics.

THE CHARACTERISTICS/COMMITMENTS
OF PROPHETIC POLITICS

By prophetic politics I mean a pattern of politics characterized by four commitments.[7] There is, initially, a commitment to prophetic values: life, love, peace, human rights and social justice, economic well-being, ecological health, and human excellence. Second, there is a commitment to social scientific analysis and fearless criticism of all existing orders in the light of the prophetic paradigm. Third, there is a commitment to prophetic constitutional breakthroughs in order to narrow the gap between ideal and reality. And finally there is a commitment to continuous prophetic scrutiny and futuristic projection (via imaginative scenarios, positive and negative) to illuminate future problems and prepare us, in advance, to deal with them.

For the political theorist these commitments translate into a set of values and norms for judging goals, principles, and behavior in politics and society; into scientific investigation and criticism of existing communities in the light of those values and norms; into creative breakthroughs (bold but prudent public policy proposals and constitutional action) to narrow the gap between ethical ideals and existing reality; and into sane and humane imaginative efforts to deal with future problems. Those committed to a more prophetic politics would, consequently, endeavor to fulfill prophetic values universally; to study the politics of all political communities with an eye to reasons for fulfillment, or nonfulfillment, of those values; to articulate and implement those policies that might prudently narrow the gap between prophetic promise and actual political performance; and to anticipate both difficulties and opportunities in the future.

It is important to emphasize that the proponents of the model of prophetic politics seek to avoid the vices of competing models—for example, Machiavellian, utopian, or liberal democratic politics—while incorporating their virtues. Since the meaning of a prophetic politics can better be understood in terms of the dialogic relationship of prophetic to Machiavellian, utopian, and liberal democratic politics, it is helpful to examine that relationship. Exploring that relationship helps to clarify the principles of prophetic politics—and, particularly, to stress its superior ethical vision, its generous and realistic understanding of political reality, its farsighted sense of political becoming, and its sanely imaginative view of the future.

I understand Machiavellian politics as the "lion and fox" politics of the nation-state. It is premised on the need for political leaders to protect the political community's vital interests in the often beastly and deceitful struggle for power that is politics. I understand utopian politics as the harmonious politics of earthly salvation. It is characterized by a vision of overcoming the struggle for power, a vision that presupposes the ultimate possibility of an earthly harmonious community marked by voluntary cooperation. I understand liberal democratic politics as the conservative politics of pluralistic balance. This patterns seeks to blend realism and idealism. It is characterized by a commitment to constitutionalism and to democratic, pluralistic, balance. Each of these patterns has strengths and weaknesses. Prophetic politics seeks to retain the strengths, while avoiding the weaknesses of each. Prophetic politics constitutes a superior radical democratic and constitutional pattern of politics, one that seeks to move beyond nationalistic idolatry, utopian hubris, and liberal democratic complacency.[8]

Thus prophetic politics is, initially, characterized by a superior ethical vision. This vision is universal and applicable to all people. Unlike Machiavellian politics, prophetic politics does not stop with the protection of the vital interests of the sovereign nation-state. Unlike utopian politics, the model of prophetic politics is not premised on earthly perfection, harmony, and salvation. Unlike liberal democratic politics, moreover, prophetic politics does not use its understanding of human and social limitations as an excuse for not continuing the battle on behalf of peace, freedom, justice, prosperity, and excellence. Those faithful to the model of prophetic politics recognize vital interests, but they see such vital interests as the vital interests of all peoples and all political communities—not simply as those of the powerful, of whites, of men, of the United States or the Soviet Union. Those in the tradition of prophetic politics see the vital interests of all people being secured best within a framework of global and national limitations wisely accepted by fallible human beings capable of working out the more detailed rules of a superior constitutional order to ensure civilized life, healthy growth, and creative fulfillment.

Prophetic politics is, secondly, characterized by a generous and yet realistic understanding of political reality. Perfect earthly salvation is impossible. But a world nourished by realistic prophetic endeavors is not. An earthly hell is quite possible; consequently, effort is required to avoid dreadful and massive violations of human rights. Conflict may not be eradicable, but success in overcoming the most disastrous warfare is possible. Superior levels of accommodation among inevitably contending interests can be achieved. And a prophetic sensitivity to the least free requires criticism of all political orders (whether liberal democratic, democratic socialist, Communist, West or East, North or South, "developed" or "developing," white or black or brown) in which the least free are struggling for emancipation and fulfillment. Prophetic standards sensitize us, ethically, to what to look for as social scientists: the necessary and sufficient conditions of peace, freedom, justice, prosperity, and excellence. The tools of social science make possible a penetrating assessment—an accurate appraisal—of the gap between prophetic standards and contemporary reality. Thus the tension between "what ought to be" and "what is" is maintained, and the complacency of liberal democratic politics is avoided.

Thirdly, those committed to prophetic politics possess a more far-sighted sense of political becoming than that possessed by those practicing Machiavellian, utopian, or liberal democratic politics. Action is commanded. Long before Marx wrote Thesis XI on Feuerbach, the biblical prophets demanded action to change the world, action based on an ethical commitment to prophetic values—but action that could only be justified and safe within a framework of convenantal or (what we today would call) constitutional limits. Such action, then, had to be creative, sane, and superior covenantal or constitutional action. Those in the prophetic tradition are buoyed by the hope that creative breakthroughs in this spirit are possible. They affirm that it is possible to move beyond the frequently timid constitutional conservatism of liberal democratic politics.

Fourthly, given the commitment to futuristic projection, we can do more than simply picture a messianic age, where swords will be beaten into ploughshares. We can begin to do what in the past we have only rarely done: project the scenarios (positive and negative) of the world that we would like to create (or avoid) and (by anticipating problems) work through differences we now foresee—and perhaps even uncover some not currently in sight. This fourth commitment underscores the importance of an open and self-correcting political and scientific system.

In this fashion, then, those committed to the model of prophetic politics can protect genuine vital interests and harness the struggle for power while avoiding idolatrous worship of the nation-state and the worst uses of force and craft. In this fashion, too, prophetic politicians can again provide us with an inspiring image of a future world, a fruitful and powerful image that can enlighten the past, orient the present, and illuminate the future while avoiding the sin of hubris. Prophetic politics may also assist us in our national political communities to move generously toward the more nearly perfect union, pursuant to notions of limited, representative, responsible, and welfare-oriented government and in accord with a mandate to balance human equities while avoiding the limited vision, deficient understanding, and timid assessments of liberal democratic politics.

The fuller meaning of the model of prophetic politics will become even clearer as I turn now to sketch the roots and flowering of the tradition of prophetic politics.[9]

THE RELIGIOUS AND SECULAR ROOTS AND FLOWERING OF THE TRADITION OF PROPHETIC POLITICS

The pattern or standard I shall employ does have—in Western civilization—historically discernible religious and secular roots, and an historically discernible religious and secular flowering. The inspiration for the model came from my interest in, and attraction to, the ethical teaching of the biblical prophets of ancient Israel. Their message, however—tied to divine revelation, a living God, a Chosen People, a covenant, mandatory commandments—conveys a commitment (however unsophisticated, however incomplete) to (1) life-affirming values of righteousness, justice, peace, freedom, love, and well-being for all humanity, (2) fearless criticism of actual conduct deviating from those values, (3) action in accord with a covenant—an embryonic constitution—to fulfill prophetic values, and (4) a long-range and hopeful concern for the future.[10]

The development of the model has been influenced by those in religion, philosophy, social science, and science who have deepened our understanding of these four commitments in history. Christianity has incorporated the Hebraic prophets; Islam has greatly respected them. Thus the perspective of the Hebraic prophets becomes a part of three great world religions. Philosophical perspectives on justice and virtue, on the constitutional idea, on the value of the rule of law, on natural law as higher law, on criticism of this world in accord with a higher standard, on the value of reason, on righteous action in accord with philosophical and constitutional mandates, on a concern for the future—these ideas have reinforced the ideas of the biblical prophets at key points. Political communities, in the Western world especially, have been strongly influenced by both these religious and these philosophical ideas. Political theorists have reflected on the ways by which the idea of covenant or contract or constitution can ensure political legitimacy, make clear the requirements of political obligation, achieve those known, public rules by which people in communities might live: by which the power of rulers are to be limited, restrained, guided; by which the ends and means of political life are to be rationally understood and accepted. Science, too, has strengthened the prophetic commitment to truth, to free inquiry, to due process, and emphasized the value of knowing consequences as a crucial part of making assessments. Both the bible and science could agree that by their fruits you shall know them.

To be maintained, prophetic values must appeal to human reason, must be free of contradictions, must be accepted by people freely, must produce results that enhance life, growth, and higher development. Those theologians, philosophers, humanists, social scientists, scientists, statesmen, and citizens who have struggled with the development of a sophisticated prophetic model have not always been conscious of their contributions to that model. But it is undeniable that in Western civilization they (1) have deeply probed questions about the values by which people should live in the political community; (2) have noted the values by which they do live, and have asked about the reasons for the gap; (3) have attempted in various ways (some unsuccessful, some partly successful, some more fully successful) to work out sensible rules for their political affairs as circumstances permitted, and to optimize preferred values; and (4) have at least tried to keep before themselves and the public a vision of a future and of the need to anticipate future problems.

To make the points above is not to deny that most often the actual patterns of prevailing politics have been most strongly influenced by the dominant forces of the day—religious, political, or economic; and that, in fact, prevailing interpretations and applications of justice, peace, freedom, love, and prosperity have been most often the interpretations and applications of the interest of the stronger! Yet in both the religious and secular domains, the idea persists in humane minds (and for good and cogent reasons) that certain values are preferable: that justice as fairness is not the interest of the stronger; that peace is preferable to war; that freedom means control over one's mind and body; that economic well-being is desirable for all; that caring is a humane response to human beings and the earth itself afflicted by misfortune or degradation; that excellence in all things is meritorious. Of course, the powerful have made war, enslaved other human beings, ruled tyrannically, condoned poverty. Yet a prophetic minority has always refused to endorse war as a human ideal, or as a necessary evil; has refused to accept slavery as inevitable; has refused to endure tyranny; has refused to tolerate poverty as an ineradicable condition rooted in religious, or biological, or social fate.

Moreover, there has taken hold in Western civilization the obligation to criticize the existing order for its shortcomings. This criticism has involved a sophisticated exploration of operative values that are to constitute the standards by which shortcomings can be detected. This criticism has also involved keener and more systematic empirical findings of violations of mandated values. This criticism has involved, too, explanations of these violations, explanations of the reasons for the gap between ideal and reality.

Additionally, this criticism has also led to calls for action—action to prevent the violations of values; action to strengthen sensible rules and policies in political affairs; action, in brief, to strengthen the existing constitution, to reform an old constitution, to usher in a radically new constitution.

Again, to say this is not to deny that those concerned with political values, those engaged in criticism of the existing order, and those seeking a superior constitutional order may not often be articulating the views of burgeoning economic, political, religious, or other forces and interests. Political actors (or forces)—interests of all kinds—do seek to protect their lives and vital interests, their healthy growth, and creative development, and will, consequently, seek rules and policies in political affairs that enhance and safeguard their vital interests.

But it is also the case that constitutionalism has deep roots in the apparently natural tendency of people and interests to protect themselves, and has been strongly reinforced by covenantal ideas. A religious covenant that endeavors to provide sensible rules for human conduct, to guard against the abuse of power, to establish limits upon human action—is also an historical reality (as much as self-interest) and has been assimilated (in its essentials) into a secular structure also concerned with the preservation of human life and sane human activity. Historically, the Judaic-Christian contribution to the development of constitutional government in the West is clear. Most important, by insisting that human rulers must be limited in their exercise of power, certain religious voices have kept open the domain of freedom, initially in the realm of religion, and then in the realm of politics. Constitutionalism has thus provided a sensible framework for positive policies to optimize preferred values.

Finally it seems reasonably clear that religious eschatology—religious visions of the future—has significantly influenced political visions of the future. Such political visions have also been influenced by philosophical and secular concerns for the future, concerns indirectly, if not directly, indebted to the Judaic-Christian religious tradition. Whether nourished by Platonic notions of a genuinely just and harmonious Republic, or by Judaic-Christian visions of the end of days and the reign of the Messiah, or by secular or scientific utopian notions, concern for the future, and for the problems of the future, has historical roots and an historical flowering in our civilization.

Illustrations of the wide-ranging generalizations in the paragraphs above (given my limited objective in this chapter) must necessarily be selective. However, such examples may, nevertheless, be persuasive on two key points: (1) that prophetic politics has roots in the biblical prophets of Israel, and (2) that the model of prophetic politics that I outlined in the preceding section of this chapter has religious and secular roots and flowering in Western civilization.

The biblical prophets were not modern liberal democrats or democratic socialists. Yet they continue to speak to modern men and women. They articulate, within the framework of the prophetic faith of Israel, religious and ethical ideas many of which are to become central to the democratic, socialist constitutional tradition. They affirm life and quality of life, divine love as a model for human relationships, the commandment to do justice, the imperative to enhance freedom (particularly for the least-free), the surpassing importance of securing peace. They criticize violators of the covenant and warn of God's wrath and punishment. They both warn of the dreadful prospect of disaster and hold out hope for redemption. They call for action to avert the threatened catastrophe. They demand a higher level of worship at a higher level of human behavior. They keep before humankind the vision of peace and the end of fear, of justice and the end of oppression, of love and the end of hate.

The biblical prophets first develop forthrightly the concept of a superior universal order that constitutes a superior standard of judgment. They first articulate the key values of prophetic politics. Thus, of peace: "And they shall beat their swords into plowshares, And their spears into pruning hooks; Nation shall not lift up sword against nation, Neither shall they learn war any more." And justice: "do justice, and . . . love mercy. . . ." And freedom: "let the oppressed go free. . . ."[11] The universalistic element in the prophetic tradition is unmistakable; and so, too, is the prophetic concern for the least-free. The commandment is to "loose the fetters of wickedness," to "undo the bands of the yoke," to "break every yoke," to "deal thy bread to the hungry," to "house the poor, to cover the naked."[12]

The biblical prophets also illustrate some cardinal features of fearless criticism. They criticize the existing order in the light of the covenantal model. They do not hesitate to criticize pharaoh or king. They warn of doom but hold out hope of redemption. They are commanded to speak out and particularly against those who would "eat the flesh of my people," who would "make the fatherless their prey." The prophets see themselves as watchmen—warning humankind but holding out the promise of a better world. They unmistakably attack idolatry and complacency. They adumbrate, if they do not elaborate, a philosophy of history that can provide "meaning to the past," "urgent importance to the present," and "ultimate significance to the future."[13]

The biblical prophets also call for action to fulfill the commandments of the covenant. They call for faithfulness to God's word. The turning that is *teshuvah* or repentance is part of that action; but the action means living a righteous life in very practical terms in this world.

The biblical prophets, finally, hold before humankind an inspiring vision of the future—of love of God and love of neighbor, of peace and righteousness, of freedom and justice, of prosperity and the end of fear—and affirm that future difficulties can best be overcome if people remain true to the covenant.

These key ideas have been carried over into Christianity. Indeed, Jesus is perceived by Christians as prophet as well as priest and king and lord. Although the prophetic impulse is sometimes obscured by an other-worldly emphasis in Christianity, and by Christianity's tendency to obey the powers that be, the prophetic impulse remains a vital, if sometimes hidden, part of Christianity, ready to burst out when (as in the Protestant Reformation) there is reason to criticize the established Church, or when those of religious conviction (whether Protestant or Catholic) seek to defend their right to religious (and sometimes political) truth against the religious or political Establishment.[14]

Both John Calvin and John Knox illustrate the recovery of the prophetic in the Protestant Reformation. Calvin did not deny that rulers must be obeyed, but he insisted "certain of the saints have a special office to rebuke their evil doings."

"Why are prophets and teachers sent? That they may reduce the world to order; they are not to spare their hearers, but freely to reprove them whenever there may be need; they are also to use threatenings when they find men perverse . . . prophets and teachers may take courage and thus boldly set themselves against kings and nations, when armed with the power of celestial truth."[15]

John Knox, exiled Puritan in Geneva, also revived the prophetic mission. Knox saw himself as a "trumpet" of God. The prophet of God may even "teach treason against kings."[16] The prophet, wrote Knox, viewed the world in the "spirit of righteous judgment."[17] Godly men were urged to overthrow idolators.[18]

We may quarrel with the interpretation by Calvin and Knox of the prophetic mission, but there can be little doubt that they served to revive that mission. The prophetic tradition thus gained a new lease on life in the Protestant Reformation. The continued life of that tradition, especially in the leftwing Protestant movements of the sixteenth and seventeenth centuries, demonstrates the continued vitality of prophetic values, criticism, action, and concern for the future.

In the eighteenth century the characteristics of the prophetic tradition emerged, in a secular variety, in a number of Enlightenment figures, and served to fashion the modern, democratic, constitutional, secular version of prophetic politics. This version was reinforced in the nineteenth century and thus passed into the modern world. In the nineteenth century, both a prophetic Judaism and a prophetic Christianity emerged as self-conscious traditions, rediscovering the ethical insights of the biblical prophets, and reinforcing (and being reinforced by) secular movements of reform. Frank Manuel calls his study of some influential Enlightenment figures *The Prophets of Paris*.[19] Whether they were fully in the prophetic tradition—or were more utopian than prophetic—need not be debated here. What is crucial is that they incorporated aspects of the prophetic tradition and made them important characteristics of modern thought: universal values, critical sensitivity to the gulf between promise and performance, recognition of the need for constitutional action, an invigorated curiosity about the future. Both the battles against slavery and on behalf of working people illustrate prophetic characteristics. As "an heir to the Romantic movement," as influenced by the "Faustian-Promethean motif," as a child of "the rationalist, determinist Enlightenment," as a philosopher and social scientist with a burning passion for freedom,[20] Marx unquestionably shared most, if not all, of these characteristics. The character, extent, and fuller meaning of that sharing we shall be exploring in the following chapters of this book.

The tradition of prophetic politics—in both its religious and secular manifestations—remains vital in the twentieth century. The prophetic impulses in prophetic Judaism and prophetic Christianity, in liberal democracy and democratic socialism, carried over from the late nineteenth to the twentieth century.[21] The tradition can be seen at work in the domains of both religion and politics. It can be seen, for example, in the continuation of the social gospel movement; in the writings of the protestant theologian, Reinhold Niebuhr; in the theological, ecumenical, and church reforms of Pope John XXIII; in a number of Jewish writers, activists, and organizations. One of its most dramatic exemplars in the United States was Martin Luther King, Jr. Political, social, and economic reform movements in the twentieth century (especially reforms involving working people, the poor, women, blacks, American Indians) illustrate the prophetic tradition at work. A contemporary secular illustration is the work of Ralph Nader. Illustrations abound. Several of the documents of the American bishops in the 1980s—for example, on nuclear weapons, on the economy—illustrate the prophetic tradition at work. So, too, the prophetic tradition can be seen at work in Liberation Theology in Latin America, in the work of the liberal wing of the Catholic Church on human rights in Latin America and elsewhere in the world, and in key aspects of the work of a number of Protestant religious groups, such as the Protestant World Council of Churches. A host of other political, social, and economic movements also clearly reveal that the prophetic impulse is alive and vital.[22]

MARX AND THE PROPHETIC: THE CONTINUING CONTROVERSY ABOUT LINKAGE

To sketch the tradition of prophetic politics is, at the least, to suggest this model as one we might reasonably use in any appraisal of Karl Marx. But what more needs to be said about the linkage between Marx and the prophetic? In dealing with that linkage one needs to be careful and critical. Different observers have seen that linkage in different ways. Some have seen a direct or indirect link between Marx's Jewish ancestry and heritage and his prophetic stance. Others see Marx's prophetic stance mediated through the influence of his early Christian upbringing. Still others call attention to Marx's Western intellectual heritage which, of necessity, included the prophetic tradition. Moreover, some critics see only some prophetic ingredients in Marx, while others see falsely messianic or apocalyptic or foolishly utopian elements in Marx's outlook. Finally, we should appreciate, there are those who would deny Marx either a religiously prophetic mantle (because he was an atheist) or a secular prophetic mantle (because of his deviation from a liberal democratic constitutional tradition).

Let me begin with Julius Carlebach's scholarly, balanced, and nuanced understanding of both the biblical prophets and of Marx.

Carlebach notes that Marx himself provides us with "some evidence, both positive and negative," of his being "a prophet-like figure." Clearly, Marx did not see himself in an orthodox Judaic prophetic tradition. He did not discuss biblical law—nor did he (I must add) affirm God and Torah. He seemed to suffer from a "blockage on all things Jewish." However,

Carlebach writes, the "remainder of the Old Testament, however, was sufficiently detached from any Jewish reality and sufficiently integrated in general European life for Marx to enjoy reading it, to use it constantly and often sympathetically in his philosophical and historical writings, and sufficiently meaningful to serve as a model, provided only that its use was properly circumscribed." Carlebach notes that "Marx's sympathy for Hebrew prophets may be gauged from the information his daughter Eleanor conveyed to Max Beer: 'He told mother that if she wanted edification or satisfaction of her metaphysical needs, she would find them in the Jewish prophets.' "[23]

In the *Eighteenth Brumaire*, Carlebach notes, we find a "more direct evaluation of the prophets." Marx argued there that Cromwell and the English had "borrowed the language, emotions and illusions for their bougeois revolution" from the Old Testament. Marx, Carlebach maintains, "seems to have seen the prophets as sponsors of ancient revolutionary ideas, and felt a certain kinship with their problems and their tasks."[24]

Drawing upon Jewish and non-Jewish sources, especially Max Weber and Yehezkel Kaufmann, Carlebach supports his views on Marx and the prophets by examining "the character of prophecy, the character of the prophets, the historical background of prophecy, and the tasks of the prophets."[25] He notes, following Weber, that the prophets uttered "emotional invective against political overlords." They fought against false prophets. "They spoke for the 'little people' and tended to attack the rich and the mighty." "They fiercely objected to impious ways of life, advocated a return to simple living, and attacked the use of religion and religious ritual as substitutes for social justice." The biblical prophets, however, differed from Marx "in that they were concerned not with man's role as a citizen but only as a religious person, and did not advocate revolutions or propose means for the masses to help themselves. They offered no sociopolitical programmes, did not champion democratic ideals and often found their main support amongst pious traditionalists. They rejected world politics *per se*, worldly wisdom and aesthetic values as alien to the Jewish tradition."[26]

"Like Jeremiah, Marx might well have felt his mission to be to show humanity that [in Martin Buber's words] 'the only way to salvation is by the steep and stony path over the recognition of reality. The feet of those who take it bleed, and there is always the threat of dizziness, but it is the one and only way.' "[27]

Focusing on the sociohistorical context with the help of Yehezkel Kaufmann, Carlebach "shows why Marx might have been so attracted to the role of the prophet." "Kaufmann saw the distinctive feature of prophecy in its 'vehement denunciation of social corruption.' " "The indignation of the prophets was born out of the rift between the ideal society stipulated in

Jewish law and the reality which faced them. The social crisis created the new prophets.''[28]

Carlebach finds resemblances as well as contrasts between Marx and the prophets. "Marx thus resembled the prophets in that he was a product of a historical situation, that he displayed a sense of dedication which suggested a mission and in his deep concern for the dispossessed and exploited." However, Carlebach maintains, he "differed from them in his exclusive interest in systems rather than in people, his philosophy of destruction before construction and his baseless assumption that a change of system would *ipso facto* bring about a change in people." The prophets, Carlebach argues, "were indifferent to systems and concerned solely with the rules of justice within systems." In contrast to Marx, they "demanded justice as an expression of religion," even though "they refused to recognize religion *per se* as an expression of justice." They differed too on the question of universalism. "While Marx's universalism ignored national boundaries," the prophets saw such boundaries "as a presupposition of universalism. . . ." Carlebach does, however, see a resemblance in style. Marx resembled the prophets in style "inasmuch as, like them, he advocated axiomatic economic laws as the pivotal structure from which social change must take its directions, just as they predicated their entire message on the absolute and binding validity of God's law." Carlebach notes other resemblances and contrasts. Thus, "like the prophets, Marx predicted doom and destruction for certain societies or sections of society, although unlike them, for whom there was always a choice," Marx's "message of doom was wholly deterministic." In addition, Marx resembles the prophets "in his 'Messianic' concepts, though these rarely withstand the tests of either time or historical analysis."

Carlebach concludes that "Marx shared distinct similarities" with biblical prophets, but emphasizes that "on the whole the similarity is with the *role* of biblical prophets." He notes that there is "little that is essentially *Jewish*" in Marx, and emphasizes that there are others "from many other nations whose historical situation and modes of action cast them in a similar" prophetic role. Carlebach notes that where "in his prophetic role Marx is most Jewish, he is also mistaken." He cites as an example a passage from *The Poverty of Philosophy* (1847): "The working class, in the course of its development will substitute for the old civil society an association which will exclude classes and their antagonism, and there will be no more political power properly so called, since political power is precisely the official expression of antagonism in civil society." Carlebach maintains that there "is nothing 'scientific' about this prediction," and then adds: "In its optimism and apodictic certainty it is Jewish in the best sense of the word, but Marx did not speak as a Jewish prophet and his message lacks the realism which he valued so highly and which the Jewish prophets understood so well." Carlebach then notes: "In the Bible there are true prophets and false prophets, Jewish prophets and non-Jewish prophets. Whether Marx was a true or a false prophet is a matter of personal belief, but there is not enough Jewish content in his message to make him more than an admirer of the vigour and realism and perhaps also of the pain and misery of the great prophets of biblical Judaism."[29]

If Carlebach is correct, Marx shares some but not all the aspects of the Hebraic prophetic mode and challenge. Some similarities—but not all—can be noted. We may, then, conclude that an effort to examine Marx within the framework of the tradition of prophetic politics—with "prophetic" understood here religiously—has some plausibility. And, as I have indicated, the plausibility will increase if we look also to a secular tradition of prophetic politics, one which draws inspiration from the biblical prophets, but which incorporates key constitutional and democratic ideas in Western thought.

Other observers also link Marx and the prophetic. Thus, Joseph Carlebach (Julius Carlebach's martyred father), although expressing regret about Marx's aberrations, nonetheless wrote: "Yet there can be no doubt that the holy anger with which Marx pursued and flayed social injustice, which gave him the moving words of the *Communist Manifesto*, is the heritage of Jewish prophets, those mighty adversaries of large-scale land ownership and economic self-seeking."[30] Gustav Mayer, the historian of socialism, claims that "Marx, though he did not know it, was in his innermost psyche a Jew cast in the mould of the prophets."[31] Julius Carlebach writes that both Arnold Kunzli and Albert Massiczek "have made the Jewishness of Marx the all-pervasive principle of their biographical studies." Both view Marx as a secular nineteenth century prophet. Kunzli "argued [writes Julius Carlebach] that Marx unconsciously identified himself with Moses."[32] Massiczek "named no less than thirty-six authors in support of the contention that Marx was like an Old Testament prophet. . . ."[33] Erich Fromm contends that Marx's socialism—particularly the humanist socialism of the early Marx—is "essentially prophetic Messianism in the language of the nineteenth century."[34]

Murray Wolfson finds a model (and a parallel) for the dualism that he detects in Marx—determinism on one hand, free will on the other hand—"in the role of the prophets of the Old Testament." Wolfson notes that the "dualism that runs through the Hebrew Bible is the omnipotence of God on the one hand, and the freedom of the will of men implicit in the injunction to obey the commandments of the Covenant."[35] He emphasizes that the "message of the prophets was of the unity of the contingent and necessary view of human action." Practice and necessity, Wolfson contends, "were themes that the Old Testament sought to unite in the transcendental being of God, just as Marx did in the materialist science of society which he intuited in his own exile."[36]

Wolfson argues that Marx, despite his intention, "had reached for the Jewish paradigm, and cast himself in the role of the prophet." Wolfson compares the prophets' obedience to divine commandments to Marx's belief in the historical process, and notes the emphasis in both Marx and the prophets on earthly practice. "The prophet's injunction is not pure faith, good works, or universal love, as ends in themselves, but as part of obedience to divine commandments. The struggle of the pious against the unrighteous was right because it was the divine will which was to work itself out with inexorable finality. The very definition of moral behaviour in Marx is expressed in terms of the workings of the inexorable historical process, just as it was defined for the Jews as the commandments of God, ultimately to be obeyed. The prophet serves to expound God's will, to be his instrument, to denounce iniquity. He serves as one of the means by which [the people of] Israel will internalize the Law in their ethical behaviour, and convince God to support Israel and, through her, the rest of mankind." Wolfson maintains that "Eschatology, morality and prophecy in the Old Testament, reappear in Marx as historical materialism, activism, and the new science of society. For both the key is not Pauline faith, but earthly practice. That practice reflects human purpose—perhaps free to err in the short term—but ultimately to conform to divine or historical law."[37]

Wolfson is aware of the Christian (Evangelical or Lutheran) influences on Marx the schoolboy, and of the Hegelian influences on Marx the university student. Yet he insists on underlining "the Hebraic elements in Marx's construction."

"It is, of course, true [Wolfson writes] that Old Testament conceptions had been embodied in the Evangelical religion in which Marx had been educated, and certainly the notion of history as the instrumentality of the Absolute was a leading Hegelian thesis, to which Marx acknowledged his indebtedness. Nevertheless it is the emphasis on practice by human beings, and the immediate response of God to the activity of men that serves to underline the Hebraic element in Marx's construction. The whole point of the prophetic injunction to Israel was that the ultimate criterion was neither sacrifice nor even worship at the temple, both of which implied belief in the existence and power of God. The basis for God's judgment was the practical behavior of the Jews. The instrumentality of God's response was practical earthly retribution, say, in the form of the Assyrian invasion."

"While it certainly is the case [Wolfson argues] that these Jewish viewpoints could have reached Marx through any number of non-Jewish intermediaries, the point is that in Brussels [1845–1847] he opted for them against his earlier secular Christianity. It is not likely that he consciously conceived of his evolving viewpoint as converging to the Jewish paradigm. Yet it is also the case that he did not reject it as Jewish as he had done in the past. Feuerbach had been mistaken to think of practice as "dirty-Jewish";

for Marx practice was the means by which humanity was forged in history, and (expressing the same inconsistency as Scripture) the means by which man made himself."[38]

Other critics, however, such as Edmund Silberner, as Julius Carlebach notes, "see no justification for invoking Marx's Jewish origins to trace a line backwards from him to the prophets of the Bible."[39]

In another recent study, Bruch Mazlish notes that Marx is "squarely in the redemptive tradition," and asks: "Is that tradition Christian or Jewish?" Mazlish, of course, is aware that some argue that Marx is "heir of the tradition of the great Jewish prophets, thundering forth at mankind." He concedes that insofar "as the Jewish tradition becomes part of the Christian, as it does in the Bible, I would agree (after all, Christ, too, was born a Jew)." But Mazlish argues that "Marx received that tradition . . . in its Lutheran form, as a result of being raised as a believing Christian," even though he did not remain a believing Christian. Mazlish agrees with Abraham Rotstein's assertion that what Marx and the prophets "share is a rhetorical structure, namely the characteristic articulation of the apocalyptic tradition that moves step by step . . . from the original condition of domination and oppression to the culmination of perfect community." Mazlish contends that the "rhetorical structure which Marx received in his Lutheran upbringing underlies his creation of a secular religion."[40]

In another passage, Mazlish acknowledges the Hegelian influence, while affirming the Christian influence. ". . . Marx was very much a religious thinker, even though his thought takes the form of a secular religion, and, even more to the point . . . it was his Christian upbringing that supplied him with his world view (in the form, or transformation, subsequently, of the Hegelian critique of religion), rather than his Jewish background. The Jewish heritage was important, but more for psychological than for intellectual reasons."[41]

Other observers, exploring the relationship between Marxism and Christianity, have largely bypassed the question of the origins of Marx's alleged prophetic ideas and, instead, have focused on the ideas themselves. Thus Howard L. Parsons has argued explicitly on behalf of "The Prophetic Mission of Karl Marx." He maintains that Marx fits the designation as prophet insofar as a prophet is a radical realist, perceives an ultimate order of goodness, criticizes and judges the existing social order, is committed to action and demands that others commit themselves to action.[42]

David McLellan, Marx's biographer and a keen student of Marx's thought, looks beyond the question of religious linkage to emphasize the Western intellectual heritage of which the prophetic tradition is a part. "Some students of Marx believe they have found the key to Marx's whole system of ideas in his rabbinic ancestry; but although some of his ideas—and even life-style—have echoes of the prophetic tradition, this tradition itself is more or less part of the Western intellectual heritage; and it would be too simplistic to reduce Marx's ideas to a secularized Judaism."[43] Kolakowski, it will be remembered, also calls attention to that Western intellectual heritage—especially emphasizing the influence on Marx of the Romantic movement, the Faustian/Promethean motif, and the rationalist, determinist character of the Enlightenment.[44]

Of course not all critics link Marx and the prophetic, or link Marx exclusively to the prophetic. Mazlish, as we already noted above, called attention to the apocalyptic strain in Marx. Others have seen Marx in the apocalyptic, millenarian tradition.[45] A number of scholars have identified Marx in the utopian tradition. Crane Brinton says we see in Marx "the most widely known of all" modern utopias.[46] Paul Tillich writes that "Marxism has never, despite its animosity to Utopia, been able to clear itself of a hidden belief in Utopia."[47] George Kateb, Frank and Fritzie Manuel, and A. J. Talmon have also placed Marx in the utopian tradition.[48] Talmon saw Marx articulating a falsely messianic position that Talmon calls "political Messianism" and that he links to totalitarian democracy. "The totalitarian democratic school . . . is based upon the assumption of a sole and exclusive truth in politics. It may be called political Messianism in the sense that it postulates a preordained, harmonious and perfect scheme of things, to which men are irresistibly driven, and at which they are bound to arrive." Talmon sees Marx as illustrating yet another nineteenth century scheme for "universal regeneration," a scheme "purporting to offer a coherent, complete and final solution to the problem of social evil."[49]

Still others, of course, argue that Marx is clearly not in the prophetic tradition—religious or secular—but that he is in a humanist, materialist, atheist, naturalist tradition, a tradition that rejects a belief in God, revelation, covenant, commandments, inalienable rights, a higher law doctrine.

I call to mind these various views on the linkage between Marx and the prophetic, Marx and Western thought, and Marx and the utopian to underscore the difficulty and complexity of trying to place Marx within a given tradition. Clearly, the linkage between Marx and these various traditions still calls for further exploration, an exploration that might, indeed, find room for parts of all these explanations. My task in this book is to advance that exploration by examining Marx, carefully and critically, within the framework of the model of prophetic politics. In this chapter we cannot resolve these conflicting interpretations of Marx and the tradition of prophetic—or utopian or Western—politics. But we are, at least, encouraged to explore the thought of Marx more fully. In conclusion, I turn again to my model of prophetic politics.

CONCLUSION

How valuable is this model in general, and in particular how valuable is it as a framework for analyzing and criticizing Marx's thought? I suggest that it is a helpful model for analyzing and criticizing a political (or social and economic) theory insofar as it highlights the critical exploration of the values of such a theory; insofar as it directs our attention to such a theory's scientific ability to illuminate the real world (as it has been, is, and will be); insofar as it requires us to ask about the theory's understanding of the relation of theory to practice, of ideas to action, of knowledge to wise judgment; and, finally, insofar as it looks to the future and addresses future problems.

The model of prophetic politics seems particularly appropriate as one to analyze and criticize Marx. This is the case, initially, because Marx's thought is unquestionably influenced by such cardinal (and prophetic) values as universal human emancipation, the overcoming of alienation, the achievement of harmony within the community and of peace between nations, abundant production in the service of human needs, and opportunity for rich human development. Secondly, Marx—like those in the prophetic tradition—is committed to scientific investigation and radical criticism of conditions that enslave, degrade, or stunt human beings; he is acutely conscious of the gap between his conception of human beings as they are capable of being and their existential reality. Thirdly, Marx is indeed committed to action to break through to a new order—for him, an emancipating communist order—to achieve his normative objectives for humankind. Finally, Marx—again like those in the prophetic tradition—is very much concerned with the future of humankind.

However, as the differing assessments of Marx as a prophet—or as a utopian or as a Western thinker—make clear, it still remains to determine how solidly he is in the tradition of prophetic (or utopian or Western) politics, or if he is genuinely in that tradition (or any of those traditions) at all. It also remains for us to determine, independently, whether Marx is a true or false secular prophet. A complete or a flawed prophet? A soundly utopian or a falsely utopian thinker? And what kind of a Western thinker?

It seems, then, entirely appropriate to use the model of prophetic politics to explore the thought of Karl Marx. In Chapter 2 I explore Marx's values as they illuminate his understanding of the meaning of a superior universal order.

NOTES

1. In setting forth my understanding of prophetic politics I draw upon, but supplement, an earlier study. See Neal Riemer, *The Future of the Democratic Revolution: Toward a More Prophetic Politics* (New York: Praeger, 1984). I am also indebted to the papers presented by Michael Walzer, Paul D. Hanson, Arthur Waskow, J. Mitchell Morse, Cornel West, and Rosemary Radford Ruether in a Graduate School Colloquium on "The Prophetic Mode and Challenge in Religion, Politics, and Society" at Drew University, April 18-19, 1985. These papers, along with my introductory essay, were subsequently published in a special double issue with that title in *The Drew Gateway* (Neal Riemer, Guest Editor) 55, Nos. 2 & 3 (Winter 1984/Spring 1985).

2. Julius Carlebach, *Karl Marx and the Radical Critique of Judaism* (London: Routledge & Kegan Paul, 1978), p. 316.

3. For a fuller understanding of the prophetic, and of this distinction, see Abraham J. Heschel, *The Prophets* (1962) (New York: Harper & Row, Torchbook Edition, 1969-71); Gerhard Von Rad, *The Message of the Prophets* (New York: Harper & Row, 1967); Joseph Blenkensopp, *A History of Prophecy in Israel* (London: SPCK, 1984); Walter Brueggemann, *The Prophetic Imagination* (Philadelphia, PA: Fortress Press, 1978). These scholars reveal the complexity of the prophets and put us on guard against easy generalizations.

4. For more on the distinction between the prophetic and the apocalyptic, see Paul Hanson, *The Diversity of Scripture: A Theological Interpretation* (Philadelphia, PA: Fortress Press, 1982), his *The Dawn of the Apocaplytic* (Philadelphia, PA: Fortress Press, 1975), and his *The People Called: The Growth of Community in the Bible* (New York: Harper & Row, 1986). See also Gordon M. Freeman, *The Heavenly Kingdom: Aspects of Political Thought in the Talmud and Midrash* (Lanham, MD: Univ. Press of America/The Jerusalem Center for Public Affairs, 1986).

5. On the distinction between the prophetic and the utopian, see Riemer, *The Future of the Democratic Revolution.*

6. For the development of this model one may consult Neal Riemer, *The Revival of Democratic Theory* (New York: Appleton Century Crofts, 1962); *Political Science: An Introduction to Politics* (New York: Harcourt Brace Jovanovich, 1983); and *The Future of the Democratic Revolution.*

7. My summary here draws on my account in *The Future of the Democratic Revolution*, pp. 223-26.

8. Ibid., pp. 4-6, and Chapters 2-4.

9. And it is but a sketch! The fuller history of the prophetic—in both its religious and secular manifestations—remains to be written.

10. Michael Walzer distinguishes between a domestic prophet and an international prophet. Jonah, for example, would be an international prophet. Amos was both a domestic and an international prophet. The domestic prophet—presupposing a common ground with his audience (the people of Israel) in a common religious tradition and a common law (God, Exodus, Covenant, Torah)—could take a more radical line and hold his people to a higher standard (freedom from oppression), one that they were familiar with and traditionally subscribed to. The international prophet, appealing to non-Israelites, could not assume that common ground; hence, his appeal (against general wickedness and violence) had to be a more minimal appeal to a kind of "international" law. Walzer notes (p. 26) that international prophecies "tend toward universality" and that what I have called domestic prophecies tend toward "particularity." Walzer concludes: "It is a mistake, then, to praise the prophets for their universalist message. For what is most admirable about them is their particularist quarrel, which is also God's quarrel, with the children of Israel" (p. 26). Walzer does note, however, that we "can . . . abstract the rules and apply them to other nations," but adds "that's not the 'use' that Amos invites"

(p. 26). See Michael Walzer, "Prophecy and Social Criticism," in *The Drew Gateway*, special issue on "The Prophetic Mode and Challenge," pp. 13–27. Regardless of whether the message of the great biblical prophets was particularistic or universalistic, it is the case that most of those in the prophetic tradition have emphasized the universalistic message. This fact, however, does not resolve the problem of the appeal of the prophetic message to peoples who do not share common ground with the prophet or resonate historically, or religiously, with the prophetic message.

11. The quotations are from Mic. 4:3; Isa. 2–4; Mic. 6–8; Isa. 58:6–7.

12. Isa. 58:6–7.

13. See Mic. 3:3; and Isa. 10:2. And in the same vein, see Amos 8:4; and Isa. 3:15; 10:1–2; 59:8–9, 14–15. The phrase on past, present, and future is Fred L. Polak's in *The Image of the Future*, 2 vols. (New York: Oceana, 1961).

14. On prophetic Christianity, see, for example, Rosemary Radford Ruether, *The Radical Kingdom: The Western Experience of Messianic Hope* (New York: Harper & Row, 1970); and Walter Brueggemann, *The Prophetic Imagination*.

15. Quoted in Michael Walzer, *The Revolution of the Saints: A Study in the Origins of Radical Politics* (1965) (New York: Atheneum, 1968), p. 63. The quotation comes from Calvin, *Jeremiah*, lecture 2:I, 44.

16. Quoted in Walzer, *The Revolution of the Saints*, p. 99. The quotation comes from Knox, *Godly Letter, Works*, vol. III, p. 184.

17. Quoted in Walzer, *The Revolution of the Saints*, p. 103.

18. Ibid., p. 105.

19. Frank E. Manuel, *The Prophets of Paris* (Cambridge, MA: Harvard Univ. Press, 1962). And see also Frank E. Manuel and Fritzie P. Manuel, *Utopian Thought in the Western World* (Cambridge, MA: Belknap Press of Harvard Univ. Press, 1979). Some, if not many, of the philosophes were often hostile to religion, which—historically—has often been associated with intolerance, bigotry, superstition, or oppression. The philosophes were not consciously fulfilling a religiously orthodox prophetic position. Yet if they were, in a sense, modern pagans—as Peter Gay argues—they illustrated key aspects of a secular prophetic impulse. As Gay writes in *The Enlightenment: An Interpretation* (New York: Knopf, 1966), p. 3: "The man of the Enlightenment united on a vast ambitious program, a program of secularism, humanity, cosmopolitanism, and freedom, above all, freedom in its many forms—freedom from arbitrary power, freedom of speech, freedom of trade, freedom to realize one's talents, freedom of aesthetic response, freedom . . . of moral man to make his own way in the world." We must not forget that Jefferson and Madison also illustrate the Enlightenment, and some remarkable prophetic breakthroughs. They translated prophetic constitutional theory into constitutional practice. See Neal Riemer, *James Madison* (1968) Rev. ed. (Washington, D.C.: Congressional Quarterly Press, 1986); *The Democratic Experiment* (Princeton, N.J.: Van Nostrand, 1967); and *The Future of the Democratic Revolution*.

20. See Leszek Kolakowski, *Main Currents of Marxism: I: The Founders* (Oxford: Oxford Univ. Press, 1981), esp. pp. 409, 412, 414.

21. See Rosemary Radford Ruether, *The Radical Kingdom; Liberation Theology: Human Hope Confronts Christian History and American Power* (New York: Paulist/Newman, 1972); and *The New Woman/New Earth: Sexist Ideologies and Human Liberation* (New York: Paulist Press, 1975); Michael Walzer, *Radical Principles* (New York: Basic Books, 1980) and *Exodus and Revolution* (New York: Basic Books, 1985); Cornel West, *Prophesy Deliverance! An Afro-American Revolutionary Christianity* (Philadelphia, PA: Westminister Press, 1982); and Arthur Waskow, *The Rainbow Sign: The Shape of Hope* (New York: Schocken, 1985). See also Arthur Waskow, "The future of prophecy and the future (or fate) of the Earth: Addressing the danger of nuclear holocaust from a prophetic perspective"; Rosemary Radford Ruether, "Prophetic tradition and the liberation of women: A story of promise and betrayal"; and Cornel West, "The prophetic tradition in Afro-America," all in

Neal Riemer (Guest Editor), "The Prophetic Mode and Challenge in Religion, Politics, and Society," *The Drew Gateway*.

22. See U.S. Catholic Bishops, *Pastoral Letter* on *Nuclear Weapons* (1983) and *Pastoral Letter on Catholic Social Teachings and the Economy* (First draft, 1984); Pope John XXIII, *Pacem in Terris* (1963); Martin Buber, *The Prophetic Faith* (1949) (New York: Harper Torchbook, 1960) and *Paths in Utopia* (1949) (Boston: Beacon Press, 1958); Reinhold Niebuhr, *The Nature and Destiny of Man* (2 vols., 1941) (New York: Scribner's, 1944); Abraham J. Heschel, *The Prophets*; and Martin Luther King, Jr., *Stride Toward Freedom* (New York: Harper, 1958); *Why We Can't Wait* (New York: Harper & Row, 1964); and *Where Do We Go From Here: Chaos or Community?* (New York: Harper & Row, 1967).

23. Julius Carlebach, *Karl Marx and the Radical Critique of Judaism*, pp. 324–25.

24. Ibid., p. 325.

25. Ibid.

26. Ibid., p. 326.

27. Ibid.

28. Ibid., pp. 326–27.

29. Ibid., pp. 327–28.

30. Ibid., p. 281.

31. Ibid., p. 285.

32. Ibid., p. 315.

33. Ibid., pp. 314–15.

34. Erich Fromm, *Marx's Concept of Man* (New York: Ungar, 1961), p. 5; and also Erich Fromm (ed.), *Socialist Humanism: An International Symposium* (Garden City, NY: Doubleday, 1965).

35. Murray Wolfson, *Marx: Economist, Philosopher, Jew: Steps in the Development of a Doctrine* (New York: St. Martin's Press, 1982), p. 194.

36. Ibid., pp. 195–96.

37. Ibid., pp. 196.

38. Ibid., pp. 196–97.

39. Julius Carlebach, *Karl Marx and the Radical Critique of Judaism,* p. 316.

40. Bruce Mazlish, *The Meaning of Karl Marx* (New York: Oxford Univ. Press, 1984), pp. 37–38.

41. Ibid., pp. 5–6.

42. Howard L. Parsons, "The prophetic mission of Karl Marx," in Herbert Aptheker (ed.), *Marxism and Christianity* (New York: Humanities Press, 1968), Ch. VII, esp. pp. 145–55.

43. David McLellan, *Karl Marx: His Life and Thought* (New York: Harper & Row, 1973), p. 6.

44. See Kolakowski, *Main Currents of Marxism*.

45. See Norman Cohn, *The Pursuit of the Millennium: Revolutionary Millenarians and Mystical Anarchists of the Middle Ages* (London: Secker and Warburg, 1957; Rev. ed., New York: Oxford Univ. Press, 1970). Cohn may have changed his mind in the revised edition of his book!

46. Crane Brinton, "Utopia and Democracy," in Frank Manuel (ed.), *Utopias and Utopian Thought* (Boston: Beacon Press, 1967), p. 51.

47. Quoted in Martin Buber, *Paths in Utopia*, p. 11.

48. See George Kateb, *Utopia and Its Enemies* (New York: Free Press, 1963); Frank Manuel and Fritzie Manuel, *Utopian Thought in the Western World* (Cambridge, MA: Belknap Press of the Harvard Univ. Press, 1979). See also the judgment of Jon Elster, *Making Sense of Marx* (Cambridge, U.K.: Cambridge Univ. Press, 1985) on Marx's utopianism, esp. pp. 91, 456, and 526–27.

49. See A. J. Talmon, *The Origins of Totalitarian Democracy* (London: Secker and Warburg, 1952), p. 252; and *Political Messianism: The Romantic Phase* (London: Secker and Warburg, 1960), p. 516. For an analysis of Talmon's thesis see John Dunn's Chapter 5, "Totalitarian democracy and the legacy of modern revolutions: explanation or indictment?" in Dunn's *Rethinking Modern Political Theory* (Cambridge, U.K.: Cambridge Univ. Press, 1985), and also pages 6–7 of his Introduction. See also Richard N. Hunt's *The Political Ideas of Marx and Engels: I: Marxism and Totalitarian Democracy, 1818–1850* (Pittsburgh, PA: Univ. Pittsburgh Press, 1974). Hunt rejects the argument that Marx was a totalitarian democrat.

2
Marx's Guiding Values and the Superior Universal Order

INTRODUCTION

In this chapter I should like to explore Marx's guiding values. They help us to understand his conception of a superior universal order. What are Marx's guiding values? And what is Marx's vision of such an order? And will these values and this vision illuminate his standard for analysis and evaluation as a philosopher, political economist, social scientist, and strategist of revolution? In exploring these interrelated questions in the second section of this chapter, I attempt some answers to the problem of Marx's guiding values and his conception of a superior universal order.

I structure my answer around a cluster of interrelated values to be found in Marx's writings: freedom, integration, humanity and community, and development. In illuminating Marx's vision and values I draw heavily, but not exclusively, upon his early writings. I think this can be safely done because, as a number of scholars have affirmed, Marx's guiding values and vision remained fundamentally the same throughout his life, despite some shifts in vocabulary and emphasis during his philosophical and political evolution.[1]

In the third section I attempt a critique of Marx's guiding values and vision, which do, I argue, indeed constitute a standard of a superior universal order, a standard that significantly influences Marx's own analysis and evaluation of bourgeois, capitalistic society, and his call for a communist community.[2] Finally, in the fourth section I sum up my findings and appraisal and set the stage for Chapter 3, which focuses more sharply on Marx's radical criticism of the existing bourgeois order of his day.

MARX'S VALUES AND VISION FOR HUMANITY

A number of interrelated, reciprocally interacting, values help us to understand Marx's vision of a superior universal order. They are the values of (1) universal human freedom, (2) integration, harmony, and peace, (3) the truly human being and community, and (4) rich individual and social realization. These are truths, Marx holds, to be discovered in the unfolding of human history. Their triumph will usher in real happiness for humankind. I link integration, harmony, and peace because they speak to the several dimensions of a life—and a community and a world—in which divisions and conflicts have been overcome, in which unity and concord have been achieved. I link the truly human individual and the genuine community because Marx sees the possibility of an authentic humanity only in a social, cooperative, communist community; only there will selfishness and egoism be overcome; only there will people be truly human beings. For similar reasons I link rich individual and social realization: individual and social development are interdependent and mutually reinforcing; one without the other is inconceivable. I turn now to Marx's own testimony on these interrelated values.

Universal Human Freedom

Freedom is central to Marx's thought, and is intimately related to his other values. Freedom will be advanced by—as well as advance—integration. Freedom is a precondition of individual and social authenticity and realization. Marx sees freedom in the abolition of those conditions that obstruct self-determination and human realization. Freedom must be understood in terms of the realization of human potentialities. Here Marx stands squarely in the tradition of the European Enlightenment.

Philosophers throughout history have attempted to unmask the illusions that restrict freedom. And, according to Marx, bourgeois critics have in fact fought and partially achieved emancipation for the bourgeoisie. Such efforts, however, have been incomplete. Emancipation must be total, effective, and universal. To be so, freedom must be understood, centrally, as emancipation from alienated and exploited labor in a capitalistic society. The proletariat must be seen as the key to universal human emancipation. Only the emancipation of working people from private property and capitalism can bring freedom to all and in all spheres. The young Marx opts for the *"total redemption of humanity."*[3]

Political emancipation is not enough. Religious freedom is not enough. Only universal human emancipation will do. Political emancipation is limited if it only liberates the state from constraints without liberating human beings from constraints. A "state may be a *free state* without man himself being a *freeman.*"[4] Freedom from religious constraints imposed by church or state does not free people from religion.[5] The bourgeois freedoms, as illustrated by the French Declaration of the Rights of Man and of the Citizen—the rights of equality, liberty, security, property—do not carry one far enough in the process of universal human emancipation. Why not? Because: "None of the supposed rights of man, therefore, go beyond the egoistic man, man as he is, as a member of civil [i.e., bourgeois, economic] society; that is, an individual separated from the community, withdrawn into himself, wholly preoccupied with his private interest and acting in accordance with his private caprice."[6]

Marx insists that the bourgeois revolutions did not bring complete liberation, and certainly not for the proletariat. This failure can best be seen by contrasting political and human emancipation, and by looking to the working, everyday life of people. Political emancipation may free one as a citizen, as one who participates in *"community* life"[7] but it also frees the bourgeois individual and permits him to carry on his economic activities in civil society. The egoistic individual and the moral citizen have been separated. Complete human emancipation calls for the re-uniting of the real individual and the citizen. Such an emancipation, Marx insists, is impossible in a bourgeois capitalistic society; it is only possible under communism.

"Political emancipation [Marx writes] is a reduction of man, on the one hand to a member of civil society, an *independent* and *egoistic* individual, and on the other, to a citizen, to a moral person."

"Human emancipation [Marx insists] will only be complete when the real, individual man has absorbed into himself the abstract citizen; when as an individual man, in his everyday life, in his work, and in his relationships, he has become a *species-being*; and when he has recognized and organized his own powers (*"forces propres"*) as *social* powers so that he no longer separates this social power from himself as *political* power."[8] Marx later moves away from the language of "species-being," but not from the idea that an authentic human being will emerge under communism.

Thus Marx can write of bourgeois revolutions and freedoms: "Thus man was not liberated from religion; he received religious liberty. He was not liberated from property; he received the liberty to own property. He was not liberated from the egoism of business; he received the liberty to engage in business."[9]

In brief, true, complete human emancipation will come when man is liberated from the chains of religion, private property, and capitalistic business enterprise, and specifically from egoistic need, huckstering, and money—all illustrations of human alienation.

Very early in his life Marx underscored "the *categorical imperative to overthrow all those conditions* in which man is an abased, enslaved, abandoned, contemptible being."[10] Put positively, this suggests that man must be lifted up, freed, found, and treated with dignity. But very quickly, in his intellectual development, Marx comes to focus on emancipation from *alienated* labor as the key to all human emancipation. Later, there will be more emphasis on *exploited* labor, but the commitment to free working people from enslavement, servitude, and despotism under bourgeois private property and capitalism persists.

Marx's view of alienation, which will be developed more fully in the next section on integration, illuminates in a negative way the nature of freedom. Alienated workers are not free. Freedom means that people are in control of their work-product, enjoy their work-activity, have recovered their humanity, and are re-united with other human beings. Emancipation involves overcoming the conditions of alienation.

This emancipation involves, especially, emancipation of the proletariat. It involves a concern for the character of emancipation—a concern for *"what kind of emancipation* is involved."[11] Marx formulates a preliminary answer to the problem of emancipation/alienation very early in his life; and he is to work at the more complete answer the rest of his life.[12] "From the relationship of estranged labour to private property it further follows that the emancipation of society from private property, etc., from servitude, is expressed in the *political* form of the *emancipation of the workers*; not that *their* emancipation alone was at stake but because the emancipation of the workers contains universal human emancipation—and it contains this, because the whole of human servitude is involved in the relation of the worker to production, and every relation of servitude is but a modification and consequence of this relationship."[13]

Although freedom will come with the emancipation of the worker from alienated and exploited labor, Marx holds that the "true realm of freedom" must be understood as that realm wherein people are more completely emancipated from the "realm of necessity," or necessary labor. "In fact, the realm of freedom actually begins only where labour which is determined by necessity and mundane considerations ceases; thus in the very nature of things it lies beyond the sphere of actual material production."[14] Communism would create a basis for the "true realm of freedom" through its rational economic and human processes, which involve "favourable" conditions, and specifically the "shortening of the working day."[15] The "true realm of freedom" will "blossom" in this more favorable "realm of necessity."[16]

As we have already noted, Marx holds that the right kind of community is crucial to freedom. Such a community is important in overcoming alienated and exploited labor. Such a community is vital in creating a more favorable economic basis for labor not "determined by necessity," for labor concerned with "the development of human energy" as "an end in itself";[17] and in enhancing the cultivation of "gifts in all directions." Thus: "Only in the community [with others has each] individual the means of cultivating his gifts in all directions; only in the community, therefore, is personal freedom possible. . . . In the real community the individuals obtain their freedom in and through their association."[18] Here, too, we see again the link between freedom, community, and development.

The individual and social freedom that Marx envisages requires the human ability to overcome the enslaving illusions of religion, of society, and of politics, and especially the illusions of bourgeois freedoms. The proletariat is the key to victory in overcoming the enslaving conditions in economics, society, and politics.

Integration, Harmony, and Peace

Closely related to universal human freedom—and, indeed, almost inseparable from such freedom—is a cluster of values I have identified as integration, harmony, and peace. To overcome the alienation of the worker—to overcome exploiting, enslaving, despotic capitalism—it is essential to overcome the estrangement or separation of the worker from his product, from his work-activity, from his humanity or species-being, and from other people. This overcoming underscores a pattern of integration. It emphasizes a triumph over conflicts and antagonisms. The integration, harmony, peace—or return, resolution—involves this natural world only, involves humans only.

In the *Economic and Philosophic Manuscripts of 1844* Marx first identifies and analyzes the four interrelated aspects of alienation and their relationship to freedom. As we have noted, the worker is alienated from his product, from his work-activity, from his humanity, and from other human beings. First, labor "is *external* to the worker, i.e., it does not belong to his essential being." The worker is "estranged from the product of his labour." The "product of labour is alien" to him and "confronts" him "as an alien power," an "alien object exercising power over him." The worker is simply not in control of his work or the product of his work.[19] Second, the worker sees his life-activity as "alien activity," as "not belonging to him." He finds no joy in his work. He is not comfortable or at home in his work.[20] Third, the worker is estranged from his "species-being." In "estranging from man (1) nature, and (2) himself, his own active functions, his life-activity, estranged labour estranges the *species* from man." Estranged labor turns man's "species-being . . . into a being *alien* to him. . . ."[21] The worker has become dehumanized. Workers are turned into appendages to machines. Fourth, human is estranged from human. "An immediate consequence of the fact that man is estranged from the product of his labor, from his life-activity, from his species-being is the *estrangement of man from man*."[22] He is estranged from his capitalistic employer and, given the competitive nature of capitalism, also frequently from his fellow workers.

Indeed, Marx also maintains that alienation is to be found pervading all of bourgeois society: in politics, religion, and bourgeois culture in general, as well as in economics.[23]

Marx argues that communism is the "re-integration or return of man to himself, the transcendence of human self-estrangement. . . ."[24] Marx sees *"Communism* as the *positive* transcendence of *private property*, or *human estrangement*, and therefore as the real *appropriation of the human essence* by and for man; communism therefore as the complete return of man to himself as a *social* (i.e., human) being. . . ."[25] This communism, which Marx equates with "fully-developed naturalism," is "fully developed humanism." Marx sees such a communism as "the genuine resolution of the conflict between man and nature and between man and man—the true resolution of the strife between existence and essence . . . between freedom and necessity, between the individual and the species." "Communism," Marx triumphantly affirms, "is the riddle of history solved, and it knows itself to be this solution."[26]

Initially, then, the integration Marx sees in communism involves the resolution of a number of conflicts. The intellectual road from this position in 1844 to the vision of a classless society, a harmonious society, is clear. So is the road to world peace, which follows from the overcoming of class conflict within nations as within the factory. Political harmony will follow economic and social harmony. Peace among nations will follow peace within nations and between classes.

Integration involves overcoming the division of labor, the division between town and country, the division between workers, and a host of other divisions. Integration involves overcoming the division of civil society and politics, of private and public, of the egoistic individual and the social community.

Radical integration, harmony, and peace will only come with the end of classes in the new communist community. Marx is insistent that the "issue cannot be . . . the smoothing over of class antagonisms but the abolition of classes, not the improvement of existing society but the foundation of a new one."[27] Marx looks to the end, the total disappearance, of class antagonisms, and of classes, with the end of "exploitation of one part of society by" another.[28] The end of domestic class conflict presages the end of international conflict. "In proportion as the exploitation of one individual by another is put an end to, the exploitation of one nation by another will also be put an end to. In proportion as the antagonism between classes within the nation vanishes, the hostility of one nation to another will come to an end."[29]

The Truly Human Being and Community

If, for Marx, freedom requires integration, both freedom and integration are linked to a truly human being and a truly human community.

Hitherto, economic, societal, political, and religious conditions have obstructed the emergence of the truly human being and the truly human community. Religion has been too concerned with another world; religion has not been concerned enough with this world. In bourgeois society there has been a separation of economic man, egoistic man, selfish man *from* political man, man as a moral citizen. And the working man, the key to universal human emancipation, has in the bourgeois society been alienated from his product, his work-activity, his species-being or humanity, and from other humans. Freedom and integration will both be served when working people have control over their product, enjoy their working hours, regain their humanity, and participate in a genuine community. Then humankind's needs—sensuous and mental—will be satisfied.

Humankind's real humanity, moreover, lies in its social character. The truly human being and the truly human community require an educated, social person. They require a rational plan of existence; they require honesty; they require a human being who has found himself, is integrated, and lives under favorable conditions. The truly human society is a social, cooperative community.[30]

The emphasis, Marx insists, must be on humankind as *"the supreme being for man."*[31] The truly human being and the truly human community require conditions that elevate, free, and affirm humankind, and treat people with dignity.[32] The *"true* and *authentic* man" must get beyond the egoism of bourgeois society.[33] He does so in a community whose interests do not clash with the interests of the selfish egoistic individual because such a community is composed of social, cooperative, unselfish humans.[34]

Rich Human Individual and Social Development

Rich human and social development is a characteristic of the truly human being and community. The process of such development can be discerned in history. Marx sees the "labor of the entire history of the world to the present" in the *"forming* of the five senses." He is also concerned with the development of the "mental senses" by human beings. He is concerned with the "objectively unfolded richness of man's essential being." Marx looks to a society that "produces man" in the "entire richness of his being—produces the *rich* man profoundly endowed with all the senses. . . ." It would appear that Marx's vision is a vision of history moving toward rich human development in a community emancipated from "crude practical need."[35]

Human "realization," Marx maintains, is "an inner necessity." "The *rich* human being . . . [is] . . . the human being *in need of* a totality of human life-activites—the man in whom his own realization exists as an inner necessity, as need." The "*rich* human being" has rich human needs.[36] The satisfaction of these human needs rests upon the right kind of productive community. In "a higher phase of communist society . . . after the productive forces have also increased with the all-round development of the individual, and all the springs of cooperative wealth flow more abundantly . . . then . . . society [can] inscribe on its banner: From each according to his ability, to each according to his needs!"[37]

Marx thinks in developmental terms. The "*entire so-called history of the world* is nothing but the begetting of man through human labour, nothing but the coming-to-be of nature for man. . . ."[38] The developmental sequence, in which human labor plays so important a part, is outlined and illustrated throughout Marx's writings.[39] "Communism," Marx argues in 1844, "is . . . the . . . phase necessary for the next stage of historical development in the process of human emancipation and recovery." "*Communism* is," he maintains, "the necessary pattern and the dynamic principle of the immediate future"; but then he adds: "but communism as such is not the goal of human development. . . ."[40] What, then, we might ask, is "the goal of human development"? Marx does not provide us with an explicit answer. We can only infer that the goal is the fulfillment of human richness in a genuinely human, social, and rich community.

Other Interrelated Values in Marx's Vision: Truth and Happiness

The intimately interrelated values treated in the foregoing four sections constitute truths to be discovered in history. These are cardinal values for Marx. They are related to other important values, for example, truth and happiness. These are not, of course, Marx's only values, but they are clearly cardinal values that illuminate Marx's vision of a superior universal order. A very brief treatment of the values of truth and happiness will underscore both that my treatment of Marx's values is by no means exhaustive, and that Marx's values must be seen as a related whole.

Although Marx develops no sophisticated epistemology, there can be no doubt that he is dedicated to the search for, and establishment of, truth—truth that he sees as being confirmed in practice in history. The task involves the unmasking of illusions, of falsehoods, and—as we have already seen—of the enslaving, alienating, dehumanizing, stunting conditions surrounding the most important human activities. "It is the task of *history*, therefore, once the *other-world of truth* has vanished, to establish the *truth of this world*. The immediate *task of philosophy*, which is in the service of history, is to unmask human self-alienation in its *secular* form now that it has been unmasked in its *sacred* form. Thus the criticism of heaven is transformed into the criticism of earth, the *criticism of religion* into the *criticism of law*, and the *criticism of theology* into the *criticism of politics*."[41]

This is Marx's position in 1843. The "criticism of earth" means a concern for "genuine human problems." It means attention to the truth of "the relation of industry, of the world of wealth in general, to the political world." This is a "major problem of modern times."[42] It means attention to the truth that "for man the root is man himself."[43] It means attention, moreover, to the truth of class struggle and the condition of the proletariat, and to the possibility of universal human emancipation.[44]

These, of course, are only a few of the truths that illustrate Marx's concerns. They illustrate also the truth for Marx of the connection between theory and practice. The philosopher's task, the critic's task, is to demystify the world. This requires affirming the truth of materialism, but materialism of a certain kind—"active," "subjective," "revolutionary," concerned with "practice."[45] Marx is emphatic on this point, and follows up his first thesis against Feuerbach with a second: "The question whether objective truth can be attributed to human thinking is not a question of theory but is a *practical* question. Man must prove the truth, that is, the reality and power, the this-sidedness of his thinking in practice. The dispute over the reality or non-reality of thinking which is isolated from practice is a purely *scholastic* question."[46]

There is very little discussion of "happiness" in Marx's writings. Yet there can be no doubt that although we do not find in Marx any significant treatment of "happiness" per se, he early announces his concern for what he calls "real happiness" and seeks by overcoming the conditions of slavery, alienation, dehumanization, and stunted development to advance such "real happiness." "The abolition of religion as the *illusory* happiness of men, is a demand for their *real* happiness. The call to abandon their illusions about their condition is a call to abandon a condition which requires illusions."[47] Happiness—real happiness—will come with communism.

CRITIQUE

What are we to make of Marx's vision for humanity? How do we evaluate his call for universal human freedom; his plea for integration, harmony, and peace; his endorsement of the truly human being and community; and his preference for rich human individual and social development? At one level of analysis, Marx's values are, indeed, prophetic values. Let us examine the argument in support of this proposition.

Clearly, total human emancipation—the overcoming of wage slavery and other forms of bondage, the capacity of individuals to determine their own destiny free of arbitrary impediments—is in the great tradition of prophetic politics. So, too, is Marx's sensitivity to, and concern for, the least-free—the proletariat. Theoretically, Marx seeks to complete the process he sees as occurring throughout history. If it is true that more and more people were freed as society moved from feudalism to capitalism, *all* would be freed under communism. They would be freed in their most important life-activity—their work. Exploitation would come to an end. The collective resources of production would be used by people, cooperatively, to overcome substantially, if not completely, the imperious demands of Nature and necessity. Necessary labor would be reduced to a minimum, and that labor that would still have to be performed would be performed under the most favorable circumstances. A richly productive communist economic system would make possible the satisfaction of all legitimate needs.

The dehumanizing aspects of the division of labor would be overcome, and human beings would be free to develop their diverse talents and to cultivate all their richly human senses. Antagonisms and oppressions would cease in the classless society. Coercive state power would become nonexistent. Human beings would attend to their life-activities freely and cooperatively. Oppression would end not only within political communities—or nations—but between them. Freedom would prevail not only for men, but for women; not only for the proletariat but also for those who had formerly been members of the bourgeoisie; and (taking note of Marx's occasional writings about non-European people) not only for white people but for black and brown people.

Universal human freedom is, in Marx's mind, closely linked with the values of integration, and harmony and peace. These values, too, rest upon overcoming alienation, exploitation, antagonism, oppression. Alienation would be overcome under communism because then the worker would have control over his product (and thus a most crucial part of his life), would work joyously, would be in touch with his social and most humane qualities, would be joined together, not separated from, his fellows. Work would cease to be exploitation. The worker's hostility to the economic system would cease. Worker would no longer be competing with fellow worker. Oppression would vanish. Conflict would disappear within the community and between nation-states. Harmony would reign. Peace would have come at last to the world.

A truly human being and a truly human community would become possible under communism. Human beings would regain their humanity and be able to participate in a genuine community. Human beings would become genuinely social. Here the conflict between individual self-interest and the community interest would be overcome. Cooperation would be the keynote of the communist community. The truly humanistic community would have come into being.

The communist community, in turn, would thus make possible genuinely rich individual and social development. Human realization would now be possible. The goal of human development—which communism lays the basis for—is the fulfillment of human potentialities in a genuinely human, social, and fully rich human community.

Marx's values—freedom, integration (harmony, peace), humanity/community, rich human and social development—are an important part of the religious and secular tradition of prophetic politics. His analysis of these values is a powerful and illuminating nineteenth century contribution to the post-modern age that we might label, paradoxically, the era of universal emancipation and destruction. Marx evidences a clear concern for universal human emancipation, especially for the end of oppression of working people, those he believes to be the overwhelming majority. He evidences, too, a strong concern for peace within and between nations, for the emergence of genuine social human beings in a cooperative and caring community, and for creative human self-realization in a creative society. These concerns ring with prophetic authenticity. This is the case even if Marx's concerns are consciously divorced from a religiously prophetic commitment to God, revelation, covenant, commandment, or from a secular prophetic commitment to a transcendent higher law, or from a rational ethical imperative.

Powerful—but limited and flawed! Marx's values for a superior universal order are, unfortunately, not fully explicated or defended; they are asserted. Presumably they will be fulfilled in history. But how they are discovered in history (emerging out of an economic and social context) and why we should endorse them—these matters are not clearly and convincingly explicated. Marx, a radical Enlightenment humanist turned communist, simply asserts that his radical, democratic, socialist, Enlightenment values will prevail once the exploiting and oppressive bourgeois capitalistic society has been replaced by a communist one. With the important exception of alienation/exploitation, Marx does not ably or fully argue on behalf of his values.

Moreover, Marx does not ask about the compatibility of the several values he endorses (for example, freedom and peace, individual and communal self-realization). Nor does he inquire about crucial values that may be missing among his preferred values (for example, love, compassion, tolerance, repentance), values that may be essential to the maintenance of his preferred or historically self-fulfilling values. Of particular importance, Marx does not adequately appreciate or satisfactorily argue for the importance of constitutionalism as a value required to sustain his other values.

We miss especially a fuller articulation of the meaning of freedom. Is Marx really committed to freedom for all, especially freedom for non-communists or anti-communists? Or is Marx so persuaded that he has arrived at the truth of the worth of communism as a way to overcome alienation, exploitation, and despotism that he cannot seriously entertain disagreement on the truth of freedom under communism, and that he therefore need not face up to freedom for anti-communist or non-communist dissenters? I believe that Marx's conception of freedom is too limited, that he seriously underestimates the importance of protecting freedom for such dissenters. This serious underestimation is related to Marx's belief in integration, harmony, and peace.

Marx's values of integration, harmony, and peace reflect a foolishly utopian conviction that alienation can be completely overcome. We have good reason to doubt whether the "whole of human servitude is involved in the relation of the worker to production"; and whether "every relation of servitude is but a modification and consequence of this relationship."[48] Because of his concentration on economic alienation, and his faith in the ability of a communist system to overcome such alienation, Marx fails to address other varieties of alienation—rooted for example in the human psyche, in the recognition of our own mortality, finiteness, fallibility, in the anomie that may afflict some people in any society, in the estrangement individuals may feel in large, unresponsive economic/political/social organizations. Marx fails to see the alienation resulting from human rejection of even a communist system. Marx fails to see that freedom, particularly freedom to think and explore the world around us (including a communist world), can produce great anxiety. Creatively coping with, if not overcoming, alienation in its many dimensions calls for a more sophisticated understanding of freedom (its promise and its perils), of the extent of anomie in modern society, of the alienating aspects of large organizations, and of certain traditional religious beliefs. Marx—given his own social scientific position as a humanist, materialistic; and given his stance as a critic of liberal democracy—is not prepared to seek such a more sophisticated understanding.

Specifically, Marx is not prepared to see that freedom can only be sensibly exercised within the framework of a clearly articulated covenant or constitution. Such a constitution recognizes diversity of interests, struggle among contending interests, and the need for wise patterns of conflict and accommodation (as well as cooperation). Such a constitution realistically concedes the dangers of, as it guards against, the abuse of human power, whether by individuals, groups, or states.

Marx furthermore does not appreciate that the opposition to idolatry or false gods carries beyond opposition to the fetishism of commodities under capitalism, and beyond the opposition to private property and money, and must include opposition to making any earthly idol—whether the proletariat or communism—into a god. It is not that Marx himself makes the proletariat, communist power, or communist party into a god. Rather his conviction that communism, ushered in by the proletariat, would produce universal human emancipation makes it easy for others to deify those who, and that which, advances such emancipation.

The concept of a classless, conflictless—an harmonious—society is a defective, if attractive, utopian idea. No one, of course, can quarrel with the end of exploitation of one class by another, with the end of warfare among nations. The end of oppression and war is a prophetic imperative in both the religious and secular interpretations of the prophetic. But is it not foolishly utopian to believe in the possibility of a conflictless society and world? Is Marx indulging in hyperbole when he talks about a classless, conflictless society, about the ultimate abolition of the state (as a coercive instrument), and about universal peace? It is hard to believe that Marx seriously holds that *all* conflicts will disappear under communism. It is more reasonable to assume that he holds that *basic* conflicts—and *basic* alienation, exploitation, oppression, and despotism—will disappear.

However, even this more reasonable proposition calls for critical examination. No one can fault this proposition on ethical grounds. However, we can ask whether this conviction prevents Marx—as I believe it does—from affirming the need for an explicit and well-developed constitutional theory to deal (both domestically and internationally) with persisting basic conflicts. This conviction seems to lead Marx to ignore (in his communist society) the persistence of those factors—in human beings, among interests, in any community or government, among nations—that make for conflict, strife, competition, and therefore militate against harmony, peace, and integration.

Thus, if Marx fails to explore the fuller meaning of freedom (both within and beyond the realm of necessary labor)—as economic control over one's destiny in work as one's primary life-activity, as civic control in a thoroughly democratic polity, and as the cultivation of one's gifts in all directions in a supportive community—he also fails to explore the fuller meaning of, and obstacles to, harmony within and between political communities. If politics is a pattern of constitutional cooperation, conflict, and accommodation, it seems to be the case that Marx fails to deal adequately with conflict and accommodation under communism. His values of integration, harmony, and peace remain vague, if desired, goals; and his failure to deal with ongoing problems of conflict and accommodation—indeed, even of cooperation—is a serious flaw in his understanding of values.

Marx's commitment, to thinking, reflective, conscious, social human beings who in a cooperative and supportive community have overcome their selfish and egoistic natures, is an attractive ideal, and is quite in accord with the prophetic vision of caring individuals in a caring community. We must, however, note Marx's failure to clarify more fully his early understanding of "species-being," and to reflect upon the dangers of the sin of pride in making man "the supreme being for man," especially in the absence of safeguards against the abuse of power.

To make this point is to raise a serious question about the soundness of Marx's view of the essential goodness of all humans. This criticism is prompted by a religious recognition of the *yetzer hara*, the evil inclination in humans (in the Jewish tradition) or of human sinfulness (in the Christian tradition), or by a secular and historical suspicion of the abuse of power. This criticism takes on additional meaning for twentieth century observers who have lived through Stalin's terror or the Holocaust and who appreciate the dangers of the abuse of power, even by those in the communist tradition who may have had the best of intentions. Indeed, as Reinhold Niebuhr has effectively argued, the dangers posed by those with good intentions may sometimes be the greatest precisely because those with power have good intentions!

The sensible transformation of the environment (in overcoming alienation, in enabling people to have control over their primary life-activities, in creating a productively rich economy, in reducing the hours of necessary labor, in opening up opportunities for the creative use of freedom in the hours beyond necessary labor) can undoubtedly help to create a new human being in a new society. But the danger of abuse of power remains a danger in that process of transformation. The freedom to criticize that abuse of power is crucial. The need to be aware of the *yetzer hara* is imperative. And the importance of having a higher standard of judgment to appeal to in making such criticism, and of having a model of the contrast between the higher and lower (whether we call it divine and human or natural law and human law), is vital.

These observations also apply to Marx's commitment to rich human and social development. The fulfillment of human potentiality in all senses is an admirable value, as long as we insist (as I believe Marx would) that such realization be good, humane, sensible. This then requires a standard of good, humane, sensible, a standard that is barely articulated and never fully developed by Marx. It is, largely, assumed. Again, freedom in exploring that standard, freedom in order to assess current applications of that standard, is indispensable. Freedom, here, means the ability to speak, write, assemble, vote, worship, in order to accept or to challenge such a standard and its application. Similarly, the protection of such freedom, such basic rights—and therefore of genuine control over government by people—calls for a constitution that provides effective and regularized restraints on those who exercise power.

In dealing with all of Marx's values, then, there seems to be no escape from three conclusions: (1) Marx's key values, although superficially attractive, remain distressingly vague and undeveloped; (2) Marx fails to articulate a full-fledged theory of constitutionalism as a concept to ensure that his values will be fulfilled; (3) Marx fails to identify other key values—whether love or fellow-feeling, compassion, tolerance, repentance—necessary to guide his individuals and to hold his communist community together. These affective, intellectual, and religious values are, for the most part, strikingly absent in Marx.

CONCLUSION

We must conclude that serious shortcomings mar Marx's values and humanistic vision—values and vision that are, in important respects, consonant with the prophetic tradition. Do these shortcomings lead us to conclude that Marx's vision is utopian and not genuinely prophetic? Is is possible to rescue the soundly utopian elements in Marx's humanistic vision?

Marx's concept of universal human emancipation takes seriously the prophetic commitment to the least-free, particularly the proletariat, and to the fuller dimensions of freedom. His concept of alienation—and of integration via communism—is radical, thought-provoking, and illuminating. His concepts of humanity/community and individual and social realization seem to be in the tradition of a secular prophetic politics, calling as they do for human fulfillment in a fulfilling community. Marx's vision, then, seems to be a prophetic vision of the necessary and sufficient conditions for life, growth, and development.

Yet, as my analysis has suggested, serious shortcomings appear to characterize those values and that vision. We are led to ask if, in important respects, those values and that vision are foolishly utopian and not genuinely prophetic. Are universal human emancipation, integration/harmony/peace, a humane community, and rich realization really possible? And, if possible, how probable? And, if we have realistic doubts about both political possibility and probability, must we be alert to the dangers facing those who—even with the best of intentions—may be tempted, as they seek to achieve such values, to commit or condone great evil done in the name of great good?

Or is it the case that we can rescue the soundly utopian—the genuinely prophetic—elements in Marx's values? That we can overcome the *hubris* in his vision? Let us postpone for now our fuller answer to these questions and concerns until we have the opportunity to explore Marx's social science, his theory of revolutionary action, and his fuller understanding of the communist future. We start first, in the next chapter, with his social science.

NOTES

1. See, for example, Bertell Ollman, *Alienation: Marx's Conception of Man in Capitalist Society* (Cambridge, U.K.: Cambridge Univ. Press, 1971); Robert C. Tucker, *Philosophy and Myth in Karl Marx* (Cambridge, U.K.: Cambridge Univ. Press, 1961); David McLellan, *Karl Marx: His Life and Thought* (New York: Harper & Row, 1973); Tom Bottomore (ed.), *A Dictionary of Marxist Thought* (Cambridge, MA: Harvard Univ. Press, 1983); Leszek Kolakowski, *Main Currents of Marxism*, 3 Vols. (1978) (Oxford Univ. Press, paperback edition, 1981); Bruce Mazlish, *The Meaning of Karl Marx* (New York: Oxford Univ. Press, 1984); Eugene Kamenka, *The Ethical Foundations of Marxism* (New York: Praeger, 1962).

2. Despite the argument of those (for example, Ollman, *Alienation*, esp. pp. 47–51) who maintain "that Marx did not have an ethical theory," I see no way of avoiding the proposition I have affirmed in the text. Ollman contends that Marx would "maintain that in knowing something, certainly in knowing it well, we already either esteem or condemn it" (p. 48). I would not deny this, but would affirm that our decision to "esteem or condemn" is based upon an ethical standard that logically requires us to "esteem or condemn" on the basis of concordance or deviation of behavior from our standard. Of course, for a host of reasons we may not behave ethically or logically. Nevertheless, I would insist (contrary to Ollman's contention, p. 49) that facts do not necessarily "contain their own condemnation and a call to do something about them." For example, without an ethical standard that condemns slavery as evil, the fact of slavery does not contain its own condemnation. Think of the millions and millions who have approved or tolerated slavery over several thousand years. The "different appreciation of the facts" (Ollman, p. 49) that leads some, for example, to condemn slavery and others to approve slavery rests upon an ethical standard of the evil or good, unacceptability or acceptability, of slavery. Prudence, of course, may still dictate what practical course to take in given circumstances. To make this argument is not to deny that such a standard may be affected by class or other factors. But the decisive element in shaping that standard is an ethical judgment, and not necessarily class. Contrary to Ollman's contention that "in asserting that workers are degraded, Marx is not making an evaluation on the basis of what he sees but describing what the workers are" I would insist that Marx is indeed making an ethical evaluation when he holds that workers are degraded! On Marx's ethical position, see also Eugene Kamenka, *The Ethical Foundations of Marxism*. Kamenka notes (p. 70): "Marx expounds no moral 'principles' or standards according to which political economy is tried and found wanting." Further (p. 72): "It is because Marx rejects the concept of ethical criticism as being the application of 'ideal' standards and treats his ethico-logic as grounded in the way things occur, that he can insist that his criticism is purely empirical." This may, indeed, have been Marx's own view, but I believe that he was deceiving himself; I believe his values did constitute a standard of judgment for him. Moreover, logically, his criticism could not be "purely empirical." Kamenka does note (p. 95) that the early Marx did have a conception "of that which ought to be" (Marx's words), linked—Kamenka notes—to "that which is reality's final aim" (Marx's words again); that Marx failed "to rid himself entirely of normative conceptions" (p. 96). See also Robert C. Tucker, *Philosophy and Myth in Karl Marx*, p. 3: "Far from deciding that a communist revolution would be desirable after discovering that it would be inevitable, he became convinced as a young man of its desirability and then embarked on a life-long effort, materialized in *Capital*, to prove that it must come."

3. From *Contribution to the Critique of Hegel's* Philosophy of Right: *Introduction* (1844) in Robert C. Tucker (ed.), *The Marx-Engels Reader*, 2nd ed. (New York: Norton, 1978), p. 64. (Unless otherwise specified, future references to the Tucker edition of Marx's writings will be to this collection. I will usually indicate the specific work of Marx being cited.) Marx's introduction was written at the end of 1843 and published in 1844. The larger critical commentary on Hegel's *Philosophy of Right* was first published in 1927.

4. From *On The Jewish Question* (1843) in Tucker, *The Marx-Engels Reader*, p. 32.

5. Ibid.

6. Ibid., p. 43.

7. Ibid., p. 41.

8. Ibid., pp. 46–47.

9. Ibid., p. 45.

10. *Contribution to the Critique of Hegel's* Philosophy of Right: *Introduction,* in Tucker, p. 30.

11. *On the Jewish Question*, in Tucker, p. 28.

12. See Ollman, *Alienation*, pp. xii–xiii, xiv, and all of Part III, esp. pp. 168, 176, 188, 197, 217, 227–28. See also Eugene Kamenka, *The Ethical Foundations of Marxism*, esp. pp. 30, 144, 191. Thus: "The distinction between freedom and alienation . . . was the ethical *leit-motif* of Marx's philosophical and political development" (p. 144); "For the social conditions that would produce the freeman Marx was to struggle for the next forty years [1843–1883]" (p. 30); and "Marx's belief in the rational, free and completely cooperative society of the human spirit . . . was the foundation and driving force of his intellectual and political development" (p. 191).

13. *Economic and Philosophic Manuscripts of 1844*, in Tucker, p. 80.

14. *Capital*, Vol. III, in Tucker, p. 441.

15. Ibid.

16. Ibid.

17. Ibid.

18. *The German Ideology: Part I* (written by Marx and Engels in 1845/46, first published in 1932), in Tucker, p. 197.

19. From *Economic and Philosophic Manuscripts of 1844*, in Tucker, p. 74 and 77.

20. Ibid., pp. 75, 77.

21. Ibid.

22. Ibid., p. 77.

23. Ibid., pp. 84–85: "This *material*, immediately *sensuous* private property is the material sensuous expression of *estranged* human life. Its movement—production and con-sumption—is the *sensuous* revelation of the movement of all production hitherto—i.e., the realization or the reality of man. Religion, family, state, law, morality, science, art, etc., are only *particular* modes of production, and fall under its general law. The positive transcendence of *private property* as the appropriation of *human* life is, therefore, the positive transcendence of all estrangement—that is to say, the return of man from religion, family, state, etc., to his *human*, i.e., *social* mode of existence."

24. Ibid., p. 84.

25. Ibid., p. 85.

26. Ibid.

27. *Address of the Central Committee to the Communist League* (Marx and Engels, 1850), in Tucker, p. 505.

28. *Manifesto of the Communist Party* (Marx and Engels, 1848), in Tucker, p. 489.

29. Ibid., pp. 488–89.

30. Marx does not clearly and fully spell out his understanding of the truly human being and the truly human community. As points 1 and 2 in this section make clear, we have to look to the opposite of slavery (freedom) and of alienation (integration) to get at Marx's positive meaning of freedom and integration. Both concepts, as I have argued, illuminate his under-standing of the truly human being and community. We also have to look to the opposites of other objectionable features that Marx finds in the existing society, even in the political democracy of a perfected Christian state, to get at one of his early key terms, *"real* species-being." Thus: "Political democracy is Christian in the sense that man, not merely one man but every man, is there considered a sovereign being, a supreme being; but it is uneducated,

unsocial man, man just as he is in his fortuitous existence, man as he has been corrupted, lost to himself, alienated, subjected to the rule of inhuman conditions and elements, by the whole organization of our society—in short man who is not yet a *real* species-being." *On the Jewish Question*, in Tucker, p. 39.

31. *Contribution to the Critique of Hegel's* Philosophy of Right: *Introduction*, in Tucker, p. 60. See also: "The emancipation of Germany is only possible in practice if one adopts the point of view of that theory according to which man is the highest being for man" (Ibid., p. 65). And: "*Every* emancipation is a *restoration* of the human world and of human relationships to *man himself*." (*On the Jewish Question*, in Tucker, p. 60).

32. *Contribution to the Critique of Hegel's* Philosophy of Right: *Introduction*, in Tucker, p. 60.

33. *On the Jewish Question*, in Tucker, p. 43.

34. Ibid., p. 45. And also, p. 51: "Only under the sway of Christianity, which *objectifies all* national, natural, moral and theoretical relationships, could civil society separate itself completely from the life of the state, sever all the species-bonds of man, establish egoism and selfish need in their place, and dissolve the human world into a world of atomistic, antagonistic individuals."

35. *Economic and Philosophic Manuscripts of 1844*, in Tucker, pp. 88–89.

36. Ibid., p. 91.

37. *Critique of the Gotha Program* (written in 1875, published in 1891), in Tucker, p. 531.

38. *Economic and Philosophic Manuscripts of 1844*, in Tucker, p. 92.

39. For example, in *The Germany Ideology: Part I; Manifesto of the Communist Party; Capital,* all in Tucker.

40. Economic and Philosophic Manuscripts of 1844, in Tucker, p. 93.

41. *Contribution to the Critique of Hegel's* Philosophy of Right: *Introduction*, in Tucker, p. 54.

42. Ibid., p. 57.

43. Ibid., p. 62.

44. Ibid., pp. 62–65.

45. *Theses on Feuerbach* (written in 1845, published in 1888), from thesis number I, in Tucker, p. 143.

46. *Theses on Feuerbach*, thesis number II, in Tucker, p. 144.

47. *Contribution to the Critique of Hegel's* Philosophy of Right: *Introduction*, in Tucker, p. 54.

48. *Economic and Philosophic Manuscripts of 1844*, in Tucker, p. 80.

3
Marx and the Radical Social Scientific Analysis and "Criticism of Everything Existing"

INTRODUCTION

Marx's values and vision, explored in Chapter 2, sensitized Marx to what to look for in the real world. They particularly sensitized him to investigate the plight of the proletariat as the least free, to explore the scientific reasons explaining that plight, and to uncover a theory of social change that would clarify the action required to overcome that plight. Marx argued that his values and vision are, in fact, in the process of being fulfilled in history. Marx's social scientific approach employs a particular logical, historical, and scientific method. His logic is strongly dialectical. His history emphasizes the primacy of material and economic forces. His science seeks to go beyond superficial and illusory appearances to the truth of the world.

In presenting Marx's social science I focus primarily, but not exclusively, on his analysis and criticism of the existing nineteenth century bourgeois, capitalistic order. I attempt to do so by addressing myself, in the second section of this chapter, to three major interrelated points: (1) Marx's conception of criticism, (2) Marx's materialist conception of history, and (3) Marx's substantive criticism of the bourgeois, capitalist order.

For Marx, inheriting as he did the philosophical tradition of Kant and Hegel, *kritik* or *critique* (criticism) is a powerful tool of philosophical and social scientific analysis. Marx's criticism focuses on the radical truth of human earthly existence, explores the reasons for the alienation and exploitation of the great mass of human beings (the proletariat), and directs his findings toward revolutionary change.

Marx's materialistic conception of history provides a valuable guiding philosophy for his criticism. His theory of history, despite its sometimes puzzling ambiguities and its seeming contradictions, supports and illuminates his criticism.

It makes sense to focus on two important aspects of the bourgeois, capitalist order—its economic foundation and its superstructure—because Marx does precisely that. He is a radical critic because he sees a huge gap between the fulfillment of his preferred values (those explored in the preceding chapter) and their condition in the nineteenth century bourgeois, capitalist order. He is eager to demonstrate the social scientific analysis that reveals the real reasons for that gap and, moreover, what action can be taken to bridge that gap.

In the third section of this chapter I attempt a critique of Marx's critique, and finally, in the fourth section, I sum up my findings and render an appraisal of Marx's radical "criticism of everything existing." I attempt to answer the question: Is Marx's social scientific analysis and criticism within what I have identified in Chapter 1 as the tradition of prophetic politics?

MARX'S CRITICISM OF THE BOURGEOIS CAPITALIST ORDER

Marx's Concept of Criticism

Very early in his life Marx, influenced by the philosophical tradition in which he had been schooled, adopts the habit of criticism. "The watchword of the young Karl Marx, as of his Young Hegelian associates generally, was *Kritik*—criticism."[1] Technically, criticism involves analyzing the ideas of other thinkers. David McLellan points out that the term "critique" "had a great vogue among the Young Hegelians," and that the "approach it represented—reflecting on and working over the ideas of others—was very congenial to Marx, who preferred to develop his own ideas by critically analyzing those of others."[2] In 1844 Marx wrote that "what we have to accomplish . . . [is a] . . . *ruthless* criticism of everything existing. . . ." The criticism must be "ruthless in two senses: The criticism must not be afraid of its own conclusions, nor of conflict with the powers that be."[3] Marx, in his criticism, attempts to get at the fundamental truth of human beings and the real world in which they live. He seeks not only to understand the world truthfully and fully, but also to point toward that change in the world that would bring it in accord with that truthful understanding. "The philosophers have only *interpreted* the world, in various ways; the point, however, is to *change* it."[4]

Marx holds that criticism must be radical and must focus on man. "To be radical is to grasp things by the root. But for man the root is man himself."[5] A radical criticism must focus on man's "*real* happiness," full human universal emancipation. It must "unmask human self-alienation" by criticizing conditions on this earth, enslaving conditions, that perpetuate such alienation and prevent emancipation. Religious, social, or political illusions that prevent people from establishing *"the truth of this world,"* the truth of their real condition in the only real world humans can know, must be dispelled by criticism. Criticism must not hesitate to be indignant, to denounce. Unafraid, criticism must look forward to destroying the alienating order, to overthrowing abasing conditions.[6]

In seeking to explore "universal human emancipation" criticism must focus on "genuine human problems," in an empirical, practical way. Criticism, insists Marx, must deal with "social and political reality," and especially with the most important and neglected reality, the condition of a universal suffering class, the proletariat.[7] This, of course, calls for a penetrating investigation of the bourgeois, capitalist order.

Criticism must also use the "dialectic method."[8] For Marx the dialetic "includes in its comprehension an affirmative recognition of the existing state of things, at the same time also, the recognition of the negation of that state, of its inevitable breaking up; because it regards every historically developed social form as in fluid movement, and therefore takes into account its transient nature not less than its momentary existence; because it lets nothing impose upon it, and is in its essence critical and revolutionary.[9] The "dialectic method"—whose logic emphasizes negation, contradiction, change, and resolution in history—thus enables Marx to examine capitalism and its conflicts, and to understand how communism would emerge out of capitalism.

Marx's critical method—which thus relies upon both logic and history—is also scientific in the sense that it seeks to go beyond superficial appearances, beyond what has been called brute empiricism, in order to grasp the deeper meaning of reality. Only in this way could deceiving appearances be unmasked. Only in this way could illusions be dispelled. Only in this way could one get at the real truth of the world, uncover the true explanation, for example, of exploitation. Indeed, Marx even contends in Volume III of *Capital* that "all science would be superfluous if the outward appearance and the essence of things coincided."[10] Howard and King sum up Marx's position as follows: "In Marx's view . . . appearances are illusory; 'reality as it appears' to social actors is deceptive. He talks of 'reality' as hidden or concealed by 'appearance.' . . . It is the role of scientific political economy to penetrate through appearances to the reality, and to make appearances scientifically comprehensible. . . ."[11]

It is, therefore, reasonably clear that Marx's philosophical concept of criticism calls upon him (1) to analyze and criticize the existing order within the framework of his ethical values (especially his concern for universal human emancipation), (2) to seek to understand the conditions of human alienation and exploitation (and especially that of the most oppressed class, the proletariat), and (3) to utilize his criticism to illuminate that action required to alter those conditions and achieve that emancipation. His criticism is, therefore, simultaneously ethical, scientific, and action-oriented. Moreover, as we next see, his criticism is guided and tremendously strengthened by his materialistic conception of history—a conception that takes Marx's social science critique considerably beyond the sometimes empty analysis of the Young Hegelians.

Marx's Materialistic Conception of History

To understand more fully Marx's criticism of the nineteenth century bourgeois, capitalist order we must clearly understand his theory of history, and particularly his materialistic conception of history. This theory helps us to understand where that bourgeois order comes from, why it functions the way it does, and why (in Marx's judgment) it must give way to a future communist order. Marx's conception of history is not free of ambiguities and seeming contradictions. Yet, recognizing these, it is possible to articulate his general orientation and significant emphases.[12]

Marx sees a pattern at work in history, a pattern that reveals important relationships about human life in history. He also sees change in history. Understanding this pattern and such change helps to link theory and practice; such understanding sets the stage for the fulfillment of universal human emancipation. Let us first examine the interrelated elements of this pattern—life, material forces of production, economic and social relations of production, society, state, and the rest of the superstructure—before turning to Marx's view of change in history.

In emphasizing life as the "first premise" in his pattern Marx's general materialistic emphasis is unmistakable. For Marx the "first premise of all human existence and, therefore, of all history" is the premise "that men must be in a position to live in order to be able to 'make history.' But life involves before everything else eating and drinking, a habitation, clothing and many other things. The first historical act is thus the production of the means to satisfy these needs, the production of material life itself."[13] Human beings thus engage in material production to satisfy the basic needs of life. In engaging in such production they begin to create their own lives, and their history.

To understand human history it is therefore very important to understand material productive forces. Marx writes that what individuals "are, therefore, coincides with their production, both with *what* they produce and with *how* they produce."[14] It is thus especially important to understand the productive forces in human history and the economic and social relations that correspond to, and that emerge to protect and advance, those forces. By productive forces Marx understands the means of production and labor power. The nonhuman means of production include such instruments of production as machinery and tools. Labor power also involves the strength, skill, and knowledge of workers. The relations of production involve the economic and social patterns of control of those productive forces. These relations involve the economic ownership of productive forces, and those property and legal relations affecting control of productive forces.[15]

According to Marx, the interrelated forces and relations of production provide the foundation for society's superstructure. More precisely, "The sum total of these relations of production [which themselves "correspond to a definite stage of development of their material productive forces"] constitute the economic structure of society, the real foundation, on which rises a legal and political superstructure and to which correspond definite forms of social consciousness."[16]

Society (especially civil society) is a concept, used early by Marx but not subsequently developed, that is nonetheless very helpful in understanding his view of bourgeois society. Marx identifies society with the totality of economic and social relations. More precisely he holds: "The relations of production in their totality constitute what are called the social relations, society, and, specifically, a society at a definite stage of historical development, a society with a peculiar, distinctive character. *Ancient* society, *feudal* society, *bourgeois* society are such totalities of production relations, each of which at the same time denotes a special stage of development in the history of mankind."[17] As he uses it, civil or bourgeois society is closely related to nineteenth century forces and relations of production. Marx thus understands civil society as the "sum total" of the bourgeois "material conditions" of life. Here Marx follows Hegel and the English and French thinkers of the eighteenth century. Marx holds that the "anatomy of civil society is to be sought in political economy."[18]

Civil society, Marx writes, is "determined by . . . existing productive forces." Civil society "embraces the whole commercial and industrial life of a given stage." Civil society is "the social organization evolving directly out of production and commerce." Civil society "forms the basis of the State and the rest of the idealistic superstructure." So understood, civil society is closely related to the productive forces and relations of society. It seems in large part synonymous with the economic structure of society and a significant part of the foundation on which the state and other aspects of the superstructure rest. Civil society is thus fundamentally the economic world of bourgeois society, beyond the family, but yet contrasted to political society or the state. Civil society is characterized by material, economic self-interest, by bourgeois property relations, by the actions of egoistic, atomistic, selfish individuals. It is a fragmented society full of conflicts and misery.[19] Peculiar to bourgeois society in the nineteenth century, it will be abolished with the advent of communism.

As we noted above, the "sum total" of the relations of production constitutes the economic structure of society, the real foundation, on which rises a legal and political superstructure and to which correspond definite forms of social consciousness." For Marx the "mode of production of material life conditions the social, political and intellectual life process in general."[20] It seems reasonably clear moreover that the superstructure also includes, in addition to the "legal and political," the "religious, aesthetic" and the "philosophic" aspects of human life.[21]

Marx's language about the relationship between foundation and superstructure does not enable us to say that Marx is a rigid technological determinist, or a rigid economic determinist, but it is unmistakably clear that, for Marx, technological and economic factors are primary and powerful in all aspects of human life.[22] Generally, but not invariably, Marx sees "the executive of the modern State" as "but a committee for managing the common affairs of the whole bourgeoisie.[23]

Although Marx sometimes notes that the elements of the superstructure may influence the foundation, that there is, in other words, a complex reciprocal relationship at work, the main weight of his argument emphasizes the powerful and abiding influence of productive forces and relations on politics, religion, philosophy, and ethics. Marx emphasizes and reemphasizes this point.

"The production of ideas, of conceptions, of consciousness, is at first directly interwoven with the material activity and the material intercourse of men, the language of real life. Conceiving, thinking, the mental intercourse of men, appear at this stage as the direct efflux of their material behavior. The same applies to mental production as expressed in the language of politics, laws, morality, religion, metaphysics, etc., of a people. Men are the producers of their conceptions, ideas, etc.—real, active men, as they are conditioned by a definite development of their productive forces and of the intercourse corresponding to these, up to its furthest forms."[24]

And again: "Morality, religion, metaphysics, all the rest of ideology and their corresponding forms of consciousness, thus no longer retain the semblance of independence. They have no history, no development; but men, developing their material production and their material intercourse, alter, along with this their real existence, their thinking and the products of their thinking. Life is not determined by consciousness, but consciousness by life."[25]

And again: "Does it require deep intuition to comprehend that man's ideas, views and conceptions, in one word, man's consciousness, changes with every change in the conditions of his material existence, in his social relations and in his social life. . . .What else does the history of ideas prove, than that intellectual production changes its character in proportion as material production is changed? The ruling ideas of each age have ever been the ideas of its ruling class."[26]

Elsewhere, however, and to the chagrin of those who cannot accept inconsistency or complexity in Marx's position, Marx argues for an active role for people in changing circumstances. People, he seems to be contending, are not powerless puppets, shaped irresistibly by circumstances. "The materialist doctrine that men are products of circumstances and upbringing, and that, therefore, changed men are products of other circumstances and changed upbringing, forgets that it is men who change circumstances and that it is essential to educate the educator himself."[27] This suggests clearly a positive, somewhat independent role for purposive people in changing circumstances that influence ideas and other elements of the superstructure. However, the limits to, and conditions of, people's changing their objective circumstances are not set forth. We have to conclude, on the basis of Marx's general philosophy of history, that the changes that people can make can only be in accord with the shaping forces of history.

The pattern that Marx sees in history—life, material productive forces, relations of production, society (civil society for the bourgeois age), state and superstructure—is dynamic and involves change in history. Changes in material productive forces lead to changes in the economic and social relations of production. Thus: "The social relations within which individuals produce, *the social relations of production, change, are transformed, with the change and development of the material means of production, the productive forces.*"[28] Changes in productive forces and relations, as we have seen, lead in turn to changes in society, and to changes in the state, in law, religion, philosophy, and ethics.

Marx's most famous formulation of his understanding of the process of change—part of the "guiding thread for my studies"—is as follows: "At a certain stage of their development, the material productive forces of society come into conflict with the existing relations of production, or—what is but a legal expression for the same thing—with the property relations within which they have been at work hitherto. From forms of development of the productive forces these relations turn into their fetters. Then begins an epoch of social revolution. With the change of the economic foundation the entire immense superstructure is more or less rapidly transformed."[29]

But, Marx insists, change only takes place when the old economic and social order is fully developed. For example, feudalism had to ripen before it was replaced by capitalism; and, similarly, capitalism will have to ripen before being replaced by communism. "No social order ever perishes before all the productive forces for which there is room in it have developed; and new, higher relations of production never appear before the material conditions of their existence have matured in the womb of the old society itself. Therefore mankind always sets itself only such tasks as it can solve; since, looking at the matter more closely, it will always be found that the task itself arises only when the material conditions for its solution already exist or are at least in the process of formation."[30] In brief, change can only occur when the material conditions for such change are ripe.

Marx sees a number of stages in historical development, and maintains that the bourgeois stage, the existing stage for Western civilization, will be succeeded by communism, first in Europe and then throughout the world. "In broad outline Asiatic, ancient, feudal, and modern bourgeois modes of production can be designated as progressive epochs in the economic formation of society. The bourgeois relations of production are the last antagonistic form of the social process of production. . . ."[31] Marx argues that "productive forces developing in the womb of bourgeois society create the material conditions for the solution of that antagonism." And then he adds, strikingly: "This social formation brings, therefore, the prehistory of human society to a close."[32]

Marx detected new and developing capitalist productive forces in feudal society coming into conflict with feudal economic and social relations that fettered those forces. Incipient capitalists wanted to be free of wage, price, guild, and trade restrictions. These restrictions inhibited productive growth. Enhanced capitalist production and trade only became possible when restrictive feudal economic and social relations were removed, and replaced by capitalistic relations—corresponding to the new, developing capitalist productive forces, and sustaining and facilitating those capitalist forces.

Capitalism, too, in time will cease to expand productive forces. Capitalism calls forth a working class and exploits it. Capitalism engenders socialized production as well as a socially conscious and organized working class. Capitalism significantly centralizes, as well as socializes, the production process. Capitalism is beset by productive difficulties in periods of economic depression and crisis. Rational in important respects, capitalism is anarchic in other respects. Capitalist economic and social relations, in turn, fetter a new and developing system of socialized production, and inhibit and exploit the proletariat, a crucial productive force in that system of socialized production. Communism will then emerge as the resolution of capitalism's difficulties—freeing the productive system to expand and meet human needs in a more rational way.[33] This is the pattern of change Marx saw at work in modern history.

Antagonism, conflict, struggle—especially class struggle—are key ideas in Marx's understanding of this pattern of economic and social change. In *The German Ideology: Part I* he summarizes his conclusions about the process of change from the bourgeois to the communist stage. This early formulation highlights the linkage between changing productive forces, the proletariat, and revolutionary activity.

"In the development of productive forces there comes a stage when productive forces and means of intercourse are brought into being, which, under the existing relationships, only cause mischief, and are no longer productive but destructive forces (machinery and money); and connected with this a class is called forth, which has to bear all the burdens of society without enjoying its advantages, which, ousted from society, is forced into the most decided antagonisms to all other classes; a class which forms the majority of all members of society, and from which emanates the consciousness of the necessity of a fundamental revolution, the communist consciousness. . . ." The revolutionary struggle of the proletariat is directed at the bourgeois class in power. In previous revolutions private property remained "unscathed." The communist revolution will abolish private property and "the rule of all classes, with the classes themselves. . . ."[34]

Thus Marx sees "a historical movement going on under our very eyes."[35] Forces in this movement are rooted in the "material means of production"—in the productive forces of society. They are rooted, too, in the "civil society"—the social "relations of production in their totality"—that develop from the "material means of production." This movement is characterized by class struggle, a clash between changing "material means of production" and capitalist relations of production. In the bourgeois period, this struggle will culminate in the demise of the bourgeoisie, the victory of the proletariat, and the advent of a new economic and social system: communism.

The fuller operation of this revolutionary struggle we will examine in Chapter 4. Here we can conclude our treatment of Marx's materialistic conception of history by emphasizing Marx's view of history as class struggle, of the nineteenth century culmination of that struggle in the battle between bourgeoisie and proletariat, and the inevitable triumph of the proletariat.

In a remarkably sweeping generalization Marx holds: "The history of all hitherto existing society is the history of class struggles." He maintains that "Freeman and slave, patrician and plebian, lord and serf, guild-master and journeyman, in a word, oppressor and oppressed, stood in constant opposition to one another, carried on an uninterrupted, now hidden, now open fight, a fight that each time ended, either in a revolutionary reconstitution of society at large, or in the common ruin of the contending classes."[36]

Marx emphasizes that "Our epoch, the epoch of the bourgeoisie, possesses, however, this distinctive feature: it has simplified the class antagonisms: Society as a whole is more and more splitting up into two great hostile camps, into two great classes directly facing each other: Bourgeoisie and Proletariat."[37] Moreover, Marx insists: "The essential condition for the existence, and for the sway of the bourgeois class, is the formation and augmentation of capital; the condition for capital is wage-labour. Wage-labour rests exclusively on competition between the labourers. The advance of industry, whose involutary promoter is the bourgeoisie, replaces the isolation of the labourers, due to competition, by their revolutionary combination, due to association. The development of Modern Industry, therefore, cuts from under its feet the very foundation on which the bourgeoisie produces and appropriates products. What the bourgeoisie, therefore, produces, above all, is its own grave-diggers. Its fall and the victory of the proletariat are equally inevitable."[38]

Let us turn next to Marx's fuller criticism of the economic foundation and superstructure of the bourgeois, capitalist order. In examining this fuller criticism, we return again—as we must—to Marx's social scientific understanding of why it is that capitalism will give way to communism.

Marx's Substantive Criticism of the Bourgeois Capitalist Order

As we have already seen, Marx holds that criticism must focus on real, human problems, on how people produce, on economic and social relations, on the proletariat, on private property, on capitalists. Criticism must be truthful and radical, unafraid to engage the capitalist powers-that-be, unafraid to drive toward the goal of universal human emancipation. Criticism, moreover, must be richly empirical and scientific—revealing the actual conditions of the working class, penetrating beyond superficial appearance to the underlying reality of the actual operation of the capitalist economy and the bourgeois social and political order; revealing too, the newly emerging (communist) productive forces that are in conflict with capitalist economic and social relations and that point toward a new communist society. Criticism must also use the "dialectic method" in order better to understand the process of change rooted in changing material, economic, and social conditions. As Marx's concept of criticism constitutes a powerful tool for analysis, so his materialistic conception of history provides him with a theory that significantly guides his criticism.

Marx's criticism is guided by an outlook that sensitizes him not only to examine the actual condition of the working class and the actual functioning of the bourgeois capitalist order, but also to look for the "natural laws of capitalist production," of those "tendencies working with iron necessity toward inevitable results."[39] As Marx writes in the Preface to the first German edition of *Capital*, his "ultimate aim" is to lay bare the economic law of motion of modern society."[40] Beyond revealing the plight of the proletariat, Marx seeks to answer, scientifically, two key questions: Why and how does exploitation of the worker take place? Why and how will exploitation be overcome? These questions guide the following analysis.

We can examine Marx's substantive criticism of the bourgeois capitalist order under two interrelated headings: (1) his criticism of the bourgeois economic foundation, and (2) his criticism of the bourgeois superstructure.

First, we set forth Marx's description of the lot of workers under capitalism, his theoretical understanding of the reasons for the exploitative operation of capitalism, and his scientific view of why and how exploitation would be overcome. Second, we focus on Marx's scathing criticism of the bourgeois superstructure and emphasize particularly his reasons for rejecting non-Marxist alternatives. This presentation sets the stage for Marx's theory of social action and his revolutionary advocacy of communism as the way to usher in freedom.

Marx's Criticism of the Economic Foundation of Bourgeois Capitalism

The Condition of the Working Class.—Marx is most concerned with the condition of the working class under capitalism. His empirical description of working class conditions, influenced early by Engels' 1844 study of *The Condition of the Working Class in England*, and reinforced later by reports of official British investigations, is vivid and indignant. Marx makes no effort to conceal (what I would call) his ethical judgments about what he is reporting. Factual description and evaluatory characterizations of what is being reported are mingled. The concepts Marx employs to characterize the condition of the proletariat under capitalism are not difficult to name; they are wage-slavery, despotism, robbery, alienation, exploitation, dehumanization, stunted development. Regardless of Marx's own characterization of these terms, they are clearly ethical evils. Of course, in making his argument, Marx also develops seemingly value-free concepts such as the labor theory of value, surplus value, the distinctions between labor and labor-power, between socially necessary and surplus labor, between variable and constant capital, between use value and exchange value, and so on. We cannot—and need not—present here all aspects of his complex analysis of capitalism; but we can and must focus on those ideas most relevant to our concern to explore Marx within the tradition of prophetic politics.

As early as 1844, and before he had begun his more detailed and systematic empirical research into the operation of capitalism in Britain, then the most advanced capitalist country in Europe, Marx had noted the worker's estrangement and had articulated the disturbing contrast between poor worker and rich capitalist. "*Political economy conceals the estrangement inherent in the nature of labour by not considering the direct relationship between worker* (labour) *and production.* It is true that labour produces for the rich wonderful things—but for the worker it provides privation. It produces palaces—but for the worker, hovels. It produces beauty—but for the worker, deformity. It replaces labour by machines—but some of the workers it throws back to a barbarous type of labour, and the other workers it turns into machines. It produces intelligence—but for the workers idiocy, cretinism.''[41] Very early, then, in his analysis—as we saw very clearly in Chapter 2—Marx holds that the worker's estrangement, or alienation, is rooted in the very nature of capitalist production. What is additionally required is a more thorough, and more scientific, account and explanation of the proletariat's exploitation. This Marx attempts in his masterwork, *Capital*.

In *Capital* Marx spells out more graphically the practical details of the worker's exploitation, and, additionally, presents his economic explanation for such exploitation. First, let me set forth Marx's vivid account of the dreadful working conditions of the proletariat. He writes of the "horrors of overwork," which Marx, ironically and sardonically, calls the "civilised horrors of overwork";[42] about what an English investigator whom Marx quotes calls "'unmitigated slavery, socially, physically, morally, and spiritually'";[43] about "'ragged, half-starved, untaught children''";[44] about "'Death from simple overwork''";[45] about "'getting 18 hours' work out of their men for 12 hours' wages'''";[46] about "'working to death''' as "'the order of the day.'''"[47]

Marx's account of the working day is worth quotation in full. It reveals Marx's passionate and outraged ethical concern as well as his social-scientific analysis. The following passage makes unmistakably clear the link between the young Marx who wrote about alienation and estrangement in *The Economic and Philosophical Manuscripts of 1844* and the mature Marx of *Capital*. This passage also emphatically underscores Marx's passion to pursue an answer to the "why" and "how" of exploitation.

"'What is a working day? What is the length of time during which capital may consume the labour-power whose daily value it buys? How far may the working-day be extended beyond the working-time necessary for the reproduction of labour-power itself?' It has been seen that to these questions capital replies: the working-day contains the full 24 hours, with the deduction of the few hours of repose without which labour-power absolutely refuses its services again. Hence it is self-evident that the labourer is nothing else, his whole life through, than labour-power, that therefore all his disposable time is by nature and law labour-time, to be devoted to the self-expansion of capital. Time for education, for intellectual development, for the fulfilling of social functions and for social intercourse, for the free-play of his bodily and mental activity, even the rest time of Sunday (and that in a country of Sabbatarians!)—moonshine! But in its blind unrestrainable passion, its werewolf hunger for surplus-labour, capital oversteps not only the moral, but even the merely physical maximum bonds of the working-day. It usurps the time for growth, development, and healthy maintenance of the body. It steals the time required for the consumption of fresh air and sunlight. It higgles over a mealtime, incorporating it where possible with the process of production itself, so that food is given to the labourer as a mere means of production, as coal is supplied to the boiler, grease and oil to the machinery. It reduces the sound sleep needed for the restoration, reparation, refreshment of the bodily powers to just so many hours of torpor as the revival of an organism, absolutely exhausted, renders essential. It is not the normal maintenance of the labour-power which is to determine the limits of the working-day; it is the greatest possible daily expenditure of labour-power, no matter how diseased, compulsory, and painful it may be, which is to determine the limits of the labourers' period of repose. Capital cares nothing for the length of life of labour-power. All that concerns it is simply and solely the maximum of labour-power that can be rendered fluent in a working-day. It attains this end by shortening the extent of the labourers' life, as a greedy farmer snatches increased produce from the soil by robbing it of its fertility.

"The capitalistic mode of production (essentially the production of surplus-value, the absorption of surplus-labour), produces thus, with the extension of the working-day, not only the deterioration of human labour-power by robbing it of its normal, moral and physical, conditions of development and function. It produces also the premature exhaustion and death of this labour-power itself. It extends the labourer's time of production during a given period by shortening his actual lifetime."[48]

Marx's criticism of the worker's life in the factory is mordant. Factory work, he writes, "exhausts the nervous system to the uttermost"; "it does away with the many-sided play of the muscles, and confiscates every atom of freedom, both in bodily and intellectual activity."[49] Of the "material conditions under which factory labour is carried on," Marx declares: "every organ of sense is injured in an equal degree by artificial elevation of the temperature, by the dust-laden atmosphere, by the deafening noise, not to mention danger to life and limb among the thickly crowded machinery, which, with the regularity of the seasons, issues its list of the killed and wounded in the industrial battle. Economy of the social means of production, matured and forced as in a hothouse by the factory system, is turned, in the hands of capital, into systematic robbery of what is necessary for the life of the workman while he is at work, robbery of space, light, air, and of protection to his person against the dangerous and unwholesome accompaniments of the productive process, not to mention the robbery of appliances for the comfort of the workman."[50]

Capitalism thus operates to dominate, exploit, and estrange the worker. During work the worker is subject to despotism—to slavery, misery, brutality. The following passage in *Capital* is also worth quotation at length—illustrating as it does the important link between the deplorable condition of the worker and the operation of the capitalistic system, an operation that connects labor's hours of work and productiveness with surplus-value (a key term that we will examine shortly), and with the worker's slavery, alienation, dehumanization, and stunted development, in brief, the worker's exploitation.

"We saw . . . when analysing the production of relative surplus-value: within the capitalist system all methods for raising the social productiveness of labour are brought about at the cost of the individual labourer; all means for the development of production transform themselves into means of domination over, and exploitation of, the producers; they mutilate the labourer into a fragment of man, degrade him to the level of an appendage of a machine, destroy every remnant of charm in his work and turn it into a hated toil; they estrange from him the intellectual potentialities of the labour-process in the same proportion as science is incorporated in it as an independent power; they distort the conditions under which he works, subject him during the labour-process to a despotism the more hateful for its meanness; they transform his life-time into working-time, and drag his wife and child beneath the wheels of the Juggernaut of capital. But all methods for the production of suplus-value are at the same time methods of accumulation; and every extension of accumulation becomes again a means for the development of those methods. It follows therefore that in proportion as capital accumulates, the lot of the labourer, be his payment high or low, must grow worse. The law, finally, that always equilibrates the relative surplus-population, or industrial reserve army, to the extent and energy of accumulation, this law rivets the labourer to capital more firmly than the wedges of Vulcan did Prometheus to the rock. It establishes an accumulaton of misery, corresponding with the accumulation of capital. Accumulation of wealth at one pole is, therefore, at the same time accumulation of misery, agony of toil, slavery, ignorance, brutality, mental degradation, at the opposite pole, i.e. on the side of the class that produces its own product in the form of capital."[51]

The Why and How of Capitalist Exploitation.—The depiction above is without doubt a powerfully damning indictment of capitalism as it operated in Marx's lifetime. However, to understand more fully the reasons that explain the "slavery," "exploitation," "domination," "robbery," and "alienation" that Marx sees in the capitalist system, we must examine more fully and precisely Marx's analysis of capitalism. We must understand the way in which it accumulated capital; the meaning and key role of surplus value; capitalism's contradictions, difficulties, and weaknesses. We must especially highlight certain key aspects of the operation of capitalism. We must appreciate the progressive socialization of certain aspects of capitalist production and yet its unplanned, anarchic character. We must perceive the significance of the centralization of capital and monopoly; the growth of the industrial reserve army; unionization; the continuing misery of workers under capitalism; capitalistic crises related to competition, overproduction, industrial depression, the falling rate of profit. We must see the global reach of capitalism. And we must especially comprehend the failure of a capitalist economic and social order to permit the development of productive forces to satisfy human needs.[52] These same factors, we shall subsequently see, also illuminate the why and how of the overcoming of capitalism.

Capitalism, Marx argues, makes for the slavery, estrangement, alienation, dehumanization, and stunted development—in brief, the exploitation—of the worker because it is driven to accumulate capital and profit. It must use the worker—his labor power—to produce capital and surplus value (the source of profit). Beyond his subsistence wage, however, the worker contributes extra hours of labor (surplus labor) for free to the capitalist; these free extra hours produce surplus value, commodities that the capitalist profits from. Marx holds that "the accumulation of capital presupposes surplus-value; [that] surplus-value presupposes capitalistic production; [that] capitalistic production presupposes the pre-existence of considerable masses of capital and labour-power in the producers of commodities."[53]

But how did capitalist accumulation get started? Marx's answer is instructive because it makes clear that exploitation has always characterized capitalism. Marx argues that the breakup of feudalism, slavery, and early imperialism all played crucial roles. A "primitive accumulation" of capital preceded capitalistic accumulation.[54] And such "primitive accumulation" was "anything but idyllic."[55] In such accumulation "conquest, enslavement, robbery, murder, briefly force," played "the great part."[56]

"The economic structure of capitalistic society has grown," Marx writes, "out of the economic structure of feudal society. The dissolution of the latter set free the elements of the former." Marx sees "primitive accumulation" as "the historical process of divorcing the producer from the means of production."[57] This divorce came with the "dissolution" of feudal society. Producers became "wage earners" when they were emancipated from serfdom "and from the fetters of the guilds." The "new freedmen became sellers of themselves," but only "after they had been robbed of all their own means of production, and of all the guarantees of existence afforded by the old feudal arrangements." This "expropriation" was "written in the annals of mankind in letters of blood and fire."[58]

Money and commodities could now be transformed into capital: the owners of money could buy "other people's labour-power."[59] The starting point of "the development that gave rise to the wage-labourer as well as to the capitalist, was the servitude of the labourer. The advance consisted in a change of form of this servitude, in the transformation of feudal exploitation into capitalist exploitation."[60] This transformation occurred when the peasant was driven from the soil; peasants were "suddenly and forcibly torn from their means of subsistence, and hurled as free and 'unattached' proletarians on the labour market."[61] This was the "prelude of the revolution that laid the foundation of the capitalist mode of production"; it occurred "in the last third of the 15th, and the first decade of the 16th century."[62]

Marx notes that the primitive accumulation and development of capitalist production was aided by human slavery. The "development of capitalist production during the manufacturing period" in England, for example, was characterized by human slavery: African slavery. "Liverpool waxed fat on the slave-trade. This was its method of primitive accumulation."[63] British cotton manufacturers processed American cotton produced by slave labor. Moreover, the "cotton industry introduced child-slavery in England," and stimulated in the United States "the transformation of the earlier, more or less patriarchal slavery, into a system of commercial exploitation." "In fact, the veiled slavery of the wage-workers in Europe needed, for its pedestal, slavery pure and simple in the new world."[64] Capital, Marx concludes, comes into the world "dripping from head to foot, from every pore, with blood and dirt."[65]

The "rosy dawn of the era of capitalist production," Marx writes sardonically, was "signalized" by the "discovery of gold and silver in America, the extirpation, enslavement and entombment in mines of the aboriginal population, the beginning of the conquest and looting of the East Indies, the turning of Africa into a warren for the commerical hunting of blackskins."[66]

Marx holds that early capitalism passed through several stages, through "manufacture" to "modern industry," as capital relations clearly emerge. In the stage of "manufacture," as Howard and King put it, we find "the emergence of exploitation and surplus value, which forms the basis of the capitalists' profit. . . . " In the stage of "modern industry" there emerges "the social relations of free competition between all capitalists in *all* industries." "It is here [write Howard and King] that Marx seeks to show how values are 'transformed' into prices of production, and surplus value into profit on total capital. . . . " "Modern industry," brought on by an industrial revolution, "is characterized by factory production, power machinery and rapid technical change."[67]

But why does the operation of capitalism necessitate, in Marx's judgment, the worker's slavery, alienation, dehumanization, and stunted development—his exploitation? Here we come again to the concept of surplus value and the secret of capitalist accumulation. The capitalist maximizes his profits, increases his capital, and his surplus value, by paying his workers only a subsistence wage and by extracting from his workers hours beyond "necessary working time," hours put in to earn that subsistence wage. The capitalist, that is, extracts from his workers additional hours beyond what the workers put in to obtain their subsistence wage, hours of work that produce commodities (and therefore value) for the capitalist. The surplus value created by labor power uncompensated beyond subsistence wages is the secret of capitalist accumulation.[68]

Given this analysis, Marx could argue that capital "is dead labour" and "vampire-like, only lives by sucking living labour, and lives the more, the more labour it sucks."[69] "The directing motive, the end and aim of capitalist production, is to extract the greatest possible amount of surplus-value, and consequently to exploit labour-power to the greatest possible extent."[70] Under capitalism, Marx declares, "the wage-worker has permission to work for his own subsistence, that is, *to live*, only in so far as he works for a certain time gratis for the capitalist." According to Marx, "the whole capitalist system of production turns on the increase of this gratis labour by extending the working day or by developing the [worker's] productivity, that is, increasing the intensity of labour power, etc." Consequently, "the system of wage labour is a system of slavery, and indeed of a slavery which becomes more severe in proportion as the social productive forces of labour develop, whether the worker receives better or worse payment.[71]

Thus since it is in the interest of the capitalist to accumulate in this way, he has a financial self-interest in keeping the working day as long as possible, in intensifying the activity of the laborer (to obtain more production by the worker in the same number of working hours), and in introducing machinery that facilitates "more work done in a shorter time." Such a situation inevitably involves exploitation of the worker.

The key formula for the rate of surplus value Marx puts as follows:

"the ratio $\dfrac{\text{surplus working time}}{\text{necessary working time}}$ determines the rate of surplus value."[72]

Wage slavery, then, is the inevitable lot of the worker under capitalism, an economic system that lives on, and profits from, stolen labor. The capitalist's control over the worker is, moreover, despotic. The worker is clearly exploited. All these ideas—wage-slavery, despotism, exploitation—are related to the concept of alienation. In treating alienation earlier in his life, Marx had argued that the worker does not have control over his product, is not free in his work (his primary life) activity, is estranged from his species-being (his humanity), and is separated from his fellow men. These aspects of alienation are also visible in the worker's "slavery," in the capitalist's despotic control over the worker, and in the worker's exploitation.

The worker makes slave-like, despotically controlled, exploited contributions through his surplus-labor to surplus-value, to the production of commodities over which he has no control, to products from which he has been effectively separated. The slave-like, despotically treated, exploited worker is also separated from joyous work-activity; he is, in this work-activity, subjected to dreadful, most unfavorable work conditions; and the long hours of surplus labor only intensify his lack of freedom. The worker, in his slave-like, despotic, exploited labor is divorced from his own humanity, what makes him truly human, and this divorce is underscored by the oppressive, dehumanizing conditions under which he labors. Finally, he is estranged from his fellow human beings: from the capitalist who employs and exploits him; and from his fellow workers. The estrangement from his fellow workers is intensified by the competition which, in a capitalist system, pits worker against worker for jobs and subsistence wages, and inures the worker to his enslaved, despotic, exploited life.

Capitalism thus exploits, oppresses, enslaves the worker. This accounts for the gap between the values of freedom, integration, humanity, and development, *and* the miserable reality of the proletariat. If my presentation is accurate, there can, then, be little doubt that Marx's values, expressed early in his life in *The Economic and Philosophic Manuscripts of 1844*, continue to inform his more mature years, and that his economic analysis in *Capital* makes clear the umistakable violations of those values.

Marx's advance in his later writings is in making clear (especially in *Capital*) the reasons for these violations. Here he reveals the why and the how of exploitation in the operation of capitalism. Here he emphasizes (for example, in *Capital* and in the *Manifesto of the Communist Party*) those features of capitalism that characterize its operation and point toward its demise. These are the features that explain why and how exploitation will be overcome. Let me turn now to some of those key features that reveal the richness of Marx's criticism.

Why and How Capitalism Would Be Overcome.—Fundamentally, Marx holds, capitalism is not able to produce abundantly and rationally and consistently to satisfy universal human freedom and needs. Capitalism, Marx readily acknowledges, has made enormous progress—compared to early productive systems—in increasing human productivity, and it has brought a measure of freedom to the bourgeoisie. But it has remained plagued by contradictions, difficulties, weaknesses that prevent it from developing productive capacity further in a genuinely free society. His social scientific analysis, deeply influenced by his values and vision, affirms that capitalism will fall, and capitalistic exploitation will be overcome, because new and developing productive forces are incompatible with existing capitalist economic and social relations.

Marx argues that capitalism has increasingly centralized, and in certain important technical ways socialized, production: Capitalism has brought the proletariat into existence, and with it proletarian consciousness, organization, unionization. Capitalism has intensified class struggle between the two major classes of the nineteenth century—capitalists and workers. Capitalism has required surplus labor to produce profits for capitalists, and an industrial reserve army of workers ever ready to contribute that surplus labor. But capitalism, Marx holds, operates unevenly, irrationally, in an anarchic fashion. Capitalism is characterized by competition, over-production, industrial crises, monopoly, a declining rate of profit, the continuing misery of the proletariat, global reach. All these features of capitalism call attention to weaknesses that, Marx believes, will lead to its downfall and its replacement by a freer, more rational, and more productive system.

Thus competition among capitalist producers heightens the exploitation of workers. Driven to produce and accumulate surplus value, the capitalist overproduces, and this leads to a glut on the market, unemployment, and industrial crises. Capitalists are driven toward monopolistic practices. Capital becomes centralized. Centralization, moreover, is not only economic but political. The activities of the bourgeoisie also enhance urbanization. In addition, the bourgeoisie seeks global markets and gives "a cosmopolitan character to production and consumption in every country."[3] The bourgeoisie universalizes the capitalist mode of production. "It compels all nations, on pain of extinction, to adopt the bourgeois mode of production; it compels them to introduce what it calls civilisation into their midst, i.e., to become bourgeois themselves. In one word, it creates a world after its own image."[4]

In his critical analysis of capitalism's weaknesses, Marx emphasizes the ironic conflicts and crises of modern capitalist production and modern capitalist society. He emphatically stresses the conflict in capitalism between its productive forces and the maintenance of an economic and social system of private property.

"Modern bourgeois society with its relations of production, of exchange and of property, a society that has conjured up such gigantic means of production and exchange, is like the sorcerer, who is no longer able to control the powers of the nether world whom he has called up by his spells. For many decades past the history of industry and commerce is but the history of the revolt of modern productive forces against modern conditions of production, against the propery relations that are the conditions for the existence of the bourgeoisie and of its rule. It is enough to mention the commercial crises that by their periodical return put on its trial, each time more threateningly, the existence of the entire bourgeois society. In these crises there breaks out an epidemic that, in all earlier epochs, would have seemed an absurdity—the epidemic of over-production. Society suddenly finds itself put back into a state of momentary barbarism; it appears as if a famine, a universal war of devastation had cut off the supply of every means of subsistence; industry and commerce seem to be destroyed; and why? Because there is too much civilisation, too much means of subsistence, too much industry, too much commerce. The productive forces at the disposal of society no longer tend to further the development of the conditions of bourgeois property; on the contrary, they have become too powerful for these conditions, by which they are fettered, and so soon as they overcome these fetters, they bring disorder into the whole of bourgeois society, endanger the existence of bourgeois property. The conditions of bourgeois society are too narrow to comprise the wealth created by them. And how does the bourgeoisie get over these crises? On the one hand by enforced destruction of a mass of productive forces; on the other, by the conquest of new markets, and by the more thorough exploitation of the old ones. That is to say, by paving the way for more extensive and more destructive crises, and by diminishing the means whereby crises are prevented.'"[75]

This analysis leads Marx to see capitalism giving way to communism. Marx holds that "capitalist production begets, with the inexorability of a law of Nature, its own negation." The process by which capitalistic private property would be transformed into "socialized property" involves the "expropriation of a few usurpers by the mass of the people."[76]

"Along with the constantly diminishing number of magnates of capital, who usurp and monopolise all advantages of this process of transformation, grows the mass of misery, oppression, slavery, degradation, exploitation; but with this too grows the revolt of the working-class, a class always increasing in numbers, and disciplined, united, organised by the very mechanism of the process of capitalistic production itself. The monopoly of capital becomes a fetter upon the mode of production, which has sprung up and flourishes along with, and under it. Centralisation of the means of production and socialisation of labour at last reach a point where they become incompatible with their capitalistic integument. This integument is burst asunder. The knell of capitalist private property sounds. The expropriators are expropriated."[77]

So it is the case—and here Marx's analysis of capitalism overlaps his theory of revolutionary action—that capitalism produces, socializes, educates, and exploits the proletariat; centralizes and "socializes" the process of production; weakens itself economically in crises; suffers from a diminishing rate of profit; is unable to overcome the contradiction between developing (partly socialized but erratic) forces of production and the economic and social relations of bourgeois society; provides allies for the proletariat in its class struggle; and in other ways sets the stage for its own demise.

" . . . [W]ith the development of industry the proletariat not only increases in number; it becomes concentrated in greater masses, its strength grows, and it feels that strength more."[78] Class conflict leads the workers "to form combinations (Trades Unions)" to protect their interests against the bourgeoisie.[79] The bourgeoisie—itself in "constant battle" with the aristocracy, with other segments of the less progressive bourgeoisie, with the "bourgeoisie of foreign countries"—asks the proletariat for its help in these battles and thus drags "it into the political arena." The bourgeoisie itself, therefore, supplies the proletariat with its own elements of political and general education, in other words, it furnishes the proletariat with weapons for fighting the bourgeoisie."[80] The bourgeoisie is also weakened from its own ranks, politically as well as economically.[81] So Marx could conclude that the "bourgeoisie . . . produces . . . its own grave-diggers," and that its "fall and the victory of the proletariat are equally inevitable."[82]

Marx's criticism of the bourgeoisie leads him to conclude that "the bourgeoisie is unfit any longer to be the ruling class in society, and to impose its conditions of existence upon society as an over-riding law. It is unfit to rule because it is incompetent to assure an existence to its slave within his slavery, because it cannot help letting him sink into such a state. . . . Society can no longer live under this bourgeoisie, in other words, its existence is no longer compatible with society."[83]

It would be a mistake, however, to complete our account of Marx's criticism of the economic foundation of bourgeois capitalism without recalling again Marx's appreciation of the positive contributions of capitalism. The role of the bourgeoisie, Marx emphasizes, has been revolutionary, indeed, "most revolutionary."[84] The bourgeoisie has destroyed feudalism. The bourgeoisie has set the stage for the appropriation of capitalism's "colossal productive forces." And by establishing capitalism world-wide the bourgeoisie has set the stage for the universal triumph of the proletariat.[85] Marx's in-depth analysis of capitalism, which clarifies the why and how of the downfall of capitalism and the triumph of communism, is in harmony with his materialistic conception of history, and also with his values and vision.

To Marx's criticism of the bourgeois superstructure we turn next in order to round out our presentation of Marx's criticism of bourgeois capitalism.

Marx's Criticism of the Bourgeois Superstructure

In his critique of the bourgeois superstructure Marx is again most concerned with illuminating the why and the how of exploitation and of overcoming exploitation. His social scientific concerns, already heightened by his values and vision, set the stage for his theory of revolutionary action. The radical character of his critique—for example, in the *Manifesto*, in *The Eighteenth Brumaire,* in *The Civil War in France,* in the *Circular Letter to Bebel*—again illustrates the continuation of the radical critique begun in such earlier writings as *The Economic and Philosophic Manuscripts.*

As we have already noted, Marx views the material means of production—the material productive forces—as the core of the foundation of society. The sum total of the relations of production, understood as the economic and social relations of production, adds up to civil society. The legal and political superstructure of society rests upon the foundation of the material and economic structure of society. Metaphysics, religion, morality, ethics, aesthetics, ideology—these are, along with state, law, and politics, parts of the superstructure of society.

Moreover, the economic struggle that Marx sees going on in bourgeois capitalist society—a struggle between workers and capitalists—is also a class struggle. The fuller understanding of the character of that class struggle requires Marx to move beyond an analysis of productive forces and relations, narrowly understood in technological and economic terms, to examine the character and operation of the bourgeois superstructure. Marx's examination drives toward, and reinforces, his earlier central conclusion: bourgeois capitalism and bourgeois society cannot be reformed to achieve the values he cherished, but must be overthrown. Again we see that Marx's social scientific analysis and criticism links up with his theory of revolutionary action. In his investigation, the sociological approach that Marx brings to economics he also brings to the bourgeois superstructure.

Critique of Bourgeois Ideas.—Marx's indictment—and it clearly is that—is vitriolic. Empirical and social scientific analysis *and* ethical appraisal are unmistakably intertwined. The dominant ideas of the larger society are the dominant ideas of the bourgeoisie. And they are employed to sustain and perpetuate the bourgeoisie. The key ideas of bourgeois liberalism—especially private property, family, religion, order—sustain capitalism, the bourgeois state, bourgeois law, the exploitative bourgeois institutions of marriage and family, and a religion that dulls the radical, man-oriented consciousness of the worker by focusing on the false consciousness of another life.

Private ownership of the means of production and exchange, as we have already seen, perpetuates the exploitation of the proletariat. The family life of the worker is dehumanized and the family life of the bourgeosie is a sham. Religion is an illusion, an opiate. Even "ideas of religious liberty and freedom of conscience" are bourgeois ideas that "merely give expression to the sway of free competition within the domain of knowledge."[86] Bourgeois morality is hypocritical. The state maintains law and order on behalf of bourgeois, capitalist values and dominance.

All bourgeois occupations are prostituted. "The bourgeoisie has stripped of its halo every occupation hitherto honoured and looked up to with reverent awe. It has converted the physician, the lawyer, the priest, the poet, the man of science, into its paid wage-labourers."[87]

Bourgeois notions of freedom, culture, law, and so on, are ideas that are "the outgrowth of the conditions" of "bourgeois production and bourgeois property," just as bourgeois "jurisprudence is but the will" of the bourgeois "class made into a law for all, a will, whose essential character and direction are determined by the economical conditions" of the bourgeois class.[88]

Marx finds bourgeois talk about the sanctity of the family and education to be as much "clap-trap" as bourgeois talk about the sanctity of private property. Always Marx contrasts bourgeois ideals with bourgeois and proletarian reality. "The bourgeois clap-trap about the family and education, about the hallowed co-relation of parent and child, becomes all the more disgusting, the more, by the action of Modern Industry, all family ties among the proletarians are torn asunder, and their children transformed into simple articles of commerce and instruments of labour."[89] The foundation of the bourgeois family, Marx observes, is "capital . . . private gain."[90] "The bourgeois sees in his wife a mere instrument of production."[91] And the bourgeois treatment of women is less than holy. "Our bourgeois, not content with having the wives and daughters of their proletarians at their disposal, not to speak of common prostitutes, takes the greatest pleasure in seducing each other's wives."[92]

Critique of the Bourgeois State.—Marx's harsh critique of the bourgeois state fits in with his equally harsh critique of other key bourgeois ideas. The bourgeois state is oppressive. Real freedom for the proletariat is not possible in the bourgeois state. Directly or indirectly, the capitalist state perpetuates capitalist rule. A dominant theme in Marx's analysis, only occasionally compromised, is that genuinely radical reform in the liberal bourgeois state, operating under the domination and perpetuation of capitalism, is not possible. This is the fundamental stress in Marx's criticism, even though he is on record as conceding that socialism might possibly occur in some progressive democratic countries.[93] Yet his general rejection of all but his own Marxist alternative, a radical revolution that would overthrow capitalism, is an emphatic and repeated note in Marx's criticism of the bourgeois superstructure.

Primarily, but not invariably, Marx understands the bourgeois state as a "committee for managing the common affairs of the whole bourgeoisie."[94] The state is an organ of coercion and oppression. Marx recognizes that the "centralized State power, with its ubiquitous organs of standing army, police, bureaucracy, clergy, and judicature—organs wrought after the plan of a systematic and hierarchic division of labour—originates from the days of absolute monarchy, serving nascent middle-class society as a mighty weapon in its struggles against feudalism."[95] But now that feudalism had been, for the most part, defeated, the state remains the bourgeoisie's weapon against the proletariat.

Only in his brilliant, if sometimes unpersuasive and sometimes inconsistent, analysis of the advent and rule of Louis Bonaparte in France, does Marx deviate from his general conviction that the bourgeoisie is fully in control of the state. This analysis merits attention—some critics have seen it as an anticipation of fascism—because it demonstrates Marx's view that if the bourgeoisie has to choose between liberalism and capitalism it will choose capitalism. The analysis certainly suggests (at least on the basis of Marx's analysis of events in France between the 1848 Revolution and Louis Bonaparte's coup in 1851) that the bourgeoisie's control of the French economy and the French state was by no means solid.

Marx seeks to explain the advent and power of Louis Bonaparte in terms of the choice by the bourgeoisie of "tranquility" and "social power" in preference over "anarchy" and "political power"; and also in terms of support for Louis Bonaparte by a diverse coalition, including the class of small peasants. Marx emphasizes that the bourgeoisie recognize that "bourgeois liberties" menace bourgeois "class rule." Marx finds the behavior of the bourgeoisie quite ironic. The bourgeoisie has to confess "that its own interest dictates that it should be delivered from the danger of *governing in its own name*; that, in order to restore tranquility in the land, its bourgeois parliament must, first of all, be given its quietus; that in order to preserve its social power inviolate, its political power must be broken; that the private bourgeois can only continue to exploit the other classes and to enjoy undisturbed property, family, religion and order on condition that their class be condemned along with the other classes to a like political nullity; that in order to save its purse, it must abandon the crown, and the sword that is to safeguard it must at the same time be hung over its own head like the sword of Damocles."[96]

Brilliant rhetoric—and marvelously ironic! If, however, this analysis is not entirely consistent with Marx's position in the *Manifesto of the Communist Party* on the bourgeois state as a "committee for managing the common affairs of the whole bourgeoisie,"[97] it does make clear Marx's appreciation of the fuller complexity of the nature of the state in mid-nineteenth century France, and it does underscore Marx's judgment that the bourgeoisie would rather sacrifice liberty than private property in the event of a clash between the two. The French bourgeoisie were willing to conclude that only Louis Bonaparte "can now save bourgeois society!" That (to rub their hypocrisy into their noses) "Only theft can now save property; only perjury, religion; only bastardy, the family; only disorder, order."[98]

This bespeaks Marx's mordant judgment about the corruption of bourgeois society. Regardless, then, of Marx's attempts to square the state of Louis Bonaparte's France with his materialistic conception of history, it is the case that Marx sees the state (whether under Louis Bonaparte or under the bourgeoisie directly) as an oppressive force.

Critique of Non-Communist Alternatives and Reformers.—Marx analyzes and dismisses a wide range of liberal and even socialist alternatives. Marx endeavors mightily to distinguish his brand of communism from these alternatives. He finds them unacceptable because they will not permit, or cannot achieve, a fundamental communist revolution. They are incompatible with the fulfillment of Marx's cardinal values, and with his social scientific analysis. Even under the best democratic republic, and its "reforms," there will not be a fundamental revolution that will give workers control over their primary life activity. Consequently, the proletariat and good communists should not be taken in by wrong-headed socialists or bourgeois reformers.

From his early commitment to communism, to the end of his life, Marx is scathingly critical of what he holds to be mistaken views in the literature of socialism and communism. He is adversely critical of what he calls "Reactionary Socialism" ("Feudal Socialism," "Petty-Bourgeois Socialism," "German, or 'True,' Socialism"); of "Conservative, or Bourgeois, Socialism"; of "Critical-Utopian Socialism and Communism."

Feudal socialism is characterized by a "total incapacity to comprehend the march of modern history."[99] Petty-bourgeois socialism (e.g., Sismondi) demonstrates some critical acuteness of modern production, but is "reactionary and Utopian in its positive aims."[100] "German, or 'True' socialism" talks of the "Alienation of Humanity," of "eternal truths," and of "Man in general": but it is reactionary and represents the German philistines.[101] "Conservative, or Bourgeois, Socialism"—as illustrated, Marx writes, by Proudhon's *Philosophie de la Misère*—desires "the existing state of society minus its revolutionary and disintegrating elements." Such socialists, as humanitarians, as do-gooders, seek to redress social grievances "in order to secure the continued existence of bourgeois society."[102]

Marx also criticizes "Critical-Utopian Socialism and Communism." Here he criticizes Saint Simon, Fourier, and Owen. They reject political and revolutionary action in favor of peaceful means. They rely, futilely, on "small experiments" and the "force of example." Their "fantastic pictures of future society" are premature because the economic situation is not ripe for the emancipation of the proletariat. They provide some valuable material "for the enlightenment of the working class," but, basically, they operate to "deaden the class struggle and to reconcile . . . class antagonisms," by means of their "castles in the air," and their miraculous belief in their social science.[103]

No one should be deceived by these "socialists." They reflect the position of the classes of which they are a part. Feudal socialists are feudal aristocrats angry with the bourgeoisie for their own reasons. "Feudal socialism: half lamentation, half lampoon; half echo of the past, half menace of the future; at times, by its bitter, witty and incisive criticism, striking the bourgeoisie to the very heart's core; but always ludicrous in its effect, through total incapacity to comprehend the march of modern history."[104] They are reactionary; they want to turn society back to a pre-bourgeois stage; they are unhappy with the bourgeoisie because "it creates a *revolutionary* proletariat.''[105] To illustrate the linkage of groups in the superstructure, Marx writes: ''As the parson has ever gone hand in hand with the landlord, so has Clerical Socialism with Feudal Socialism.'' ''Christian Socialism is but the holy water with which the priest consecrates the heart-burnings of the aristocrat.''[106]

The peasant and the petty-bourgeois are also threatened by the rise of the modern bourgeoisie and attack ''the disastrous effects of machinery and division of labour,'' ''the concentration of capital and lands in a few hands,'' ''overproduction and crises.'' They note too ''the inevitable ruin of the petty bourgeois and the peasant, the misery of the proletariat, the anarchy in production, the crying inequalities in the distribution of wealth, the industrial war of extermination between nations, the dissolution of old moral bonds, of the old family relations, of the old nationalities.''[107] But their outlook is backward-looking; they would restore the old or cramp the new means of production and exchange. Their ''last words are corporate guilds for manufacture, patriarchal relations in agriculture.''[108]

The ''German, or 'True' Socialists'' emasculate French Socialist and Communist literature. They ''write their philosophical nonsense beneath the French original.'' For example, ''beneath the French criticism of the economic functions of money, they write 'Alienation of Humanity.' . . .''[109] Their attacks on the bourgeoisie serve ''the absolute governments, with their following of parsons, professors, country squires and officials'' and thus reactionary interests, the interests of the petty-bourgeois class, the interests of ''the existing state of things in Germany.''[110] They serve to ''kill'' both the ''industrial and political supremacy of the bourgeoisie'' and the ''rise of a revolutionary proletariat.''[111]

Conservative, or bourgeois, ''socialists'' are not really interested in revolutionary change that would fundamentally ''affect the relations between capital and labour.'' They call only for ''administrative reforms.'' They want the proletariat to ''remain within the bounds of the existing society'' but to ''cast away all its hateful ideas concerning the bourgeoisie.'' What reforms do they favor? ''Free trade: for the benefit of the working class. Protective duties: for the benefit of the working class. Prison reform: for the benefit of the working class.'' Their position is summed up in the phrase ''the bourgeois is a bourgeois—for the benefit of the working class.''[112]

Critical-Utopian Socialists and Communists do not realize that historical action cannot ''yield to their personal inventive action,'' that ''historically created conditions of emancipation'' cannot yield to ''fantastic ones.'' Their ''own surroundings'' lead such socialists ''to consider themselves superior to all class antagonisms.'' ''They want to improve the condition of every member of society, even that of the most favoured.

Hence, they habitually appeal to society at large, without distinction of class; nay, by preference, to the ruling class." Although they—particularly the founders of utopian schemes—have enlightened the working class, the disciples of the "originators of these systems" have become reactionary, hold "fast by the original views of their masters, in opposition to the progressive development of the proletariat," and "violently oppose all political action on the part of the working class."[113]

Marx's criticism of other socialists in 1848 helps us to understand his criticism of German socialists in the German Social Democratic Party in the 1870s. Marx is sharply critical of reformers in the German Social Democratic party who reject "violent bloody revolution" in favor of "*reform*," who, because they are worried about offending the bourgeoisie, will abandon the class struggle.

"In order to relieve the bourgeoisie of the last trace of anxiety it must be clearly and convincingly proved to it that the Red Bogey is really only a bogey, and does not exist. But what is the secret of the Red Bogey if not the bourgeoisie's dread of the inevitable life-and-death struggle between it and the proletariat? Dread of the inevitable outcome of the modern class struggle? Do away with the class struggle and the bourgeoisie and 'all independent people' will 'not be afraid to go hand in hand with the proletarians'! And the ones to be cheated would be precisely the proletarians."[114]

Marx is opposed to the position of the reformers who favor mediation, persuasion, and submission, who are fearful of frightening the bourgeoisie, and favor "petty-bourgeois patchwork reforms which, by providing the old order of society with new props, may perhaps transform the ultimate catastrophe into a general piecemeal and as far as possible peaceful process of dissolution."[115] Communists must, therefore, oppose ideas about reform as mistaken, as "adulterating."[116]

Marx's scathing and often sarcastic criticism of his brethren in the German Social Democratic Party was designed to prevent them from abandoning the fundamental communist revolution in favor of liberal democratic bourgeois reform. His criticism illustrates clearly his conviction that even his socialist brethren are influenced by the environment of the bourgeois superstructure, particularly the reformism that is so much more compatible with the old or existing order than with a truly revolutionary philosophy.

Marx's social scientific analysis and criticism of the bourgeois superstructure adds up to the very important conclusion that the fundamental communist revolution—and with it the fulfillment of Marx's preferred values for humanity—cannot be achieved through piecemeal changes in the bourgeois superstructure. That superstructure—state, law, politics, religion, philosophy, education—reflects the values of the capitalist economic and social order, the capitalist mode of production and bourgeois society. Only in exceptional cases—cases that we will consider in the next chapter—might this be otherwise.

Understanding this criticism of bourgeois, capitalist society we are in a better position to understand and explore Marx's argument on behalf of the revolutionary breakthrough to communism. Before we turn to that argument, however, let us subject Marx's social scientific analysis and criticism to a critique.

CRITIQUE

Marx's social science is powerfully illuminating, but nonethless limited and seriously flawed in important respects. There can be no doubt, however, that Marx goes far beyond most nineteenth century secular, prophetic critics—not only in revealing the gap that existed between the proletariat's existential condition and human freedom and development, but also in throwing bright light on how this condition had come to be, why exploitation continued under bourgeois capitalism, and what might be done to overcome this gap. Moreover, his radical criticism is powerful and appealing precisely because his ethical values guide his empirical research and because his empirical theory is consciously related to revolutionary action.

In the prophetic tradition—religious or secular—Marx is unafraid to engage in radical, and fearless, social scientific analysis and criticism. He is unafraid—in the interest of speaking (if not God's word) the truth of alienation and oppression as he perceives it—to take on the powerful establishments of his day: religious, philosophical, political, economic, and particularly bourgeois capitalism. His nineteenth century analysis and criticism of the gap between liberal ideals and liberal realities is potent.

Marx's analysis and criticism goes beyond empty moralizing to seek to uncover the reasons for—explanation of—the alienation and oppression of workers in the workers' lack of control over their destiny, a lack of control rooted in the nature of the capitalist economy and its mode of operation. He sees the economic foundation of life to be crucial in explaining who gets what and how. He criticizes the way in which capitalist economic power in the nineteenth century is manifest in government, law, education, religion, and other domains of life.

His criticism of contemporary society—and of those who exercise influence in such society—is not based on a religiously historical memory of God, Exodus, freedom, the Sinai Covenant, the *mitzvot*: of a God who cares for the oppressed and leads them out of bondage, of a people called to abide by the commandments to live a more ethical life in a caring and responsible community. But Marx acts as a secular Moses in fashioning his own historical epic of the need for the proletariat to move from wage slavery to communist freedom, of inevitable progress toward freedom based on a materialistic and dynamic conception of history. In Marx's epic the bourgeois capitalist has replaced Pharaoh; Marx has replaced Moses;

the proletariat have become the chosen people; communist commandments (thou shalt understand who oppresses you and why; thou shalt overthrow thy oppressor; thou shalt march toward and eventually enter the promised communist land) have been substituted for the *mitzvot*; class struggle has replaced wrestling with God; the classless society has replaced the end of days!

Marx's social science epic—his paradigm—enables him to analyze and criticize the operation of both the capitalistic foundation and the bourgeois superstructure and lay bare, at least to his satisfaction, the contradictions of capitalism, the character of class struggle, the condition of the proletariat, the way in which capitalism will be overthrown. As social scientists we can no longer look at the world in the same way since Marx wrote. In his probing of social life Marx goes far beyond the vital, if simple, ethical injunctions of the religious prophets and their secular followers. He attempts to develop a richer and deeper social scientific understanding of the realities of oppression, and what is required to overcome such oppression.

But if Marx is a powerful social scientist, his social science is also limited and flawed. His social science is limited because of what he excluded from his range of vision; and his social science is flawed because of his scientific astigmatism.

Bourgeois, capitalistic society doesn't quite function in the way Marx said it did. It is by no means clear that the contradictions Marx saw operating in capitalism will lead to capitalism's destruction. It is by no means clear that the people in liberal democracies are unable to reform capitalism, to correct its worst abuses. It is by no means scientifically clear that communism is the inevitable alternative to capitalism as an economic system and to liberal democracy as a political system.

If Marx is right in his presentation of the often dreadful working conditions of the proletariat in the nineteenth century, and of other aspects of the operation of capitalism (especially of capitalist profits at the expense of workers), he fails (perhaps understandably) to anticipate some late nineteenth century and some twentieth century developments. He fails to appreciate in advanced liberal democratic states the viability of a regulated capitalism, the power of workers to protect their economic, political, and social interests, and the ability of a liberal democracy to address (modestly if not radically) capitalistic abuses and the call for social justice. He does not grasp the resilience, vitality, or staying power of capitalism or of liberal democracy; nor does he anticipate (or, if he appreciates, approve) the emergence of democratic socialism functioning in a still largely capitalist society as a realistic alternative to communism.

Although he may have perceived important trends toward concentrations of capitalist enterprises in the nineteenth century, he mistakenly contends that declining profits, the growing misery/organization/militancy of workers, and severe economic crises (rooted in capitalism's contradictions) will inevitably pave the way for capitalism's demise.

Moreover, if Marx is not entirely accurate in his social scientific examination of capitalism, and of the liberal democratic bourgeois superstructure, he also misses a number of other key forces because of his particular focus on the industrial proletariat. Despite some attention to farmers and peasants, he tends to slight their importance in his analysis. He tends not to pay significant attention to service workers. Despite some appreciation of the importance and power of nationalism as a key force shaping modern society, he does not fully appreciate that national loyalty will be a more important factor in shaping the allegiance of workers—and others—than class.

Moreover, Marx misses the vast importance of racism, anti-semitism, religion, and sexism in modern society—forces that cut across class lines and make clear that Marx's focus on class conflict is limited and flawed. Clearly, to miss racism, sexism, anti-semitism, religious bigotry, virulent nationalism is to miss powerful forces militating against the least-free! And despite his recognition of the rapacious operation of capitalism, its squandering of resources, its maltreatment of nature, Marx does not challenge the dominant emphasis of his age on production or question the dominant cornucopian premises of the nineteenth century. We will have more to say about these crucial omissions when we turn to Marx's vision of the future communist society.

Here we can also note again Marx's failure adequately to understand the nature of constitutionalism, and particularly its importance in guarding against the abuse of power. He correctly sees that constitutionalism in a bourgeois republic is often a shield to conceal capitalist oppression of workers. He recognizes the superficiality of merely formal constitutional protections. Yet we must acknowledge that Marx fails to explore more fully the way (however limited) that constitutionalism protects freedom, and ensures that the advance of democracy will increasingly enhance freedom in all domains. If some of Marx's social scientific ideas are in harmony with a secular prophetic paradigm, it is the case that the idea and operation of covenant, or constitution, or social contract is either absent or neglected or undeveloped in Marx's social theory.

In focusing, in his social scientific analysis, on wage slavery Marx is clearly in the prophetic tradition. However, in not doing justice to other groups among the least-free—to women suffering under patriarchy, to blacks and other people of color suffering under oppressive white domination, to Jews or other oppressed religious groups suffering persecution, forced conversions, pogroms at the hands of the dominant majority, and to all the innocent who suffer in war and revolution—Marx's prophetic stance (despite his own devotion to universal human emancipation, despite his opposition to wage slavery, despite his sympathy for women's rights, etc.) is open to serious question. To these points, and to the role of the dissenting noncommunist minority, we shall return when we examine Marx's understanding of the operation of the communist society.

CONCLUSION

Marx emerges as a powerful, illuminating, fearless, if limited and flawed, critic who is at least partially in the tradition of a secular prophetic politics. By focusing on universal human emancipation and related values, on the condition of the proletariat, on the dominant economic system of his day, on the relationship between foundation and superstructure, Marx is able to underscore—in concept and in rich detail—the gap between his ideals and goals *and* the existing reality. And because he is able, to his own satisfaction, to explain the reasons for the gap and to point toward a remedy that would close the gap, he goes beyond moral protest to social scientific diagnosis and remedy. To his credit he forces social scientists to think more radically about the necessary and sufficient conditions of freedom, integration, humanity, and community.

However, by focusing on what he does, he misses important points about those cardinal values. He neglects to explore aspects of freedom that go beyond work-activity and the realm of necessary labor. He also neglects aspects of integration beyond control over one's work product, joy in one's work activity, being in touch with one's social and humane being, and beyond a truly cooperative community with one's fellows. He neglects, too, the fuller dimensions of humanity and of community, and especially the problems of a community ushered in by violence and by the revolutionary dictatorship of the proletariat. He neglects, finally, to explore more adequately the meaning of rich human and social development.

To make these points is to say that Marx's views of freedom, integration, humanity and community, and rich human and social development are partly flawed. To so argue is also to raise doubts about Marx's theory of revolutionary communist action, and also about Marx's failure to explore the communist future more critically. To these matters I shall turn in the next two chapters. First, however, I turn to examine Marx's theory of revolutionary action.

NOTES

1. Robert C. Tucker (ed.), *The Marx–Engels Reader*, 2nd ed. (New York: Norton, 1978), p. 12.

2. See David McLellan, *Karl Marx: His Life And Thought* (New York: Harper & Row, 1973), p. 69. See also Leszek Kolakowski, *Main Currents of Marxism: I: The Founders* (Oxford: Oxford Univ. Press, 1981) who highlights Marx's critique of Hegel, Feuerbach, Proudhon, and others.

3. Article in *Deutsch-Franzosische Jahrbucher* (1844), in Tucker, p. 13.

4. *Theses on Feuerbach* (1845), Thesis XI, in Tucker, p. 145.

5. *Contribution to the Critique of Hegel's* Philosophy of Right: *Introduction* (1844), in Tucker, p. 60.

6. Ibid., pp. 54, 55, 56.

7. Ibid., pp. 57, 60, 62.

8. *Capital*, Vol. I (1867), *Afterword to the Second German Edition* (1873), in Tucker, p. 301.

9. Ibid., p. 302.

10. See M. C. Howard and J. E. King, *The Political Economy of Marx* (New York: Longman, 1975), p. 60, endnote 18. Also see Gerald A. Cohen, *Karl Marx's Theory of History* (Princeton, NJ: Princeton Univ. Press, 1978), p. 326.

11. Howard and King, *The Political Economy of Marx*, p. 39.

12. See Melvin Rader, *Marx's Interpretation of History* (New York: Oxford Univ. Press, 1979). "My impetus in writing this book," writes Rader in his Preface, p. vi, "springs from contradictions in the various interpretations and in the apparent contradictions in the writings of Marx. I have tried to find an underlying consistency in his complex vision of history, but not at the cost of glossing over real contradictions." See also Cohen, *Karl Marx's Theory of History*.

13. *The German Ideology: Part I* (Marx and Engels, 1845/46), in Tucker, pp. 155–56.

14. Ibid., p. 150.

15. See Cohen, *Karl Marx's Theory of History*, p. 32.

16. *A Contribution to the Critique of Political Economy* (1859), Preface, in Tucker, p. 4.

17. *Wage Labour and Capital* (lectures, 1847, published in 1849), in Tucker, p. 207.

18. *A Contribution to the Critique of Political Economy*, Preface, in Tucker, p. 4.

19. See *The German Ideology: Part I*, in Tucker, p. 163. See also Anne Showstack Sassoon's article on "civil society" in Tom Bottomore (ed.), *A Dictionary of Marxist Thought* (Cambridge, MA: Harvard Univ. Press, 1983), pp. 72–74.

20. *A Contribution to the Critique of Political Economy*, Preface, in Tucker, p. 4.

21. Ibid., p. 5.

22. See Cohen, *Karl Marx's Theory of History*, who "defends historical determinism" (p. ix), and states that his "version of historical materialism may be called technological" (p. 147, note 1). But see also Rader (*Marx's Interpretation of History*), who finds two models of historical explanation in Marx: "organic totality and base-superstructure" (p. 231). He notes (p. 231), that orthodox Marxism "has stressed the base-superstructure model to the nearly total exclusion of the organic model, thus doing Marx a great disservice." Rader maintains that "there is no necessary conflict [between these two approaches] if we think of them as models rather than as descriptions or social entities" (p. 232).

23. *Manifesto of the Communist Party*, in Tucker, p. 475.

24. *The German Ideology: Part I*, in Tucker, p. 154.

25. Ibid., pp. 154–55.

26. *Manifesto of the Communist Party*, in Tucker, p. 489.

27. See *Theses on Feuerbach*, Thesis III, in Tucker, p. 144.

28. *Wage Labour and Capital*, in Tucker, p. 207.

29. *A Contribution to the Critique of Political Economy*, Preface, in Tucker, pp. 4–5.

30. Ibid., p. 5.

31. Ibid.

32. Ibid.

33. See, for example (all in Tucker), *Capital*, Vol. l, pp. 396–97 and *Manifesto of the Communist Party*, p. 474, for Marx on feudal restrictions; and *Capital*, Vol. 1, pp. 437–38, for Marx's famous summary of the process by which the "expropriators are expropriated."

34. *The German Ideology: Part I*, in Tucker, pp. 192–93.

35. *Manifesto of the Communist Party*, in Tucker, p. 484.

36. Ibid., pp. 473–74.

37. Ibid., p. 474.

38. Ibid., p. 483.

39. *Capital*, Vol. I (1867), *Preface to the First German Edition*, in Tucker, p. 296.

40. Ibid., p. 297.

41. *Economic and Philosophic Manuscripts of 1844*, in Tucker, p. 73.

42. *Capital*, Vol. I., in Tucker, p. 365.

43. Ibid., p. 367.

44. Ibid., p. 368.

45. Ibid., p. 371.

46. Ibid., p. 370.

47. Ibid., p. 371.

48. Ibid., pp. 373–74.

49. Ibid., p. 409.

50. Ibid., pp. 410–11.

51. Ibid., pp. 430–31. Relative surplus value refers to the extra value resulting from the increased productivity of labor within a *set* working day, value produced, for example, by mechanization. Relative surplus value results from decreasing the length of necessary labor-time and increasing the length of surplus labor-time within a *set* working day. Absolute surplus value refers to the value produced by hours of work beyond subsistence wages—hours beyond necessary labor-time. Absolute surplus value is increased when total working hours are increased, or when workers are required (within a *set* working day) to work more intensely.

52. These themes run throughout *Capital*. Interpretations are diverse. I have found Howard and King, *The Political Economy of Marx*, cogent and persuasive. I have also found Angus Walker, *Marx: His Theory and Its Content: Politics as Economics* (New York: Longman, 1978) very helpful.

53. *Capital*, Vol. 1, in Tucker, p. 431.

54. Ibid.

55. Ibid., p. 432.

56. Ibid.

57. Ibid., pp. 432 and 433.

58. Ibid., p. 433.

59. Ibid., p. 432.

60. Ibid., p. 433.

61. Ibid.

62. Ibid., p. 434.

63. Ibid., pp. 434–35.

64. Ibid., p. 435.

65. Ibid.

66. Ibid.

67. See Howard and King, *The Political Economy of Marx,* pp. 49–50. For Marx on "manufacture" see *Capital*, Vol. 1, in Tucker, pp. 388–403.

68. See Marx in *Capital*, Vol. 1, in Tucker, p. 365: "Suppose the working day consists of 6 hours of necessary labor, and 6 hours of surplus labor. Then the free labourer gives the capitalist every week 6 x 6 or 36 hours of suplus-labour. It is the same as if he worked 3 days in the week for himself, and 3 days in the week gratis for the capitalist."

69. Ibid., pp. 362-63.

70. Ibid., p. 385.

71. *Critique of the Gotha Program* (1875, published in 1891), in Tucker, p. 535.

72. Ibid., pp. 407 and 361.

73. *Manifesto of the Communist Party*, in Tucker, p. 476.

74. Ibid., p. 477.

75. Ibid., p. 478.

76. *Capital*, Vol. I, in Tucker, p. 438.

77. Ibid.

78. *Manifesto of the Communist Party*, in Tucker, p. 480.

79. Ibid.

80. Ibid., p. 481.

81. Ibid.

82. Ibid., p. 483.

83. Ibid.

84. Ibid., p. 475.

85. Ibid., p. 477.

86. Ibid., p. 489.

87. Ibid., p. 476.

88. Ibid., p. 487.

89. Ibid., pp. 487–88.

90. Ibid., pp. 487 and 474.

91. Ibid., p. 488.

92. Ibid.

93. Marx's exceptions were Britain, Holland, and the United States. The reasons for these exceptions, and the problems they pose for Marx's theory (particularly his commitment to fundamental revolution rather than reform), will be treated more fully in the next chapter.

94. *Manifesto of the Communist Party*, in Tucker, p. 475.

95. *The Civil War in France* (1871) (published in 1891), in Tucker, p. 629.

96. *The Eighteenth Brumaire of Louis Bonaparte* (1842), in Tucker (orig. 1972 edition), p. 474.

97. *Manifesto of the Communist Party*, in Tucker (2nd edition, 1978, as cited throughout), p. 475.

98. *The Eighteenth Brumaire of Louis Bonaparte* (1842), in Tucker, p. 615.

99. *Manifesto of the Communist Party*, in Tucker, p. 491.

100. Ibid., p. 493.

101. Ibid., pp. 493–96.

102. Ibid., p. 496.

103. Ibid., pp. 497–99.

104. Ibid., p. 491.

105. Ibid., p. 492.

106. Ibid.

107. Ibid., p. 493.

108. Ibid.

109. Ibid., p. 494.

110. Ibid., p. 495.

111. Ibid.

112. Ibid., pp. 496–97.

113. Ibid., pp. 497-99.

114. *Circular Letter to Bebel, Liebknecht, Bracke, and Others* (1879), in Tucker, p. 551–52.

115. Ibid., p. 553.

116. Ibid., p. 555.

4
Marx's Theory of Revolutionary Communist Action

INTRODUCTION

In this chapter I focus on Marx's theory of revolutionary communist action, and especially on the judgments that Marx brings to questions of strategy and tactics in the making of the communist revolution. This chapter builds logically on Chapters 2 and 3. In Chapter 2 I explored the ethical component in Marx's thought: Marx's conception of what ought to be—his vision, ends, values. In Chapter 3 I explored the social scientific or empirical component in Marx's thought: Marx's understanding of what has been, is, and will be—his understanding of the realities of history, of technology, of economics, of sociology, of politics. In this chapter, by way of contrast, I propose to explore the prudential component in Marx's thought: his judgments about practical means, his judgment of what wisely can be done in practice to usher in the new communist society. Of course, Marx makes his judgments to advance his communist ends in the light of the social scientific realities that both limit and make possible the achievement of those ends. Clearly, Chapters 2 and 3 set the stage for this chapter and significantly influence the judgments that Marx will bring to practical action.

In the second section of this chapter, consequently, I explore the key question: What is Marx's theory of revolutionary action? And in the third section, my critique of that theory of action, I ask: How do we assess Marx's theory of revolutionary action?

In the second section I emphasize that call for revolutionary judgment and action. First, I especially note in Marx a significant and consistent judgment on communist ends and general preparatory means (stage 1: preparing for revolution). Second, I focus more sharply on the multiple and diverse strategies of revolution (in stage 2: making the revolution) dictated by differing circumstances in the European countries Marx was most interested in—Britain, France, Germany, and Russia. Third, I examine Marx's judgment on what is required to consolidate the communist revolution; here (stage 3: consolidating the revolution) we encounter Marx's judgment about the dictatorship of the proletariat. Fourth, in stage 4 (achieving mature communism) I examine Marx's judgments about action, policy, and problems in the period of communism.

In my critique (in the third section), I ask if Marx's theory of revolution is compatible with the theory of a prophetically just revolution. This permits me to assess the soundness of Marx's judgment about the unalterable revolutionary end of communism, and the wisdom of Marx's recommendations to facilitate preparatory means. It also permits me to appraise the practical sense of those revolutionary judgments—informing practically-effective strategic and tactical decisions—that Marx holds necessary, in differing countries, to bring the communists to power; to enable them to move through the process of consolidating the communist revolution; and to deal with crucial problems in the mature communist society itself. In my conclusion (the fourth section), I ask: How powerful and illuminating, and how limited and flawed, is Marx's theory of revolutionary, communist action? And how compatible is Marx's theory of action with the secular tradition of prophetic politics?

In dealing with Marx's theory of revolutionary action, one faces a number of complications and difficulties that interfere with the effort to articulate a clear, cogent, and consistent theory.[1] Problems of judgment (especially of prudent judgment) in action are themselves difficult. They require a thorough appreciation of the soundness of ends, and of the humaneness, rationality, and effectiveness of means. They require, putting the matter of the relationship of means to ends differently, a thoughtful balancing of costs and benefits, and thus a knowledge (not easily vouchsafed) of consequences. Moreover, when revolutionary action is involved, problems of judgment inevitably involve a thinking through of the agonizing problem of the just revolution. These problems are complicated by the fact that even the most objective revolutionary actor is beset by personal hopes and fears that influence, and often distort, humane judgment and the calm, social scientific understanding of reality, of consequences, of probability and possibility.

In addition, we as twentieth century observers are too often inclined to read back into our presentation and assessment of Marx's revolutionary theory of action our own biases influenced by our twentieth century understanding of Marxism/Leninism/Stalinism, and by our own understanding of the democratic socialist experience (whether in Britain, Sweden, West Germany, or elsewhere). Twentieth century observers find it quite difficult to call to mind the nineteenth century environment—often undemocratic, often authoritarian—in which Marx was called upon to make his judgments on strategy and tactics. Keeping these complications and difficulties in mind may perhaps help us to do justice to Marx's nineteenth century theory of revolutionary, communist action.

MARX'S THEORY OF REVOLUTIONARY COMMUNIST ACTION

We must at the beginning emphasize that judgments are required at a number of stages on the way to, and then with the achievement of, communism. Judgments must be made, for example, (1) in the period of preparation for revolution under capitalism; (2) in the period of making the revolution that would bring communists to power[2]; (3) in the period of the consolidation of communism—often with the necessary help of the still controversial dictatorship of the proletariat; and (4) in the period of the achievement of mature communism.

Marx provided no book or article exploring fully and clearly these four stages. In what he does write he informs us more about the judgments required for action in stages 1 and 2 than about stage 3, and more about stage 3 than stage 4. However, despite the difficulties of articulating a coherent theory, based on a wide variety of judgments over the course of a complex revolutionary life and recognizing the dangers of generalizing on the basis of specific responses, it is nevertheless possible to piece together in Marx a general theory of revolutionary strategy and tactics.

Stage 1: Preparing for the Revolution

In any attempt to set forth Marx's theory of revolutionary communist action—and the judgments of strategy and tactics based on that theory—one must at the outset clearly recognize in his writings certain very important judgments, about which there should be relatively little quarrel. Here I refer to judgments on key ends and certain general preparatory means. These can easily be identified in stage 1. (Of course, the judgment about communism as the end informs all four stages.) Similarly, certain preparatory means will also carry over into stages 2 and 3.

Marx's Judgment on Communism as an End

There is initially in Marx a clear-headed, constant, and unchanging judgment about communist ends. Once Marx becomes a Communist he never deviates from his judgment that a fundamental, radical, and transforming communist revolution is required to achieve freedom, integration, humanity/community, and rich development for workers. Regardless of the strategy required in a particular country at a particular time, under particular circumstances, Marx never alters his judgment that the end to be obtained by action must be a democratic communist society: based on majority worker control; requiring the abolition of bourgeois capitalism and private ownership of the means of production and exchange; producing an end of the coercive and parasitic state; capable of overcoming alienation, exploitation, oppression, the stultifying division of labor; based on the achievement of productive abundance. The communist revolution will never be complete until such a communist society comes into existence. Most of the texts to support these generalizations have been cited in Chapters 2 and 3.[3]

Marx's Judgment on Preparatory Means

Other generally uncontested ideas—crucial to Marx's judgments about preparatory revolutionary action—must also be thoroughly appreciated. These are judgments, rooted in Marx's social science, about what it takes to get ready for the communist revolution. Thus Marx insists that material and economic developments in history are required to establish the conditions for a successful communist revolution. Until these developments are ripe, a communist revolution is premature.

These judgments also help to explain Marx's rather consistent opposition (which we will encounter again in stages 2 and 3) to those insurrectionists who believed that a minority workers' *putsch* can successfully overthrow capitalism, and also to those anarchists who believed that the state will wither away immediately after the communist seizure of power. In contrast to insurrectionists and anarchists, Marx argues consistently that the material conditions for the communist revolution must be ripe. He insists that only the overwhelming majority (either of workers, or of workers, peasants, and petit bourgeoisie) can make the revolution. He maintains that minority force alone cannot make a successful revolution. He holds that majority force, legal or illegal, wielded by workers in control of the state will normally have to be employed after the revolution to ensure the achievement of communism.

I explore these judgments about revolutionary strategy and tactics more fully when I examine, in stage 2, Marx's several strategies for revolution. I introduce them here only to underscore Marx's judgments about preparing for the revolution. Preparation requires ripe material, economic, and political conditions. Preparation calls for building majority support. Preparation calls for avoiding the mistaken revolutionary judgments of insurrectionists and anarchists.[4]

Thus, although Marx believes in the historical inevitability of communism and is firmly persuaded that material and economic conditions must be ripe for communism, he strongly endorses the need for political action. Preparatory political action is needed to create the ripe situation for the communist revolution. Clearly the political battle has to be fought in conjunction with the economic battle. Indeed, Marx holds that economic exploitation is a form of political control and oppression. The oligarchic or authoritarian or bourgeois state protects bourgeois economic domination. The economic and political struggles for freedom are thus intimately related.[5]

In stage 1, workers get ready by doing the following: by understanding the march of history (at least in Western Europe) from feudalism to capitalism to communism; by understanding more fully the nature of the exploitation and oppression of the workers under capitalism; by understanding the weaknesses of capitalism; by understanding more fully the nature of class struggle; by understanding clearly the weapons that capitalism and the democratic republic place in the hands of workers. We explored this understanding in Chapter 3.[6]

Workers, in stage 1, get set by doing the following: by organizing; by unionizing; by propagandizing; by becoming politically active; by working with progressive democratic forces; by pushing aggressively within parliamentary bodies, if they are open to suasion, for key democratic reforms—for example, universal suffrage, the ten hour day; by avoiding deception by utopian socialists, bourgeois reformers, or even wrong-headed socialist reformers; by acting to prepare the proletariat, at or shortly after the revolution (depending on circumstances), to become the ruling class; by never losing sight of the need for the fundamental communist revolution. Most of these ideas have also been explored in Chapter 3.

Here one cannot overemphasize the importance that Marx (and Engels) attribute to universal suffrage. Marx writes: ". . .Universal suffrage is the equivalent for political power for the working class of England, where the proletariat forms the large majority of the population, where, in a long, though underground civil war, it has gained a clear consciousness of its position as a class, and where even the rural districts know no longer any peasants, but only landlords, industrial capitalists (farmers) and hired laborers. The carrying of Universal Suffrage in England would, therefore, be a far more socialistic measure than anything which has been honored with that name on the Continent." Marx's judgment on the crucial importance of universal suffrage holds as well for France and Germany, indeed, for all countries.[7]

If Marx's judgment about universal suffrage is clear, other judgments are less so. For example, the exact revolutionary moment depends upon a judgment about "ripeness." Judgments about ripeness vary, as we shall see shortly, with the character of the regime—oligarchic, authoritarian, liberal bourgeois, or other—and especially in the light of the economic and political development of the country involved.[8]

Before turning to examine Marx's diverse, multiple strategies for revolution in stage 2, let me illustrate a little more fully some of the key ideas in Marx's fairly consistent judgment about getting ready and set for the communist revolution: and especially his judgment on the necessity of a fundamental communist revolution rather than capitalist reform.

Historical and social scientific perspectives are crucial to sound communist judgment. Marx holds that communists "theoretically . . . have over the great mass of the proletariat the advantage of clearly understanding the line of march, the conditions, and the ultimate general results of the proletarian movement." Marx always maintains that the "advance of industry, whose involuntary promoter is the bourgeoisie, replaces the isolation of the labourers, due to competition, by their revolutionary combination, due to association." Marx insists that "what the bourgeoisie, therefore, produces, above all, is its own gravediggers." Given this perspective Marx reaches the confident judgment that the "fall" of the bourgeoisie "and the victory of the proletariat are equally inevitable."[9] Such a judgment obviously strengthens the confidence of workers and communists in the preparatory stage for revolution under capitalism. Although Marx never says so in so many words, it is clear that such confidence is crucial to a successful revolutionary strategy.

This confidence is reinforced by Marx's analysis in *Capital* and by his judgment that with the growth of "misery, oppression, slavery, degradation, exploitation" of workers under capitalism there will also grow "the revolt of the working class, a class always increasing in numbers, and disciplined, united, organized by the very mechanism of the process of capitalist production itself." Marx's materialist conception of history, buttressed by his analysis in *Capital*, supports his judgment that the clash between productive forces and relations will lead to capitalism's downfall. Marx is certain that in time the "expropriators" will be "expropriated."[10]

Rather consistently Marx insists that communists should maintain a distinct Communist identity, dedicated to a fundamental communist revolution. They might have to work with or support other progressive forces when they—that is, the communists—lack majority strength, but they should maintain their identity and independence. They should keep their attention riveted on the fight for the interests of workers. They might have to work with bourgeois allies, but they should keep their eyes always on their own ultimate victory. Experience dictates that they should distrust bourgeois allies in victory. Wherever possible, when the time is ripe they should offer their own candidates in elections, and unhesitatingly press radical demands upon the bourgeoisie in order to push them in a socialist direction. They are well advised to be organized, armed, and militant. The character of that militancy depends on the character of their opponents, their allies, and other circumstances.[11]

Marx never tires of insisting that bourgeois democrats are at best reformers seeking only to make existing society tolerable and comfortable to them. They are not interested in radical, communist revolution. For example: "Far from desiring to revolutionize all society for the revolutionary proletarians, the democratic petty bourgeois strive for a change in social conditions by means of which existing society will be made as tolerable and comfortable as possible for them."[12]

If utopian socialists are naive about the way to achieve communism, and if bourgeois reformers are certainly not interested in achieving communism, German social democrats—"socialists," according to Marx—should not be taken in by the tactic of reform. Marx admonishes them not to abandon the class struggle in favor of "patching up . . . the capitalist order."[13] Communists must never lose sight of the need for a fundamental revolution to overthrow capitalism and usher in a genuinely communist society.

Stage 2: Making the Revolution

It is helpful, initially, to point out that Marx's judgments about making the revolution cannot be understood unless we see him as a revolutionary communist in the nineteenth century, seeking ways and means to move toward a fundamental communist revolution in European countries that were by no means democratic in the liberal democratic twentieth century meaning of that term. Indeed, such countries were oligarchic or authoritarian or despotic. Suffrage was limited in all European countries, including Britain, the most liberal and the most parliamentary government. Democratic freedoms—of speech, press, and association, for example—were limited in France and Germany. Executives in France and Germany were not fully responsible to parliamentary assemblies. In brief, genuinely popular rule and genuine protection of basic rights were not to be found in any European country. Marx's judgments about making the revolution had to take these factual propositions into account.[14]

Secondly, it is helpful in understanding Marx's judgments about revolutionary strategy if we recognize that Marx is not to be seen as a modern twentieth century communist (à la Lenin or Stalin), or as a modern twentieth century Social Democrat (as a Western-style parliamentary democrat), or as either a nineteenth or twentieth century liberal democrat (since he believed in overthrowing capitalism and liberal democrats do not). It is also helpful if we reject the view that Marx is an early Communist who matures into a Social Democrat. And, as we think of his relationship to twentieth century communism—and especially Stalinism—it is helpful to recognize that Marx does not subscribe to a belief in an elite vanguard party, the minority seizure of power, a one-party dictatorship, or the systematic use of political terror.[15]

Having said all of the above, it is equally important to emphasize the judgments Marx does make. Marx certainly believes that capitalism must be overthrown. He does maintain that this overthrow requires revolutionary action. He holds that workers will play a key role in the communist revolution, although the nature of that revolutionary action might have to vary from country to country, depending on conditions. The "classic" Marxist position, which we outline next, conditions to a significant degree all revolutionary communist strategies.

Proletarian Majority Revolution

This is a strategy for "more advanced countries with a working-class majority, like Britain. . . . " And Marx believed that workers constituted two-thirds of the British population.[16] This is a strategy for countries, however, where the proletariat cannot use suffrage to achieve power legally and peacefully. Richard N. Hunt, whose work has done so much to clarify the political ideas of Marx, affirms that Marx throughout his life generally "advocated a violent, illegal, fairly swift, but nonetheless *democratic* revolution against the existing authoritarian governments." Why generally? Because, as we see later in this chapter, violence and illegality will not be necessary in genuinely democratic countries, where the workers, if they are the majority, can achieve communism peacefully and constitutionally. Unfortunately: "Where the masses could not vote, the rule of the majority—democracy—could only be imposed violently and illegally."[17]

Hunt maintains that this strategy, "appropriate for Great Britain, involved the overthrow of a propertied oligarchy by the proletarian majority of the nation."[18] Marx, he notes, "originally thought of achieving communism by means of violent revolution . . . but violent revolution by a proletarian majority against an entrenched oligarchy of wealth. . . . "[19]

Later, of course, Marx identifies Britain as a country wherein communists might come to power peacefully and legally. Apparently, before the modest expansion of suffrage that Marx saw in Britain in his lifetime, and before the advent of universal suffrage that Marx championed but did not see in his lifetime, Marx believed that the proletarian majority revolution to overthrow the entrenched oligarchy would have to be violent. The problems involved in such a majority proletarian revolution Marx does not fully explore. In my critique in the third section of this chapter I will return to these problems.

Hunt argues persuasively that Marx had initially "envisaged the attainment of communism by means of a spontaneous revolution, carried out by the masses themselves as the result of their own self-maturation, without any need for elite assistance or totalitarian-democratic devices."[20]

Although this simple early vision was not completely untouched by circumstances, it "did not change appreciably between 1843 and 1848, and indeed it remained the ideal model throughout" the life of Marx.[21] Hunt argues that "All subsequent strategies and tactical expedients were but variations on this classical theme."[22]

The revolution must be a popular revolution that would enable the workers, where they are in the majority, to come to power. As we have noted, if the revolution can be accomplished peacefully via democratic processes, based on universal suffrage and basic freedoms, that is preferable. If, however, that were not possible, the workers—the majority—must overthrow the minority ruling over them. In this way the working class becomes the ruling class.[23]

There is evidence in the *Manifesto*, as well as in other texts, to support Marx's endorsement of a proletarian majority revolution. In the *Manifesto of the Communist Party* Marx indicates that the communist revolution must be a majority revolution, based on workers: "All previous historical movements were movements of minorities, or in the interest of minorities. The proletarian movement is the self-conscious, independent movement of the immense majority, in the interests of the immense majority."[24]

Marx clearly identifies communists with workers—the interests of the immense majority. Marx insists that communists "do not form a separate party opposed to other working-class parties"; that they "have no interests separate and apart from those of the proletariat as a whole"; that they "represent" the "common interests of the entire proletariat."[25] The communist revolution is thus a democratic revolution, based on the overwhelming majority—the proletariat.

Marx insists that political action to advance the revolution is necessary. But the right time to revolt and forcibly overthrow the capitalist state cannot be predicted in advance. All that can be said is that the time must be ripe. In the *Manifesto* Marx maintains that under capitalism a "more or less veiled civil war" is going on, that such war will break "out into open revolution," and that "the violent overthrow of the bourgeoisie lays the foundation for the sway of the proletariat."[26]

The *Manifesto* does not spell out the details of such "overthrow." The character of overthrow remains vague. We are informed only "that the first step in the revolution by the working class . . . is to raise the proletariat to the position of ruling class, to win the battle for democracy." This can be interpreted as the proletariat's achieving political power. Once the "battle for democracy" is won, "the proletariat will use its political supremacy to wrest, by degrees, all capital from the bourgeoisie, to centralize all instruments of production in the hands of the State, i.e., of the proletariat organized as a ruling class; and to increase the total of productive forces as rapidly as possible.''[27] In brief, the proletariat, as the ruling class, uses the power of the State to sweep away ''by force the old conditions of production,'' and to usher in the new, and revolutionary, communist mode of production.[28]

Force is presumably necessary since bourgeois capitalists will not voluntarily accept communism. The character of that force remains a most controversial matter in Marxist strategy. Communism—of course—remains the goal of every Marxist strategy. With what speed will communism be attained? What will be the more precise process by which communism will be attained? These crucial questions—which we will return to in examining the stage of consolidating the communist revolution—are unfortunately never fully and clearly addressed.

Although Marx does not develop a theory of the just revolution, Richard N. Hunt argues that the revolution Marx had in mind would qualify as a just democratic revolution on the Mazzini model. The ''proletarian revolution would be a just cause, supported by the majority, where no other means were open.''[29] Whether Hunt's conclusion is correct is a matter we will postpone for our critique, at which time we will also ask whether Marx's revolutionary theory is compatible with a prophetic theory of the just revolution.[30]

Alliance of Workers, Peasants, and Progressive Bourgeoisie

The strategy of proletarian majority revolution, which Marx adhered to throughout his life, is not, however, Marx's sole revolutionary strategy. He also articulates a second strategy—of alliance of the majority classes. Here we turn to the strategy for ''less advanced but still essentially bourgeois countries, like France and Germany,'' a strategy involving a ''more complex process. . . . ''[31] Initially, Marx advocates a liberal bourgeois revolution (supported by workers, peasants, and petit bourgeoisie) to establish a constitutional monarchy with genuine parliamentary institutions in Germany, or a genuine parliamentary regime in France. This strategy is a modification of the strategy of proletarian majority revolution. This modification, in the 1848 period, is required ''to fit the more backward conditions of France and Germany. . . . ''[32] Marx's judgment is that this revolution will in time be followed by a communist revolution.[33]

With the failure of the liberal haut-bourgeois revolutions of 1848, Marx adopted a more radical approach, one that looked to a majority alliance of petit bourgeois, peasants, and workers to make a ''popular revolution against authoritarian government,'' a revolution that would establish a democratic republic, which would then be followed after a suitable period of preparation by communist rule. "Only after an extended period of time would the proletariat be developed enough to rule alone and implement full communism." Hunt emphasizes that even during the ultraradical period of 1850, Marx's strategy "was but a refinement of the one" he "had in mind for France prior to February 1848 and for Germany after November 1848."[34]

"The refinement," Hunt writes, "involved three new points: (1) the workers should develop their own independent organizations within the broader alliance of majority classes, so as not to fall under the shadow of the 'pale' democrats; (2) as between their two partners, the workers should count more on the peasants and expect quick betrayal from the petty bourgeoisie; and (3) in the absence of political freedoms—and only for that reason—it is necessary to work in and with secret societies and collaborate with their largely Blanquist leaders."

"Even during the ultraradical period, however," Hunt emphasizes, "Marx and Engels definitely did not accept the Blanquist prescription for a deliberate seizure of power by a conspiratorial elite, followed by the educational dictatorship of that elite and the immediate introduction of communism, with elections postponed until the classless society was a reality."[35]

Again, some elements of this strategy can be found in the *Manifesto*, where Marx indicates the importance of working with the bourgeoisie in Germany "whenever it acts in a revolutionary way" and with French republicans against the conservative bourgeoisie. "In short, the Communists everywhere support every revolutionary movement against the existing social and political order of things." They seek to labor "for the union and agreement of the democratic parties of all countries."[36] The *Manifesto*, of course, is very clear on the ultimate clash between bourgeois and proletarians. So it is quite evident that the alliance with the petit bourgeoisie and the peasants is temporary and will not save bourgeois capitalism. Pointedly, in the *Manifesto* Marx holds that "the bourgeois revolution in Germany [which he mistakenly anticipated] will be but the prelude to an immediately following [another mistaken judgment!] proletarian revolution."[37] These mistaken judgments lead Marx subsequently to place his reliance on a ruling majority alliance of peasants, petit bourgeoisie, and workers, which in turn, after a preparatory period of time, will be followed by proletarian rule.

How countries such as France and Germany, which lacked a population that had a majority of proletarians, would come to proletarian rule has led to a great deal of controversy about the genuinely democratic commitments of Marx. Is he really a totalitarian democrat, at least in the period 1848–1850? Let us, in the conclusion to this section, address this question again, with the help of Richard N. Hunt's keen analysis.

Hunt argues convincingly that Marx does not accept the idea of a vanguard party of the enlightened few. Marx's membership in the Communist League notwithstanding, Marx's judgment is characterized by an "unvarying repudiation of conspiracies."[38] "Where legal conditions permitted" Marx "preferred an open mass party such as the Chartist movement in Britain or the nationwide workers' party they tried to create in Germany in 1849."[39]

Marx also clearly favors a majority revolution; he does not support minority revolution. Hunt acknowledges that Marx's second strategy of alliance of the majority classes "may justifiably raise skeptical eyebrows when it is understood as 'permanent revolution'—initiated, to be sure, by an alliance of the majority classes in countries like France and Germany, but carried to its ultimate conclusion by the proletariat alone."[40] But, argues Hunt, Marx "envisaged a process [not of weeks or months] extending through a couple of decades at least, during which time the proletariat was expected—as a consequence of economic modernization—to develop into the majority class."[41] In our critique in the third section, below, we shall return to Hunt's interpretation and to the question of Marx's judgment.

Next, what about the troubling question of revolutionary terror? Hunt notes that both "Marx and Engels' most bloodthirsty pronouncements on the subject of revolutionary terror similarly belong to the period 1848–1850, after which they condemned terror far more often and more sharply than they ever praised it. The oft-quoted terror passages of the *Neue Rheinische Zeitung,* once set in their proper historical context, appear to be helpless cries of outrage against the physical brutality of the counterrevolution, rather than a serious program of action; in their day-to-day behavior as 'practicing' revolutionaries, the two men showed distinct cautiousness and restraint. The final and renowned invocation of terror in the March *Circular* was in all likelihood the inspiration of Willich [a German radical communist], since no similar recommendations can be found in any of Marx and Engels' other 1850 writings. While they certainly envisaged the use of force during and immediately after the revolution to 'crush the resistance of the bourgeoisie,' a systematic policy of terror was not integral to their vision of revolution, since they did not imagine a minority would be imposing its will on the reluctant majority, but quite the contrary. Only a minority of dispossessed bourgeois and their hangers-on would pose any threat to the democratic republic."[42]

What, next, of the idea of the dictatorship of the proletariat, which also troubles interpretations of Marx's revolutionary strategy and tactics? We will explore this idea more fully in a separate section. Here we can share Hunt's judgment that Marx's usage of the term "has little in common with the totalitarian notion of educational dictatorship by an enlightened elite."

"Insofar as the phrase had an exact meaning, it referred to the unavoidably extralegal [and perhaps repressive] character of an otherwise democratic government by the proletarian majority during the *Provisorium* [or interregnum] that must immediately follow any revolution."[43]

Hunt, in refuting the charge that Marx in his revolutionary strategy and tactics was a totalitarian democrat, affirms Marx's faith—and confident judgment—in the capacity of the masses. "Perhaps the key distinguishing feature of Marx and Engels' thinking . . . was precisely their conviction, their ultimate democratic faith, that the masses could and would educate *themselves*, liberate *themselves*, and rule *themselves*."[44] We will have occasion to assess this faith again—as well as the other points made above—in our critique.

Legal, Constitutional, Peaceful Revolution

As we have noted earlier in this chapter, Marx holds that a revolution to bring workers as a majority of the population to power and to communism will be necessary because those in power, including the bourgeois capitalists, will not give up their political and economic power in any other way. In the *Communist Manifesto* and elsewhere, Marx emphasizes that the communist revolution involves "violent overthrow," "force," "forcible overthrow."[45] This is not the judgment of a bloodthirsty communist revolutionary, but the realistic recognition of a sober social scientist.

Peaceful change is preferable, but it is highly unlikely. The absence of universal suffrage and of the basic freedoms of speech, press, assembly, and association makes it extraordinarily difficult, if not impossible, for workers—alone or in alliance with other progressive democratic forces—to use peaceful, constitutional, legal means to come to power. Marx, very early in his revolutionary career, acknowledges that some reforms benefiting workers—especially universal suffrage, the ten hour day, regulatory factory legislation—can be accomplished in bourgeois countries. But he never believes, in saying this, that such reforms will be enough. Such reforms, alone, will not lead to communism.[46]

Later in his life, however, Marx acknowledges that in certain advanced capitalist countries socialism might be accomplished peacefully—and constitutionally and legally. This judgment, we must appreciate, is a modification of his fundamental position with regard to means, not an abandonment of his commitment to communism and the revolutionary change that communism signifies. If such students as Hunt are correct, Marx was always committed to genuinely democratic means. Marx, however, is clearly unafraid to advocate a democratic revolution—including the use of force by the majority—if peaceful, constitutional, legal means will not work to advance communist ends. When such means would work, they are preferable. In 1871 Marx holds: "We must declare to the governments: we know that you are the armed power directed against the proletariat; we will agitate against you in peaceful ways where that is possible for us, and with arms where it is necessary."[47]

In 1872 Marx made a speech in Amsterdam that throws light on his views on the possibility of peaceful change in some countries. He stated that "we do not deny that there are countries like America, England (and, if I knew your institutions better, I would add Holland), where the workers can achieve their aims by peaceful means."[48] Even as he endorses this strategy, he notes its limitations: "However true that may be, we ought also to recognize that in most countries on the Continent, it is force that must be the lever of our revolutions; it is to force that it will be necessary to appeal for a time in order to establish the reign of labour. . . . "[49] He had also affirmed this position a year earlier in an interview with a *New York World* reporter: "In England . . . the way to show political power lies open to the working class. Insurrection would be madness where peaceful agitation would more swiftly and surely do the work. In France [by way of contrast] a hundred laws of repression seem to necessitate the violent solution of social war."[50]

Marx's judgment about the possibility of a peaceful, constitutional, legal path to socialism is hedged with reservations and characterized by fears. Marx worries about the resistance of the bourgeois ruling classes and of undemocratic states. He also worries about the lack of militancy in the working class and in social democratic working parties. He fears the counterrevolution that an authoritarian state or the bourgeois class will undertake to prevent or overturn a genuinely democratic communist revolution.

In 1880 Marx writes to an English friend that "my party . . . considers an English revolution not necessary, but—according to historic precedents—possible." He then adds that "if the unavoidable evolution turns into a revolution, it would not only be the fault of the ruling classes, but also the working class. . . . " He notes that every "pacific concession" of the ruling classes "has been wrung from them by 'pressure from without.' " The action of the ruling class keeps pace with the pressure of the working class. If the working class has "weakened," Marx maintains, "it is only because the English working class know not how to wield their power and use their liberties, both of which they possess legally."[51]

The fear of a counterrevolution, directed against the workers, is real and not imaginary. Marx had seen such counterrevolution by authoritarian states and capitalist forces—which he wrote of as a "pro-slavery" revolution—in 1848–1850 and in 1870. He had seen the failures of the haut-bourgeoisie in Germany and in France to carry through even a liberal revolution. He is very conscious of the conservative character of peasants and petit bourgeoisie in both Germany and France. Hence to hold out confident hope of a peaceful, constitutional, legal communist revolution is normally unrealistic.[52] Consequently, Marx's general judgment is that the communist revolution will not be peaceful or legal because the ruling capitalist class will not accept peaceful and legal means that threaten loss of its economic and political power.

Here it is helpful to make some distinctions about Marx's commitments to democratic, legal, peaceful, and gradual change—commitments that help to distinguish Marx's position from that of social democratic reformers whom Marx often criticized for their lack of militancy. As Hunt neatly puts the key points, Marx holds that "the workers' victory would be the conscious effort and the will of the majority—hence democratic at all events. It *might* be legal, if the other side opened and kept open a legal path to power for the majority. It *might* be peaceful, if the other side submitted to that majority without rebellion. It would be gradual only in the sense of not happening all overnight, but would certainly appear swift and decisive in comparison to the reformist vision."[53]

One cannot, of course, be sure whether Marx might have changed his opinions on the possibilities of peaceful change through the ballot box if he had lived longer. We do know that Engels, who outlived Marx by twelve years, was clearly heartened by the peaceful and legal progress that socialists were making in Europe, particularly in Germany. Although he too, along with Marx, had criticized German social democrats for their lack of communist vision and militancy, he did underscore in the very year of his death in 1895 the possibilities of peaceful change in countries that enjoyed universal suffrage. There is no reason to conclude that Marx did not substantially share Engels' position on this issue.

Engels emphasizes that the "bourgeoisie and the government came to be much more afraid of the legal than of the illegal action of the worker's party, of the results of elections than of those of rebellion."[54] He notes, "Rebellion in the old style, street fighting with barricades, which decided the issue everywhere up to 1848 was [now] to a considerable extent obsolete."[55] Street fighting might, however, still play a role later in the course of a revolution, and it might have to be "undertaken with greater forces."[56]

Nonetheless, Engels emphasizes the importance of winning the great mass of the people through "propaganda work and parliamentary activity."[57] He sees the possibility, through electoral success, of becoming "the decisive power in the land."[58] It is important to avoid a large-scale clash with the military.[59] Engels sees "irony" in the legal electoral success of socialists. "We, the 'revolutionists,' the 'overthrowers'—we are thriving far better on legal methods than on illegal methods and overthrow. The parties of Order, as they call themselves, are perishing under the legal conditions created by themselves."[60]

Although Engels is unhappy—as Marx would have been—about an impression that his position might lead people to think he is a defender of peace at all costs and one who abhors force under all circumstances, that he is a blind worshipper of legality, it seems reasonably clear that in 1895 Engels recognized changing circumstances. He recognized the difficulties of revolutionary street fighting, the power and danger of the military, the opportunities provided by peaceful propaganda, universal suffrage, parliamentary power.[61]

We cannot be absolutely sure that in 1895 Marx would have shared Engels' views 100 percent. We can only say that in his own lifetime Marx saw some possibility for legal and peaceful change in England and America; that he thought force would probably be needed on the continent; but that he was responsive to changing circumstances that might lead him, pragmatically, to alter his views on the possibility of legal and peaceful change in such countries as Germany and France. The main emphasis in his writings, even in his later years, is still the emphasis on the need for a radical and fundamental revolution—probably necessitating force—to usher in proletarian rule and communism. Such force, he never forgets, might be required to forestall a non-democratic and pro-bourgeois counterrevolution or to defeat it after a proletarian legal victory.

Marx's position, then, is that of a tough-minded but democratic communist revolutionary. Hunt summarizes the common position of Marx and Engels as follows: "It is apparent that neither Marx nor Engels 'mellowed' with age on these issues [of legal revolution, of peaceful change]; rather it was external conditions that changed, as various Western countries extended democratic institutions in a way that made 'legal revolution' a possibility in their eyes. That possibility did not extend to Germany even though the establishment of a democratically elected Reichstag there might create such an illusion among the gullible; in Germany, a legal electoral victory could be a signal for violent revolution not a substitute for it. Indeed, this might well prove to be the case even in the Western democracies, if the workers' victory produced a pro-slavery [i.e., a pro-capitalist] rebellion on the part of the bourgeoisie. Marx and Engels never supported political violence as an offensive weapon in democratic countries, and were willing to go out of their way to avoid provoking the bourgeoisie to violence. They *desired* a legal and peaceful changeover as much as any reformist; where they differed was in their *estimate of the probabilities*, and in their consequent insistence that the workers always stand ready for a forceful showdown when the class struggle reached its climax. The dichotomy here should not be drawn between revolutionaries and democrats, but between tough-minded and tender-minded democrats."[62]

So there is a possibility—but by no means a clear-cut probability—for a legal and peaceful transformation to communism in countries with "democratic institutions—not just universal suffrage to be sure, but universal suffrage combined with a competent legislature, a democratically controlled executive branch, and the usual political freedoms."[63] Again and again Marx's judgment is that "we will agitate against you in peaceful ways where that is possible, and with arms where it is necessary."[64] But Marx never tires of insisting that piecemeal reforms, per se, will not lead to communism. This provides an important clue, along with Marx's recognition of the need to be ready to defeat a counterrevolution by force, that serves to distinguish Marx from mere socialist reformers.

Hunt puts the important question here: "But if Marx . . . allowed for a peaceful and legal 'revolution' in democratic countries, if . . . [he] advocated the formation of an open mass party that aimed at winning an electoral majority, if . . . [he] rejected political violence as an offensive weapon and sought reform through legislation—then why should . . . [he] *not* be considered a reformist?"[65]

Marx is to be differentiated from "reformists" insofar as he insists militantly on carrying through the revolution—peacefully if possible, by violence if necessary—to achieve communism. Secondly, he recognizes more clearly than the reformists that workers must be armed and prepared to use violence to defeat a counterrevolution. "All this suggests strongly" that Marx was "not *looking* for violence," was "ready to go out [of his] way to avoid it, and certainly saw no need for the workers to initiate it in democratic countries." "Nonetheless, [Marx] differed from more tender-minded socialists in that [he] did not flinch at the prospect, but rather counseled workers over and over again to rely on their own military potential and to stand ready to resist and suppress any slaveowner's [counterrevolutionary] insurrection that might be attempted." As a "tough-minded" democrat he "faced up squarely to the central issue of force as the *ultima ratio* of state power."[66]

We will return again to Marx's judgment on legal and peaceful revolution, and especially to his judgment about communist force to defeat counterrevolutionary authoritarian or capitalist force in our critique. These issues remain troubling ones in the revolutionary calculus of costs and in the defense of Marx's revolutionary theory as a theory of a just revolution.

Communism via an Agrarian Revolution

Strategies one and two (proletarian majority revolution, alliance of the majority classes) are clearly the central ones in Marx's nineteenth century lifetime. Strategy three (legal, peaceful, constitutional revolution) is, in some advanced countries, a possibility, but not a strong probability. Even less probable, although considered briefly but not developed fully, is a fourth strategy based on a possible agrarian revolution in Russia. Such a communist revolution might emerge from mass peasant discontent in a country like Russia, and might be based on such a communal Russian agricultural arrangement as the *obshchina*. By the mid-1870s Marx "countenanced the prospect of a mass peasant revolution in Russia, where, because of the surviving traditions of the village community [the *obshchina*], it seemed at least possible that socialism might be constructed immediately. . . . "[67]

In Marx's last published writing, a preface to the Russian edition of the *Communist Manifesto*, he asks: "Can the Russian *obshchina*, though greatly undermined, yet a form of the primeval common ownership of land, pass directly to the higher form of communist common ownership? Or, on the contrary, must it first pass through the same process of dissolution as constitutes the historical evolution of the West?" Or, putting the matter differently, can Russia—because of the *obshchina*—skip the bourgeois, industrial stage and go directly to communism? Marx's terse and ambiguous answer is this: "If the Russian Revolution becomes the signal for a proletarian revolution in the West, so that both complement each other, the present Russian common ownership of land may serve as the starting-point for a communist development."[68]

Marx's modest elaboration on his position here, in the unsent drafts of three separate letters to a Russian revolutionary exile, Vera Sassoulitch, are not very illuminating. Marx looks to, without specifying the character of, a "necessary" Russian revolution. He writes enigmatically: "If the revolution comes at an opportune time, if it concentrates all its forces to ensure the free development of the rural commune, this commune will soon develop into an element that regenerates Russian society and guarantees superiority over countries enslaved by the capitalist regime."[69]

Marx considers the idea that a Russian revolution might be able to skip the bourgeois state and go to communism. He does not want people "to change my sketch of the origin of capitalism in Western Europe into an historical-philosophical theory of Universal Progress, fatally imposed on all peoples, regardless of the historical circumstances in which they find themselves."[70] Finally, however, Marx endorses the view, articulated by Engels, that a socialist revolution in Russia, based on a peasant revolution and the *obshchina*, will only be successful if also accompanied by a supporting proletarian revolution in the West.[71]

What is clear is that Marx's view of a social revolution in Russia is based on a mass peasant movement, not on a minority revolutionary communist vanguard. Popular emancipation, the Russian revolution—as Hunt puts it—"must be the work of the masses themselves."[72]

This strategy of an agrarian revolution as the route to communism in Russia would probably not receive the attention it gets—given its minor treatment in the corpus of Marx's writing—were it not for the twentieth century reality of the Russian Revolution and the Chinese Revolution (neither of which, of course, was crucially related to a tradition of the agricultural commune).

Stage 3: Consolidating the Revolution

Although we have touched upon Marx's judgments on consolidating the revolution, it remains now to consider this stage of the communist revolution more fully. In this section we summarize some of Marx's general judgments on this theme, and then focus more sharply on the controversial conception of the dictatorship of the proletariat, as it functions as a crucial strategy in consolidating the revolution. We pay particular attention to the emergence of a communist constitution, the use of force in proletarian rule, the status of freedom and democracy (including freedom for opponents of the communist revolution) in this period, changes in the economic domain looking toward the overthrow of capitalism and its replacement by communism, other communist political and social actions, the meaning of "permanent revolution." This presentation, therefore, develops Marx's judgments about proletarian rule, and explores more fully his views of the state, constitution, power, democracy, and party.

General Judgments About Consolidating the Revolution

As we have already noted, the communists, having come to power, must press on to abolish capitalism and ensure worker control of the means of production and exchange. They must, moreover, affect a communist transformation of society in the political and societal as well as the economic realms. The coercive and often parasitic state, used or tolerated by bourgeois capitalist interests, must be smashed, and replaced by proletarian rule and democratic institutions. Workers and their revolutionary allies must unhesitatingly use their political powers—including the coercive power of the state—to ensure the building of a communist society.

These general judgments do not answer in more detail key questions about the task of consolidating the revolution. Unfortunately, Marx never addresses this task in a full and complete way in a single text, or indeed in several texts. Hence, we have to piece together his answers from a number of sources and at considerable risk. A key danger in this enterprise is giving more prominence and significance to the concept of the dictatorship of the proletariat than it deserves in the corpus of Marx's writings.

The Dictatorship of the Proletariat

Richard N. Hunt's summary of the history of the concept provides a helpful introduction. "By tracing the history of the slogan 'dictatorship of the proletariat' through . . . eleven successive writings, we may understand the controversial idea in its proper historical setting. If not just a 'little expression,' as Kautsky would have it, neither was it 'the very essence of Marx's teaching,' à la Lenin. The phrase was never used in any of the masters' more substantial publications but was employed only to express factional compromises or distinctions in their dealings with other currents of the socialist movement: first as a compromise slogan with the Blanquists in 1850, and then as a counterposed idea of dictatorship to be distinguished from the Blanquist notion; next as an emphatic means of rebutting the anarchist call for an immediate dissolution of the state; and finally as a provocative way of striking a 'wholesome terror' into the faint hearts of Lassalleans and reformist Social Democrats. The *rule* of the proletariat was surely 'the essence of Marx's teaching,' but to label it 'dictatorship' was in truth little more than factional politics."[3] As we try to get at the meaning of the dictatorship of the proletariat, let me emphasize that my primary concern is to try to illuminate Marx's judgments about the consolidation of the revolution.

As we have seen, for Marx the communist revolution ushers in proletarian rule. But the proletarians need to consolidate their control. Presumably, in strategies one and two, and prior to the advent of a new communist constitution establishing communist legitimacy, this requires—in the process of completing the overthrow of capitalism—a "revolutionary dictatorship of the proletariat."[4] Such a proletarian dictatorship is necessary in the illegal interim stage of the revolutionary process to ensure proletarian rule and to initiate communist policy in order to prepare the way for the more genuinely communist community.

In 1875 Marx makes explicit his understanding of the interim stage of the communist revolution. "Between capitalist and communist society lies the period of the revolutionary transformation of the one into the other. There corresponds to this also a political transition period in which the state can be nothing but the *revolutionary dictatorship of the proletariat.*"[5]

But what did Marx mean by this concept? We can gain a little more insight into Marx's understanding of the dictatorship of the proletariat by examining what he had to say (without explicitly using the term "dictatorship of the proletariat") in the *Manifesto* in 1848, in his letter to his German socialist brethren in 1879, and in his *The Civil War in France* in 1871 (where the term is used explicitly). While liberal democrats have trouble with Marx's logic, it is important to understand that Marx sees proletarian rule, in the interim stage of the revolution after the overthrow of capitalism, as both democratic and dictatorial: democratic because it is based on majority and popular rule; dictatorial because it is both illegal, in the interregnum between the majority revolution and a communist constitution, and it requires revolutionary force.[76] The soundness of this argument we will return to again in our critique.

In the *Manifesto* Marx seems to have anticipated at least some of the ideas that give meaning to his concept of the dictatorship of the proletariat. In the *Manifesto* he notes that the proletariat, in becoming the ruling class in "the first step of the revolution," makes "despotic inroads on the rights of property, and on the conditions of bourgeois production," and adopts measures that, although at the beginning "insufficient and untenable," progressively revolutionize the mode of production.[77] The proletariat must sweep "away by force the old conditions of production."[78]

Marx does not explicitly say that these measures illustrate the way in which the dictatorship of the proletariat operates. And he does not indicate in the *Manifesto* that these measures will be enacted legally after the adoption of a communist constitution. They are, however, clearly measures designed to consolidate the revolution. Given Marx's language about "despotic inroads" and "force," we might, then, properly conclude that these measures do illustrate the operation of the dictatorship of the proletariat.

The measures that seemed appropriate in 1848 for "most advanced countries," but which Marx recognizes might not be applicable at other times ("measures [which] will of course be different in different countries"), include the famous Marxist decalogue. These measures illustrate concretely actions that might be required to advance the communist revolution. Presumably, if enacted prior to a new communist constitution, they would clearly illustrate the democratic, revolutionary dictatorship—or rule—of the proletariat.

Hunt argues that measures taken by the proletarian majority after the adoption of, and presumably in accordance with, a communist constitution would not be dictatorial, because the dictatorship functions only in the illegal interregnum between the majority's seizure of power and the adoption of the legitimating communist constitution. However it is not absolutely clear that the proletariat will not use coercion to consolidate communism even after the adoption of the communist constitution. Such coercion would then be legal, but it still might be considered dictatorial by, for example, the capitalists who are repressed, even if in accordance with the rule of the proletarian majority.

Marx himself did not clearly and fully develop the position (attributed to him by Hunt) that the dictatorship of the proletariat would cease once a communist constitution is adopted. And Marx did not indicate how long the dictatorship of the proletariat would last or when the new communist constitution would be written. If Hunt is correct, the dictatorship of the proletariat would not occupy the whole period between the proletarian seizure of power and the advent of mature communism—the period best understood in Marx's language as the first phase of communism.

However, if Hunt's argument is persuasive, it is not definitive. Marx's failure to clarify more adequately the nature of the dictatorship of the pro-letariat leaves open the possibility that the coercive and repressive aspects of the dictatorship of the proletariat might last even after the adoption of the communist constitution makes such action legal, might in other words linger on until the advent of mature communism and the abolition of the coercive state. This possibility, of course, would be enhanced if capitalistic and bourgeois forces resist the process of communism—particularly if they resist forcefully.

The decalogue in the *Manifesto* calls for the following:

"1. Abolition of property in land and application of all rents of land to public purposes.

2. A heavy progressive or graduated income tax.

3. Abolition of all right of inheritance.

4. Confiscation of the property of all emigrants and rebels.

5. Centralisation of credit in the hands of the State, by means of a national bank with State capital and an exclusive monopoly.

6. Centralisation of means of communication and transport in the hands of the state.

7. Extension of factories and instruments of production owned by the State; the bringing into cultivation of wastelands, and the improvement of the soil gener-ally in accordance with a common plan.

8. Equal liability of all to labour. Establishment of industrial armies, especially for agriculture.

9. Combination of agriculture with manufacturing industries; gradual aboli-tion of the distinction between town and country, by a more equitable distribution of the population over the country.

10. Free education for all children in public schools. Abolition of children's factory labour in its present form. Combination of education with industrial produc-tion, etc., etc."⁹

Some of these measures, we must note, are quite compatible with modern liberal democratic philosophy. Other measures are more radical and would probably encounter strong, if not violent, resistance from those adversely affected. Certainly, socialization of the means of production and exchange would encounter such resistance.

In brief, the proletariat, organized as the ruling class, would use the power of the State to sweep away "by force the old conditions of produc-tion," and to usher in the new, and revolutionary, communist mode of production. This would involve "despotic inroads on the rights of property." Measures to centralize all instruments of production in the hands of the workers would progressively achieve the communist revolution.

Marx's criticism of his German socialist brethren—especially their anti-reformist views—also helps us to understand Marx's concept of the revolutionary dictatorship of the proletariat. These anti-reformist views, we must remember, are also characteristic of the *Manifesto*. In a letter to Bebel, Liebknecht, and other German Social Democrats, Marx attacks the tactic of reform as a policy that abandons the class struggle in favor of "patching up . . . the capitalist order."[80]

Marx contrasts the correct communist position with that of wrong-headed Social Democratic reformists. Communists must be committed to "determined political opposition," not to "general mediation." They must "struggle against the government and the bourgeoisie," not "attempt to win over and persuade them." They must adopt a policy of "defiant resistance to ill treatment," not one of "submission and confession that [their] punishment . . . [is] deserved." They must opt for destruction of the bourgeois order, not for patching it up. They must be committed to "violent bloody revolution" not "peaceful . . . dissolution."[81]

Here, then, Marx insists that peaceful, gradual, and piecemeal reform will not do the job. A fundamental, violent revolution is necessary. This argument of Marx's is, of course, designed to illuminate the need for a fundamental, violent revolution to overthrow the bourgeois state—a strategy that we outlined in our previous section on making the revolution. However it also makes clear that revolutionary means, utilizing force, will also have to be used after that overthrow; that the revolution will have to use force not only to overthrow capitalism at the beginning but also will have to use proletarian power until the fundamental transformation to the communist order has taken place. The complete destruction of the oppressive bourgeois order presumably calls for such proletarian force against the bourgeoisie. In using such force, the proletariat—the majority of people—will clearly and unmistakably be using their power in the interests of the fundamental communist revolution.

Of course, in *The Class Struggles in France*, published in 1850, Marx had earlier identified "revolutionary socialism" ("communism") as "the declaration of the permanence of the revolution, the class dictatorship of the proletariat, as the necessary transit point to the abolition of class distinctions generally, to the abolition of all the relations of production on which they rest, to the abolition of all the social relations that correspond to these relations of production, to the revolutionizing of all the ideas that result from these social relations."[82] He sees the dictatorship of the proletariat as a device to "crush the resistance of the bourgeoisie"[83]; as constituting "the transition to the *abolition of all classes* and to a *classless society*."[84] For further amplification of Marx's understanding of the "revolutionary dictatorship of the proletariat" we turn to his analysis in 1871 of *The Civil War in France*.

If Engels is correct, the Paris Commune "was the Dictatorship of the Proletariat." Certainly Marx saw a mythic model of the Paris Commune as a possible model of a worker's revolution, if not *the* model of such a revolution.[85] The Paris Commune at least throws some light on what revolutionaries had done, and might do, after their seizure of power. Our reservations about the historical accuracy of Marx's account of the Commune need not prevent our presentation of Marx's model.

Marx sees the Commune as "essentially a working-class government, the produce of the struggle of the producing against the appropriating class, the political form at last discovered under which to work out the economic emancipation of labour."[86] He writes that the "Commune intended to abolish that class-property which makes the labour of the many the wealth of the few. It aimed at the expropriation of the expropriators. It wanted to make individual property a truth by transforming the means of production, land and capital, now chiefly the means of enslaving and exploiting labour, into mere instruments of free and associated labour."[87]

Marx views the Commune as a working person's revolutionary seizure of power. The armed people of Paris had seized political power. They then proceeded to destroy the repressive organs of the old government, especially the old standing army, and to democratize legitimate governmental organs. "While the merely repressive organs of the old governmental power were to be amputated, its legitimate functions were to be wrested from an authority usurping preeminence over society itself, and restored to the responsible agents of society. Instead of deciding once in three years which member of the ruling class was to misrepresent the people in Parliament, universal suffrage was to serve the people . . . "[88]

Destruction and restoration go hand in hand. "The first decree of the Commune, therefore, was the suppression of the standing army, and the substitution for it of the armed people."[89] The people's representatives are to be held responsible, and their powers are to be "revocable at short terms."[90] In a comparable way, the police and judges are to be held responsible, and their powers revocable.[91] Churches are to be disestablished and disendowed.[92] Education is to be free and "cleared of all interference of Church and State."[93]

The Commune is to be a "working, not a [phony bourgeois] parliamentary body"; it is to be "executive and legislative at the same time."[94] The parasitic state bureaucracy will be destroyed along with the old state's standing army. This will end irresponsible and expensive power.

"The Commune made that catchword of bourgeois revolution, cheap government, a reality, by destroying the two greatest sources of expenditure—the standing army and State functionarism."[95] The Commune thus acts to destroy, weaken, or transform the old "centralized State power, with its ubiquitous organs of standing army, police, bureaucracy, clergy, and judicature."[96]

"The Commune was therefore intended to serve as a lever for uprooting the economical foundations upon which rests the existence of classes, and therefore class-rule."[97] Moreover, the pattern of the Paris Commune serves as a model for the communist revolution throughout France. A "Communal Constitution" ensures unity in the Nation, appropriate local self-government, and national regeneration."[98] The Commune points toward a communism of "cooperative production," of "united cooperative societies" able "to regulate national production upon a common plan, thus taking it under their own control, and putting an end to the constant anarchy and periodical convulsions which are the fatality of Capitalistic production."[99]

Although the Commune was repressed by force, it establishes an example—Marx argues—and points the way. "Working men's Paris, with its Commune, will be forever celebrated as the glorious harbinger of a new society."[100] The example of the Paris Commune provides us with a little more understanding of how a communist revolution might come and how it might proceed. Workers will lead the revolution, but they will draw support from shopkeepers, tradesmen, and merchants, as well as from peasants. The revolution will require a popular exercise of armed power, the destruction of repressive forces, the construction of new democratic forces. Workers may have to return force for force, violence for violence. No miracles are to be expected. Long struggles before victory are foreseen.[101]

If, indeed, as Engels maintained, the Paris Commune illustrates the dictatorship of the proletariat, it sheds partial light on the meaning of that controversial concept. Clearly, that concept is "democratic" in the sense that workers and their allies—the people—are in control and running affairs in accord with their interests. Whether this popular "democracy" protects the civil rights of rulers of the old regime is open to serious question, a matter we will address shortly. Certainly, the economic and political power of the rulers of the old bourgeois regime will be destroyed.

How necessary is the dictatorship of the proletariat? Apparently Marx thinks it necessary because capitalistic forces and the non-democratic state will not give up without a fight. After his careful analysis Hunt is persuaded that Marx "envisaged a mass revolution to *establish* democratic institutions, preferably in the radically deprofessionalized form suggested by the Paris Commune, but once established in any event, there was no further need for violence unless provoked by the other side, and no further need for dictatorship unless to deal with such insurrections through martial law.'' For Marx, dictatorship (writes Hunt) ''was not an inherent part of workers' rule,'' and perhaps this is one reason he ''used the term so infrequently.''[102]

Hunt maintains, further, that while Marx ''sometimes spoke of the need to 'smash' the bureaucratic state,'' he ''never spoke of smashing democratic institutions of representation and self-government, even bourgeois ones.''[103] Hunt concedes that Marx ''seemed to assume a violent suppression of the bourgeois minority in which no quarter need be given, no rights or restraints acknowledged.'' But then Hunt notes that democratic use of force could be justified under a liberal democratic philosophy of revolution, especially democratic force aimed at open minority rebellion, that is, violent resistance by the bourgeois minority. The basic freedoms of speech, assembly, and association might not be extended to such violent minority rebels. One could only ask of the communist revolutionaries that they put down such a violent bourgeois minority revolt ''with the minimum force possible and with maximum humanity.''[104]

However, Hunt also notes, nowhere does Marx ''suggest that [peaceful] opponents of the revolution be denied the core political freedoms or the right to vote.'' He emphasizes that Marx never says a word in support of curtailing, for example, ''the rights of peaceful opposition under the Paris Commune.''[105] There is evidence, moreover, supporting Marx's seemingly prudential practical revolutionary dictum of restraint in exchange for restraint, and brutality for brutality, even if, in counterrevolutionary periods, his rhetoric is sometimes shrill.[106]

The dictatorship of the proletariat would, then, be required only for a limited time, most clearly in the illegal interregnum between the communist revolution and the onset of proletarian rule *and* (Hunt argues) the advent of a democratic communist constitution. However, Marx tells us too little about the legitimating communist constitution, and does not explicitly indicate that the dictatorship of the proletariat—or at least all features of dictatorial power—will cease once that constitution is in place. Hence, we remain in doubt as to the exact duration of the dictatorship of the proletariat.

Hunt sums up Marx's position on consolidating the revolution as follows: Marx ''expected the state as parasite to disappear immediately through deprofessionalization, the state as dictatorship, if required initially, to disappear by definition with the establishment of a new legality, and the state as coercive power to disappear substantially with the end of expropriations and bourgeois resistance, but only completely and absolutely after a new generation had so internalized the rules of social intercourse that no external coercion whatsoever would be required.''[107]

We will return to Marx's judgments about consolidating the revolution, and to his concept of the dictatorship of the proletariat, in our critique. There we will ask whether Marx's theory can find a place within the theory of the just revolution. There, too, we will assess Marx's revolutionary calculus of costs and benefits, with particular attention to the character of democracy and freedom in Marx's revolutionary theory.

Stage 4: Achieving Mature Communism

Now, what of the advent of communism itself and the character of, and judgments required in, the communist community? The communist revolution points toward the end of oppression for workers, the end of class antagonisms and of classes. It points not only toward fuller freedom but also toward integration, toward a more genuine humanity and community, and toward rich individual and social development. But what more does Marx tell us of the character of the process by which the revolution moves toward mature communism? And what of his judgments about communist society itself?

One famous passage in the *Manifesto* provides us with some hints. "When, in the course of development, class distinctions have disappeared, and all production has been concentrated in the hands of a vast association of the whole nation, the public power will lose its political character. Political power, properly so called, is merely the organized power of one class for oppressing another. If the proletariat during its contest with the bourgeoisie is compelled, by force of circumstances, to organise itself as a class, if, by means of a revolution, it makes itself the ruling class, and, as such, sweeps away by force the old conditions of production, then it will, along with these conditions, have swept away the conditions for the existence of class antagonisms and of classes generally, and will thereby have abolished its own supremacy as a class."[108]

Presumably, revolutionary force will have to be employed, not only to make the initial revolution but to ensure subsequent worker control of the economy, political life, and society. When the communist economy is in place and functioning, then oppressive political power will become obsolete. Presumably, in the newly created communist society, coercive police, prisons, and armed forces will no longer be necessary.

The communist revolution points not only toward the end of oppressive power, and the achievement of freedom, but also toward free development and the ability to respond to human needs.

"In place of the old bourgeois society, with its classes and class antagonisms, we shall have an association, in which the free development of each is the condition for the free development of all."[109]

"In a higher phase of communist society, after the enslaving subordination of the individual to the division of labor, and therewith also the antithesis between mental and physical labour, has vanished; after labour has become not only a means of life but life's prime want; after the productive forces have also increased with the all-around development of the individual, and all the springs of cooperative wealth flow more abundantly—only then can the narrow horizon of bourgeois right be crossed in its entirety and society inscribe on its banner: From each according to his ability, to each according to his needs!"[110]

Marx anticipates that communist society will overcome a number of divisions within society—and especially the division of labor. His most famous affirmation of this scenario is, of course, his picture of an idyllic community society that has successfully overcome the division of labor in cooperative society. Thus, in *The German Ideology* (1845/46) Marx indicates that in the "communist society, where nobody has one exclusive sphere of activity but each can become accomplished in any branch he wishes, society regulates the general production and thus makes it possible for me to do one thing today and another tomorrow, to hunt in the morning, fish in the afternoon, rear cattle in the evening, criticise after dinner, just as I have a mind, without ever becoming hunter, fisherman, shepherd or critic."[111]

Is this a romantic, utopian relapse—contrary to Marx's hostility to "castles in the air"—or does it inform us that Marx seriously believes that the stultifying division of labor could actually be overcome under communism, that freedom in diversity could actually prevail? We cannot be absolutely sure. But we can note that Marx anticipates overcoming the worst aspects of the division of labor, and other divisions—for example, the division between town and country, between the sexes, between vocation and avocation.[112] He does look to Communism as a society in which diversity in labor—aided by multiple jobs and job rotation—would end the stultifying division of labor.[113] He does seek to reduce labor time to a minimum in order to free people for their own development.[114] He does stress the importance of productive abundance as a means to ensure the satisfaction of material needs and to create the material basis for political, social, and cultural freedom and achievement.[115]

Marx recognizes that "in the first phase of communist society" there would be "defects." Equal pay for equal work, for example, would not eliminate unequal needs or unequal endowment. In brief, those needing more might not, in this first phase, be able to receive more under a system of strict equality and right. Equal right would still be bourgeois right. Marx notes that "one worker is married, another not; one has more children than another, and so on and so forth. Thus, with an equal performance of labour, and hence an equal share in the social consumption fund, one will in fact receive more than another, one will be richer than another, and so on. To avoid all these defects, right instead of being equal would have to be unequal."

Marx holds that "these defects are inevitable in the first phase of communist society as it is when it has just emerged after prolonged birth pangs from capitalist society. Right can never be higher than the economic structure of society and its cultural development conditioned thereby."[116] But, Marx maintains, in the "highest phase of communist society," needs can be satisfied. At this point, communist society will have overcome "the birth marks of the old [bourgeois] society from whose womb" it has emerged.[117]

In economics, production and the means of production are Marx's crucial concerns. Presumably, proletarian control of production, and the cooperative society that will "regulate national production upon a common plan," is the key to communist success and to the achievement of communist objectives.[118] Marx criticizes the emphasis on "distribution" as "vulgar socialism."[119] This is not because Marx is indifferent to distribution, or to consumer needs, but because he sees in worker control of production the key to freedom, integration, humanity and community, and development. Once in possession of that key, other problems—including distribution—will be more easily solved.

If worker control and fruitful productivity are crucial features of the process of movement toward mature communism, and if mature communism looks toward the free and all-round development of the individual and the more complete satisfaction of his needs, what more can we say about the character of the classless communist society?

Politically, Marx favors a radically democratic communist society. Such a society will function as a responsible, highly responsive, participatory democracy, and will be characterized by what Hunt has called "democracy without professionals." People will fulfill necessary governmental functions on a part-time and short-term basis. Thus there will be no perpetuation under communism of the bureaucracy of the parasitic or coercive or authoritarian or bourgeois state. Deprofessionalization will prevail.[120]

Beyond these democratic and freedom-enhancing hints, however, Marx seems to be adverse to depicting the more exact nature and operation of the mature communist society. Indeed, in several places he indirectly or directly criticizes those who call for spelling out a communist constitution as utopians. "They [the working class] have no ready-made utopias to introduce *par decret du peuple*."[121]

Presumably, no a priori blueprints for the communist society can be drawn up and mechanically implemented. The character of the communist constitution will presumably be worked out by working people as they free themselves from the old bourgeois society.

Yet, as we have seen, despite Marx's reservations about spelling out the blueprints of the communist society, a number of key ideas about communist society do emerge. And other key ideas are emphasized. Marx does maintain, for example, that "with the abolition of class distinctions all social and political inequality arising from them would disappear."[122] He also insists that war between nations, and exploitation of one nation by another, will also disappear under communism. "In proportion as the exploitation of one individual by another is put an end to, the exploitation of one nation by another will also be put an end to. In proportion as the antagonism between classes within the nation vanishes, the hostility of one nation to another will come to an end."[123]

But beyond his general statements about achieving worker control, overcoming divisions in society, accomplishing abundant production, enhancing participatory democracy, deprofessionalizing the bureaucracy, enhancing political and social equality, ending antagonism and war, we do not find a clear, full, explicit account of the operation of the communist constitution. We do not learn, for example, how power will be limited, granted, restrained, or how basic freedoms will be maintained. We do not find out about the conduct of elections or about the role of parties, and so on. There is little emphasis upon the fuller rules of the communist game, presumably because oppressive power will have ceased. The problem of the nature of the struggle for power, of accommodation among conflicting interests, presumably does not have to be seriously addressed because oppressive power will have ceased to be a problem. Hence, Marx does not seriously address the problem of the exercise of power within a communist constitution.

It is not the case that Marx is unaware of the question of the role of the state, or—more accurately for Marx—of legitimate governmental functions in communist society. In the *Critique of the Gotha Program* Marx himself asks the hard question: "The question then arises: what transformation will the state undergo in communist society? In other words, what social functions will remain in existence there that are analogous to present functions of the state?"[124] But although Marx criticizes the authors of the Gotha Program for not dealing "with the future state of the communist society" (or with the preceding stage of the revolutionary dictatorship of the proletariat), he does not answer his own question about functions in the communist society, or deal with the "future state of communist society."[125] We are left to assume—on the basis of his views in *The Civil War in France*—that legislative, executive, and judicial functions will remain, and that they will be carried out in a highly democratic fashion.

Marx's failure to clarify more fully the nature of communist society, and to address problems of getting there and making the communist system work well, call for further comment. Let us now turn to a critique of Marx's theory of revolutionary communist action, and attempt to speak more fully to Marx's theory and the important questions it prompts us to raise.

CRITIQUE

Perhaps the best way to address the various questions that have emerged in this chapter about Marx's judgments is to focus on the question of the just revolution, interpreted in the tradition of prophetic politics. This is, I appreciate, an exacting standard for criticism, but it should illuminate our assessment of Marx's theory of revolutionary action.

Our critique, therefore, requires us to ask about the soundness of Marx's ends, his understanding of pervasive and systemic violations of human freedom, his judgment about the possibility of peaceful means to overcome oppression, his humane calculus of costs and benefits, his exploration of the probability that the new communist society and economy will be (and will remain) democratic, free, and fulfilling. In speaking to Marx's judgments about the communist revolution as a just revolution we examine what he says about strategy and tactics in the four stages of his theory of revolutionary communist action.

The criteria for a just revolution in the tradition of prophetic politics—which also constitute a set of general propositions for a defensible calculus of costs and benefits—include the following: (1) The ends and values of the revolutionaries must be fully justifiable, clearly articulated, and thoroughly understood. (2) Violations of those ends and values must affect the overwhelming majority of people, must be widespread, systemic, and deep. (3) Lawful and peaceful means to overcome these violations must first be exhaustively tried, and found wanting. (4) Revolutionary means must be based on the actions of the majority who are oppressed. (5) Revolutionary means, even if violence is required, must still operate under standards of humanity, decency, and restraint. (6) A new constitution (or the reaffirmation of an older constitution), protecting violated and fought-for ends and values, must be a clear objective of the revolution, must be based on the popular will, and must be achieved with all reasonable speed. (7) Even in the transition to the new society, and even under the new constitution, the revolutionaries in power must not in the name of security or in the name of completing the revolution engage in acts of repression of those values and ends for which the revolution was fought, except for an emergency period of limited duration and then under the strictest safeguards. (8) It must not automatically be assumed that the ends and values of the revolution will automatically come into being; a constitutional system—open, democratic, respecting freedom, guarding against the abuse of power—must not only be established *but also jealously maintained* to assure that the revolution is not fought in vain, to provide safeguards against the abuse of power, to ensure that power is wisely exercised, and to allow for a bona fide appraisal of ends and values in the post-revolutionary era.

What of Marx's judgments in stage 1—preparing for the revolution? How sound are Marx's ends and values? Clearly, this is a question of momentous importance. If Marx's ends and values are fully justifiable, clearly articulated, and thoroughly understood, the road is open to examine the other criteria for a just revolution and thus for revolutionary action and satisfaction of the other criteria of the just revolution. Marx's means then become more persuasive. If his ends and values are not justifiable, and so on, then all revolutionary means except legal and peaceful change become suspect. (Of course, in appraising Marx's ends and values, we still have to consider whether communism does in fact usher in his own, or prophetic, ends/values.)

The ends of freedom, integration (harmony, peace), humanity and community, and rich human and social development are (in the abstract) justifiable ends. Universal suffrage and democratic governance are clearly justifiable. Greater control by people—especially workers—over their lives (in the domains of economics, politics, and society) is in theory laudable. Marx's concern for the least-free—their power, needs, development—is clearly in the tradition of prophetic politics.

What is not so clear, however, is the fuller meaning of freedom, integration, humanity/community, and development in the communist society. Is worker control of the means of production and exchange—a key end of communism as an economic system—a totally acceptable value? Or, even if desirable, not practical? Or is there a possibility that freedom (as self-determination, as enabling power in all domains) and communism (as an economic system) are not entirely compatible? Is there a possibility that a regulated capitalism (as an economic system) and liberal democracy (as a political system) are not only compatible with, but essential to, freedom? Certainly the range of economic and political options—communism, democratic socialism, liberal democracy, regulated capitalism—under which freedom and other prophetic values can best prevail should not be dogmatically foreclosed.

Integration, harmony, peace are also attractive ends and values. Overcoming the stultifying division of labor, ending class conflicts, and achieving international as well as domestic peace are powerfully attractive ideas. But again, is it clear that communism will in fact achieve these goals? As we have noted earlier, in Chapter 2, here too Marx's argument is asserted but not conclusively established. How could it be conclusively established in the absence of the practical communist experiment? There is a large ingredient of faith in Marx's value-system. Moreover, one can legitimately ask whether Marx's values—whether freedom, integration, humanity/community, rich development—do not betray in part a foolishly utopian conviction about human possibility.

Marx's ethical commitment to human beings living genuinely human lives in a genuine community, and to rich individual and social development, is laudable. His desire to overcome egoism, to recover social concern and cooperation, to enable human beings to fulfill their unique and creative potentialities in an abundant and supportive community cannot be flawed. However, the relationship between communism and the achievement of these objectives must be probed. Can Marx's vision of economic, political, and social democracy and fulfillment be accomplished under Marx's variety of communism? We simply do not have the evidence to enable us to answer that crucial question.

We can only note how attractive and justifiable at least some of Marx's ends and values are at the same time as we also note how vague they are. We can also underscore how unproved is the link between communism and those ends. We can emphasize what is missing in Marx's articulation of ends. And we can declare how impractical if not foolishly utopian some of his key ideas are.

We would be more satisfied about Marx's ends and values if we knew more about the democratic communist constitution that Marx seemingly endorses, but never fully articulates or develops. We would be happier if he had not been so morally constipated, [126] if he could have explicitly endorsed a constitutional bill of human rights, an open society, a constitution limiting and regulating the exercise of power and guarding against its abuse. We would be happier if he could have addressed the question (in communist society) of conflicts of interests, of elections, of parties, of the relationship between leaders and followers, of the operation of participatory democracy, of democracy without professionals. In the economic sphere we miss Marx's articulation of the way in which the communist economy would operate tò fulfill his objectives. We miss a clear picture of how the various divisions in society could in fact be overcome.

Consequently, we are not entirely persuaded that Marx's ends and values are, indeed, fully justifiable, clearly articulated, and thoroughly understood. Although partly in the tradition of prophetic politics, his ends and values still betray at key points some foolishly utopian conceptions. This means that we must be all the more careful in assessing the rest of his theory as a prophetically just revolution.

In examining Marx's judgments about general preparatory means, we must address the accuracy of Marx's materialistic conception of history, and of his analysis of capitalism and bourgeois society. His views here provide the social scientific basis for his judgment about violations of values, and his confidence in the inevitability of the communist revolution. If such a revolution is not historically inevitable, if Marx's judgment about violations is not accurate, we may lose confidence in Marx as a social scientist and in the cogency of Marx's revolutionary strategy and tactics. Crucial here is Marx's judgment that workers are inevitably oppressed—and massively so—by the very operation of capitalism.

As we have noted, to qualify as a just revolution in the prophetic tradition, violations of prophetic values must affect the overwhelming majority of people, must be widespread, systemic, and deep. Does the "wage slavery" of workers qualify here? Does the absence of universal suffrage in the nineteenth century qualify? Does the absence of democratic freedoms and responsible and responsive parliamentary institutions in the nineteenth century qualify? And is it the case that "wage slavery" and other violations of democratic principles are destined to be overcome?

If the absence of universal suffrage and of democratic freedoms and institutions is a crucial violation of prophetic values (as I believe to be true), then Marx has a powerful case for seeking change. Similarly, if the treatment of workers in the nineteenth century illustrates, in significant measure, wage slavery (as I believe it does), then again Marx can make a powerful case for change. Violations of fundamental values in the nineteenth century were widespread, systemic, and deep.

A key question now involves the troubling issue of whether it will take revolutionary change to communism—however democratic—to overcome wage slavery, or whether economic freedom for workers can be achieved without the overthrow of capitalism as an economic system, can be achieved by liberal democratic reforms within a capitalistic economic system.

Another key question is the question of time: how long will it take to achieve freedom for workers in the economic domain, and for all people denied universal suffrage and democratic freedoms and institutions? How patient must people in the nineteenth century denied fundamental political and economic freedom be? Given what we in the twentieth century democratic tradition believe, Marx could make a very convincing case for preparing for rapid and radical change. Whether such change must only be democratic communist change is less clear.

Certainly, however, Marx's position on change is more plausible than that of the insurrectionists, the anarchists, and the reformists of his day. Certainly Marx sees more clearly than the insurrectionists that achieving freedom will require more than a violent, minority *putsch*. Similarly he sees more clearly than the anarchists that power will have to be employed after a revolution to gain power. Moreover, more clearly than the reformists, he sees the need for more radical change achieved more rapidly.

However, whether Marx's calculus of costs and benefits is more persuasive than that of the reformists—bourgeois or social democratic—will depend on the character and speed of reform, and on the reformists' own calculus of costs and benefits. We will return to this vital issue of the calculus of costs shortly.

What of Marx's four-fold strategy of making the revolution? Let us assume, for the moment, that Marx's ends are fully justifiable, and that violations of those ends affect the overwhelming majority. Does Marx first look to legal and peaceful change? Does he first seek to exhaust legal and peaceful means, only to discover that they will not work?

We know that Marx would have preferred legal and peaceful revolution to achieve communism, if legal and peaceful means were possible and could work. His early revolutionary judgment is that these means are not available and therefore cannot work. This is why violent revolution will be necessary. Only later in his life does he entertain the possibility that in some countries—Britain, the United States—legal and peaceful revolution might be possible. But he worries about a capitalist counterrevolution. And he does not emphasize *exhaustion* of legal and peaceful means. Although he recognizes the need for economic and political ripeness for revolution, appreciates that the communist revolution requires considerable preparation, and affirms that the attainment of power would take decades, Marx does not, I believe, go along with exhausting legal and peaceful means in those countries where the majority of people are denied universal suffrage and democratic freedoms and institutions.

In Britain and the United States his responsiveness to legal and peaceful means would have been directly proportional to the reality of universal suffrage and democratic freedoms and institutions. But even here he would have pushed aggressively toward revolution, if it appeared that those ruling in a bourgeois-dominated democracy would stop short of permitting a majority of the people—the workers—to initiate communism.

The realities of the nineteenth century, however, demonstrated the absence of universal suffrage. (Truly universal suffrage, in theory and practice, had to await the twentieth century—even in the United States.) Other democratic freedoms and institutions were in Europe largely limited to Britain. Moreover, capitalism—and consequently "wage slavery"—characterized both Europe and America. Granted Marx's assumptions about massive violations of freedom, and the absence of legal and peaceful means to achieve change in most countries, Marx could have made a powerful argument for violent revolution, especially in countries like France and Germany. His case would have been weaker in Britain, and weaker still in the United States.

Marx's strategy of a proletarian majority revolution or an alliance of the majority classes is compatible with the theory of the prophetically just revolution insofar as Marx insists that the communist revolution must be based on the majority. Even Marx's concession that a communist revolution in Russia might be sparked by the peasant majority is compatible with the majoritarian principle of the just revolution.

However, questions must be asked about the facts here. (1) Is it really the case that a majority of the population (two-thirds, Marx thought) were industrial workers in Britain? (2) Even if workers were a majority, is it clear that they favored a communist revolution? Even if (1) is true as both Marx and Engels believed, was (2) true? If not, then a proletarian majority revolution could not be justified.

We have no Gallup polls in nineteenth century Britain to test these questions. But the evidence we have suggests that a majority of workers were not communists. And if we look to voting records of workers in the late nineteenth and in the twentieth centuries, we find no support for the conclusion that a majority of workers were communists. I leave open the question whether the workers were blinded by false consciousness and so on. It would seem that Marx would have a difficult time establishing in fact that a majority of people, including workers, really favored a communist revolution to redress the legitimate grievances they may have felt. If this is the case, Marx would not be able to justify his communist revolution as a majority revolution.

If such difficulties affect our appraisal of Marx's judgment about the proletarian majority revolution in a country like Britain, they also affect Marx's strategy of alliance of majority classes in France and Germany. We could assume that a majority alliance of workers, peasants, and petit bourgeoisie might come together to make a revolution to establish a democratic republic. But then our questions about the proletarian, and presumably communist, majority recur. How long after the revolution by the alliance will it take for workers to become a majority of the population in France and Germany? And assuming that they would in time become a majority, is it the case that they would be communists and favor and undertake the communist revolution?

Again, we lack demographic studies and polls that might help us to answer these questions. But again, even if workers came to be a majority of the population, it is not at all clear that workers would be communists and favor a communist revolution. This, then, would make a communist revolution unjustifiable, so long as such a revolution must be a majority revolution.

Marx's revolutionary hopes may have affected his social scientific understanding. He may have assumed, without establishing scientifically, either that workers in France and Germany would become a majority of the population or that (having become a majority of the population) they would be communists and favor a communist revolution.

The same difficulty would face a majority revolution in Russia. Even if the peasants were a majority, and assuming that they would make a revolution, is it the case that the majority of peasants were communists and desired to make a communist revolution? What evidence we have does not support an affirmative answer.

Let us next turn to the question of revolutionary means. I have stated that revolutionary means, even if violence is required, must still operate under standards of humanity, decency, and restraint. Such means must also, of course, be effective. (We shall assume here, contrary to some of our reservations expressed above but for the sake of argument, that so far all the criteria for a just revolution up to this point have in fact been satisfied.) The main emphasis in Marx's judgment here is that violence may be necessary but should operate under restraint. Restraint for restraint, force for force—this is Marx's recommendation.[127] Marx is not a believer in a brutal reign of terror, in a wholesale bloody physical purge of opponents.

However, Marx does not fully address the difficulties of revolutionary violence, or the dangers to humanity, decency, and restraint in the midst of the revolution. He *does* emphasize that dangers of violence spring from capitalists and the bourgeois or authoritarian state: because workers are oppressed under capitalism and such a state, because capitalists will not give up without a fight, and because of the pro-capitalist counterrevolution that they will initiate to defeat the communist revolution. In view of the suppression of liberal, let alone communist, revolutions in the nineteenth century, and in view of the suppression of popular, democratic, and constitutional movements in the twentieth century, Marx's argument about the source of violence is persuasive. Whether Marx himself guards against communist revolutionary excesses in his own strategy of revolutionary action is another question. In my judgment, he is not sufficiently aware of these dangers and did not adequately guard against them.

Let me turn next to the question of the adoption of the new communist constitution. Marx himself does not make the adoption of a communist constitution, identified as such, a prominent point in his revolutionary strategy. As with his talk about rights, he seems reluctant to articulate his views on a communist constitution. We can only assume, on the basis of his remarks in *The Civil War in France,* and elsewhere, that he strongly endorses key democratic ideas and institutions—universal suffrage, free elections, democratic governmental decision makers (whether legislators, executives, judges) responsible to the people, protection of the basic freedoms of speech, press, assembly, association. But he does not spell out the fuller character of the communist constitution.

Similarly, we must assume that worker control will characterize the economy—and be a cardinal feature of the communist constitution—but again the character and operation of worker control remains a mystery. In the *Manifesto* Marx emphasizes centralization of power; in *The Civil War in France* he favors decentralized ideas. We never find out about the ultimate decision-making organ (other than the people) in Marx's constitution. We do not find out about relations between a national decision-making organ and local decision-making organs.

Marx fails to answer a host of other questions relevant to both politics and economics. What about conflicts between one decision-making organ and another? How is the common economic plan worked out? How do workers make decisions in the factory and on the farm? What is the more exact relationship between leaders and followers? How does the communist constitution guard against the abuse of power? How does it protect the basic freedoms? How are elections conducted? What is the role of parties, if any, in the electoral process?

Additionally, Marx does not tell us when the new communist constitution will come into being. Will it come into existence with all reasonable speed? And what will be the process of its drafting and ratification? If it will be drafted by the people's representatives, will its ratification be by the people or their representatives? And who will be able to participate in the elections relevant to the drafting and adoption of the constitution?

The absence of answers to these questions suggests Marx's constitutional, as well as moral, constipation. In the absence of such answers we have reason to be suspicious of any claim on this point that Marx's theory of revolution is a just revolution.

In dealing with our next criterion—transition to the new society—we come to stage three of Marx's theory, consolidating the revolution, and to the troublesome issue of the dictatorship of the proletariat. Can Marx's theory of the dictatorship of the proletariat be justified as a necessary, if illegal, use of force by the proletarian majority to overthrow the oppressive minority, to smash the coercive or parasitic state, to overthrow capitalism as an economic system, to consolidate proletarian rule, to guard against the expected pro-capitalist counterrevolution? Such a dictatorship of the proletariat would only prevail (if Hunt is correct about Marx's position) in the interregnum prior to the adoption of the new communist constitution, and would presumably cease with that adoption. Hence, the dictatorship would prevail only for the emergency period of the consolidation of the seizure of power, for the smashing of the coercive bourgeois or authoritarian state, and for the overthrow of capitalism.

The degree of repression of the forces of the pro-capitalistic regime would be determined by the degree of their resistance. Because Marx expected significant resistance he was prepared to use repression as necessary. But again, presumably the policy of restraint for restraint and force for force would prevail. Presumably rights of pro-capitalist forces to dissent peacefully would exist. Marx does not elaborate on the problem of peaceful and electoral activities by pro-capitalist forces. It is, however, hard to imagine Marx allowing such peaceful activities to move to the point of counterrevolution. And whether Marx would permit, as according to his democratic commitments he should have been forced to permit, pro-capitalist forces to rally votes, gain a majority, and overturn communism in a peaceful revolution is a most important, if extremely difficult, question! He did not speak to this possibility because of his conviction (his dogmatic conviction?) that (1) the proletariat either is or will become a majority of the population, (2) the proletariat will convert to communism, and (3) the proletarian communist majority will never change. These convictions, particularly (2) and (3), need to be seriously challenged!

Next, what of the troublesome question, does the dictatorship of the proletariat really cease with the adoption of the legitimating communist constitution, or does it continue to exist during the whole period of the consolidation of communism, up until the achievement of mature communism? Hunt argues that it does cease with the advent of the communist constitution.[128] However, key coercive and repressive measures against capitalistic forces—characteristic of the dictatorship of the proletariat—will continue, Marx holds, until the advent of communism.[129] Whether such coercion or repression is now legal (because based on a legitimating communist constitution) may not be a convincing argument for those coerced or repressed. It becomes important to examine the nature of that remaining and "necessary" coercion and repression.

If such coercion and repression merely involve mopping up pockets of violent pro-capitalist (minority) resistance to the communist revolution and program, that would be one thing. If, however, such coercion and repression mean the denial of freedom of speech, press, assembly, association, if they mean the denial to anti-communist or non-communist forces of the peaceful and legal opportunity to turn out the communists in power, that would be another matter entirely. Unfortunately, Marx does not clarify the issues here.

We are, in addressing these issues, unavoidably influenced by communist revolutions in the twentieth century—in Russia, Yugoslavia, Cuba, and China; and the experience in these countries is not reassuring on the preservation of genuinely democratic freedoms for all. So, even if the coercion that continues after the end of the dictatorship of the proletariat (with the adoption of the communist constitution) does not illustrate the dictatorship of the proletariat, it may still be objectionable and in violation of the freedoms that a just revolution is designed to ensure.

Finally, we come to the criterion of the maintenance of a free, open, democratic communist constitution in the stage of mature communism. Can such a constitution be maintained? Can safeguards against the abuse of power exist and work effectively? Can power be wisely exercised? Will the communist constitution facilitate a bona fide appraisal of ends and means, so that the political, economic, and social health of communist society can be ascertained—so that one can see if freedom, integration, humanity/community, and development really are flourishing?

Here Marx provides us with little help in theory. Since no Marxist communist society comes into existence in the nineteenth century, we cannot look to actual communist experience in that century for help. And since it is by no means clear that communist revolutions and societies in the twentieth century have followed Marx's model, we are not helped by twentieth century experience.

We are, however, warned by twentieth century experience to be on guard against the danger of abuse of power by communist regimes and their failure to achieve Marx's values. We are warned against tendencies toward an undemocratic society that may flow from not keeping in mind all the criteria of a prophetically just revolution. If Marx's theory of revolutionary action does not satisfactorily fulfill all the criteria of the prophetically just revolution, how much more likely that other theories—deviating from Marx's—would fail to fulfill that standard.

CONCLUSION

The judgments in Marx's theory of revolutionary communist action emerge as powerful and illuminating, but also as limited and flawed. His judgments are powerful and illuminating insofar as they highlight the importance of both economic conditions and political power in achieving a revolutionary breakthrough for workers and their allies against undemocratic governments and economic exploitation in bourgeois state and society. In Chapter 3 we emphasized Marx's judgment about the crucial relationship between economics and freedom. In this chapter, we have concentrated more on politics and freedom.

Marx sees clearly the importance of political struggle as a way, in conjunction with economic struggle, for oppressed workers to exert pressure on behalf of their own freedom. And Marx makes a convincing case on behalf of violations of freedom, and other values, in the nineteenth century. Marx thoroughly appreciates the importance of universal suffrage and other basic democratic freedoms and institutions, when they were available, in the struggle for both political and economic power. He wisely rejects the minority *putsch* as a way to advance communism. He astutely perceives that the anarchist belief that the state could be immediately abolished is unrealistic. He persistently refuses to be taken in by bourgeois reformers not really interested in, or social democratic reformers deflected from, fundamental, radical changes that would get at the root of, and remedy, the oppression and exploitation of workers. There is evidence, then, supporting the proposition that Marx is a tough-minded, radical, democratic communist, and not a totalitarian democrat who believes in a minority revolution, a vanguard party, the systematic use of terror, and total control by the state of all aspects of life.

On the other hand, we also have reasons for seeing many of Marx's judgments as limited and flawed. Most importantly, his revolutionary theory does not fully satisfy the criteria of a prophetically just revolution. This standard is, I concede, an exacting one, and might seem to be offered in order to make impossible the justification of the communist revolution. Such, however, is not my intention. It is my intention to hold all revolutions—and all politics—to an exacting prophetic standard, and especially a revolutionary politics that would radically transform the world.

Although Marx's values of freedom, integration, humanity/community, and development are in the abstract quite compatible with the ends for which a just revolution can be fought, we must question whether communism would, in logic or experience, necessarily advance those values, and at a price we are willing to pay. Moreover, Marx assumes—again without convincing evidence—that workers will not only come to be the majority of the population in all countries, *but* that they will support communism as the way to freedom and that, consequently, there will be majority support for the communist revolution and society. Given our reservations above, we have all the more reason to probe carefully the rational, humane, effective means Marx would employ to achieve the communist revolution and society.

Marx is rightly impatient, but does he give up too quickly, especially at the end of his life, on the wisdom of legal, peaceful revolution? Does he correctly sense that communism would probably never be achievable in a legal, peaceful revolution, and therefore place his prime emphasis on violent revolution? Does he fail to calculate prudently the costs of a violent revolution, of the temporary dictatorship of the proletariat, of the continued use of coercion until the advent of mature communism as against the benefits of communism? Does he fail to articulate fully a communist constitution that would ensure the participatory democracy and worker economic control he favors; that would guard against the abuse of power; that would address the realities of the conflicts of interests and the struggles for power that characterize every society? Does Marx simply fail to face up to these issues because of his faith in the wisdom, humanity, decency of the proletarian communist majority? Because of his unwillingness to appreciate the dangers of the abuse of power even by communists with good intentions?

Does his recognition of the need for difficult judgments in the first two, or three, stages of the communist revolution tend to disappear in stage four, the stage of mature communism, because with the advent of the conflictless, classless communist society there would no longer be any need for difficult judgments? Underlying the weaknesses in Marx's judgment here there is, it would seem, a romantic, indeed utopian, predilection, a belief that with the destruction of the old capitalistic, coercive society a new harmonious communist society—a social, altruistic, caring, fulfilling society—will come into existence. A belief that egoism, selfishness, divisions, conflicts of interests, oppression, struggle, and evil will all disappear in the communist society!

Although Marx is justifiably critical of most governments in his day because they were not democratic and were often oppressive, he did not fully appreciate the reform potentialities of nascent liberal democratic regimes that were beginning to emerge at the end of his life, and that become more powerful in the twentieth century. He also fails to see the adaptive capabilities of capitalism as an economic system, an adaptive capability that would function in both the economic and political domains, permitting capitalism to survive. He had good reasons to be suspicious of most regimes in his lifetime; but although he presses hard for key reforms in his day, he still does not see that in time liberal democratic regimes might, in their own self-interest, move even more significantly to remedy some of the worst problems of an unregulated capitalism and of oligarchic political rule. Needless to say, Marx would not have been satisfied with such reforms; he would not have been satisfied with changes short of communism! Was he asking too much to press for the complete overthrow of capitalism and its replacement by communism?

Marx's theory of revolutionary communist action is only partly in the tradition of a secular prophetic politics. Marx's theory is closest to prophetic politics in Marx's theoretical commitments to freedom, in his indictment of freedom's violations, in his call for action to end those violations, in his advocacy of a democratic and fulfilling communism. His theory moves away from a secular prophetic politics when it is unable to establish the link between communism and freedom, when Marx fails to spell out more clearly a defensible calculus of costs and benefits, when he neglects to articulate a democratic communist constitution that would limit the abuse of power and preserve an open society.

We will have a further opportunity to explore Marx's judgments—as well as his ethics and social science—when we turn, as we now do, in the next chapter to Marx's view of the future of economics, politics, society, and culture.

NOTES

1. In addition to the complications and difficulties I treat in the text, there is the matter of Marx's "ambiguous legacy." The argument here is that there are different, and sometimes conflicting, views expressed by Marx in his writings, which create ambiguity as to his real meaning. See, for example, Sidney Hook, *Marx and the Marxists: The Ambiguous Legacy* (Princeton, NJ: Van Nostrand, Anvil Books, 1955); Bertram D. Wolfe, *Marxism: One Hundred Years in the Life of a Doctrine* (New York: Dial, 1965); George Lichtheim, *Marxism: An Historical and Critical Study* (New York: Praeger, 1961). But see also Richard N. Hunt, *The Political Ideas of Marx and Engels: I: Marxism and Totalitarian Democracy, 1818-1850* (Pittsburgh, PA: Univ. Pittsburgh Press, 1974), and *The Political Ideas of Marx and Engels: II: Classical Marxism, 1850-1895* (Pittsburgh, PA: Univ. Pittsburgh Press, 1984). Hunt finds less inconsistency and ambiguity in Marx than Hook and Wolfe, in large part because of Hunt's more thorough and up-to-date analysis of the corpus of the writings of Marx (and Engels) (some of it newly published) and also because of his scholarly attention to Marx's practical actions (sometimes necessitating compromise with allies on Marx's "left" and "right") and to lesser known writings of both Marx and Engels. In my own presentation of Marx's ideas I am greatly indebted to Hunt's scholarship and magnificent detective work. Hunt is particularly helpful in calling our attention to the undemocratic character of European governments in the nineteenth century, and in helping us to understand the period 1848-1850, which brought forth most of Marx's most radical revolutionary pronouncements.

2. Here I will be following, with some modifications, Richard N. Hunt's presentation of Marx's four strategies.

3. I interpret the controversial phrase, "permanent revolution," to mean persistence in adhering to the need for the fundamental change to communism. Although the "democratic" character of Marx's communist society may still be the subject of controversy, all scholars of Marx must now address Hunt's argument (and evidence) in support of Marx as a "tough-minded democrat."

4. I have emphasized preparation because I believe it highlights Marx's insistence on the relation of theory to practice and because it helps to distinguish Marx's strategy of revolutionary action from the strategies of thoughtless insurrectionists and naive anarchists.

5. Marx's recognition of the need for political action is to be found in all of his writings, and is characterized, as well, by his own involvement in politics. The recognition of economic exploitation as political control is noted in the *Grundrisse* and in *Capital*.

6. These weapons included worker consciousness and organization, certain democratic freedoms, including suffrage.

7. See Marx's article on *The Chartists: Collected Works,* Vol. 11 (New York: International Publishers, 1979), pp. 335-36. For other references on universal suffrage see also Hunt, *The Political Ideas of Marx and Engels,* Vol. I, p. 73, 78-79, 85-86, 135-38, 141-42, 208, 217-18, 229, 233-34, 301, 324-25.

8. Judgments about the ripe time for revolution—the *kairos* of revolution—constitute the most difficult, the most troubling, of revolutionary judgments.

9. *Manifesto of the Communist Party*, in Robert C. Tucker (ed.), *The Marx-Engels Reader*, 2nd ed. (New York: Norton, 1978), pp. 484 and 485.

10. *Capital*, Vol. 1, in Tucker, p. 438.

11. *Address of the Central Committee to the Communist League* (1850), in Tucker, pp. 506-11.

12. Ibid, p. 504.

13. *Circular Letter to Bebel, Liebknecht, Bracke, and Others*, (1879), in Tucker, p. 553.

14. See Hunt, *The Political Ideas of Marx and Engels.*

15. Ibid.

16. Ibid., vol. I., p. 258. As we noted earlier, Marx held that "the proletariat forms the large majority of the population" in England. See note 7 above.

17. See Hunt, vol. II, p. 133.

18. See Hunt, vol. I, p. 340.

19. See Hunt, vol. II, p. 363.

20. See Hunt, vol. I, p. 132.

21. Ibid, p. 147.

22. Ibid.

23. Ibid, p. 136.

24. *Manifesto of the Communist Party,* in Tucker, p. 482.

25. Ibid., p. 484.

26. Ibid., p. 483.

27. Ibid., p. 490.

28. Ibid., p. 491.

29. See Hunt, vol. II, p. 246.

30. Fundamentally, the justification of revolution in Mazzini is the same as that in Locke and Jefferson. For argument and justification on a related idea, see Michael Walzer, *Just and Unjust Wars* (New York: Basic Books, 1977).

31. See Hunt, vol. I, p. 258.

32. See Hunt, vol. II, p. 363.

33. See Hunt, vol. I., p. 257.

34. Ibid., pp. 257–58.

35. Ibid.

36. *Manifesto of the Communist Party*, in Tucker, p. 500.

37. Ibid.

38. See Hunt, vol. I, p. 339.

39. Ibid, p. 340.

40. Ibid.

41. Ibid.

42. Ibid., pp. 340–41.

43. Ibid., p. 341.

44. Ibid.

45. *Manifesto of the Communist Party*, in Tucker, pp. 483, 491, 500.

46. See, for example, *Circular Letter to Bebel, Liebknecht, Bracke, and Others* (1879), in Tucker.

47. Quoted in Hunt, vol. II, p. 330. Hunt also writes: "One will search the writings of Marx and Engels in vain to find any advocacy, either specific or in general, of the use of political violence as an offensive weapon in stable democratic countries." Hunt, vol. II, p. 336 (see also p. 342).

48. *Speech in Amsterdam*, in David McLellan (ed.), *Karl Marx: Selected Writings* (Oxford: Oxford Univ. Press, 1977), p. 594.

49. Ibid, pp. 594–95. On the question of the peaceful or violent achievement of communism, see also Friedrich Engels, *The Tactics of Social Democracy,* in Tucker, pp. 556–73.

50. Quoted in Hunt, vol. II, p. 329.

51. Marx to Hyndman, in McLellan, *Karl Marx: Selected Writings,* p. 594. We must emphasize that despite his realistic understanding that sometimes the workers were not militant enough, Marx expressed fundamental confidence in the working class to emancipate itself. And he didn't hesitate to scold his German Social Democratic brethren for lacking such confidence. "The emancipation of the working class must be the work of the working class itself.

We cannot, therefore, cooperate with people who openly state that the workers are too uneducated to emancipate themselves. . . . '' *Circular Letter to Bebel, Liebknecht, Bracke, and Others,* in Tucker, p. 555.

52. Hunt, vols. I and II, strongly emphasizes this point. He writes (vol. II, p. 339): ". . . even where the legal path was open it might be slammed shut at the last moment, making violence necessary to enforce the will of the majority and making it advisable for the workers even in democratic countries to be familiar with the use of weapons.'' And: "Marx and Engels wanted the workers even in democratic countries to stand ready to use arms should that be made necessary by violent or illegal actions of the other side'' (p. 339).

53. See Hunt, vol. II, p. 361.

54. Friedrich Engels, *The Tactics of Social Democracy,* in Tucker, pp. 566-67.

55. Ibid., p. 567.

56. Ibid., p. 569.

57. Ibid., p. 570.

58. Ibid., p. 571.

59. Ibid.

60. Ibid.

61. Ibid., p. 556.

62. See Hunt, vol. II, p. 360.

63. Ibid., p. 331.

64. Ibid., p. 330.

65. Ibid., p. 336.

66. Ibid., p. 342.

67. See Hunt, vol. II, p. 363.

68. In McLellan, *Karl Marx: Selected Writings*, pp. 583-84.

69. Ibid., p. 580.

70. Quoted in Hunt, vol. II, p. 309.

71. Ibid., pp. 312, 314.

72. Ibid., pp. 316 and 324.

73. See Hunt, vol. I, p. 334.

74. *Critique of the Gotha Program,* in Tucker, p. 538.

75. Ibid.

76. See Hunt, vol. I, pp. 293, 295, 296-97, 319, 334, and 341. Thus Marx wrote: "Every provisional condition of state following a revolution requires a dictatorship, and an energetic dictatorship at that'' (quoted in Hunt, vol. I, p. 293). And Hunt (p. 334): "Functioning thus outside the framework of any established consititutional law, the Commune was both democratic and dictatorial at the same time. It was a short-lived miniature prototype of the ultimate dictatorship of the proletariat.''

77. *Manifesto of the Communist Party,* in Tucker, p. 490.

78. Ibid., p. 491.

79. Ibid., p. 490.

80. *Letter to Bebel, Liebknecht, Bracke, and Others,* in Tucker, p. 553.

81. Ibid., p. 551-53.

82. In McLellan, *Karl Marx: Selected Writings*, p. 296.

83. Quoted in Hunt, vol. I, p. 315.

84. Ibid., p. 305.

85. Engels in his 1891 "Introduction" to *The Civil War in France* (1871) wrote: "Of late, the Social-Democratic philistine has once more been filled with wholesome terror at the words: Dictatorship of the Proletariat. Well and good, gentlemen, do you want to know what this dictatorship looks like? Look at the Paris Commune. That was the Dictatorship of the Proletariat.'' In Tucker, p. 629.

86. *The Civil War in France,* in Tucker, pp. 634-35.

87. Ibid., p. 635.

88. Ibid., p. 633.

89. Ibid., p. 632.

90. Ibid.

91. Ibid.

92. Ibid.

93. Ibid.

94. Ibid.

95. Ibid., p. 634.

96. Ibid., p. 629.

97. Ibid., p. 635.

98. Ibid., pp. 633, 634, 635.

99. Ibid., p. 635.

100. Ibid., p. 652.

101. Ibid., pp. 635–636.

102. See Hunt, vol. II, p. 246.

103. Ibid., pp. 84–85.

104. Ibid., pp. 185–86.

105. Ibid., pp. 194 and 195.

106. Ibid., pp. 198–205.

107. Ibid., p. 246.

108. *Manifesto of the Communist Party*, in Tucker, pp. 490–91.

109. Ibid., p. 491.

110. *Critique of the Gotha Program*, in Tucker, p. 531.

111. *The German Ideology:* Part I, in Tucker, p. 160.

112. See Hunt, vol. II, Ch. 12, and "Transcending the Division of Labor," pp. 213–31, particularly pp. 218, 219, and 224.

113. Ibid., p. 217.

114. Ibid., p. 224.

115. Ibid., pp. 224 and 226.

116. *Critique of the Gotha Program,* in Tucker, p. 531 (and also p. 530).

117. Ibid., p. 529.

118. *The Civil War in France*, in Tucker, p. 635.

119. *Critique of the Gotha Program,* in Tucker, pp. 531 and 532.

120. See Hunt, vol. II, Preface, p. xi, and p. 231ff.

121. *The Civil War in France*, in Tucker, p. 635.

122. *Critique of the Gotha Program*, in Tucker, p. 535.

123. *Manifesto of the Communist Party,* in Tucker, pp. 488–89.

124. *Critique of the Gotha Program*, in Tucker, p. 538.

125. Ibid.

126. See Hunt, vol. II, pp. 179–80, 187, 188, 210, and 211. See ibid., pp. 179–180, for Hunt's use of the phrase, "moral constipation," to describe Marx's "chronic difficulty in expressing a positive moral conviction, a disorder from which both men [Marx and Engels] suffered virtually all their lives." Hunt concludes his Chapter 6, "Individual Rights Versus Tyranny of the Majority," with this paragraph: "Surely this moral constipation, whatever its deeper roots, has been a misfortune for us all. The entire body of evidence we have now examined, private as well as public, negative as well as positive, in deeds as well as words, all points to the conclusion that underneath the tough cynicism they so often affected Marx and Engels did respect the rights of peaceful opposition and would have allowed those Victorian 'decencies' to their class antagonists after the revolution just as consistently as they demanded them for themselves before it. But their inability to say so clearly enough, loudly enough, and often

enough has made it all too easy for their putative disciples to ignore the difference between peaceful and violent opposition and to adopt a real—rather than affected—cynicism about rights in general.''

127. See Hunt, vol. II, "The Rights of Civilized Class Warfare," pp. 200–11. Hunt writes (p. 208) that there was in Marx (and Engels) a belief in a "tacit contract, with its double implication—brutality for brutality, restraint for restraint. . . ." On a style that might have led to a reduction of violence, see Hunt's suggestion on p. 362.

128. See Hunt, vol. II, p. 246.

129. Ibid.

5
Marx and the Future of Economics, Politics, Society, and Culture

INTRODUCTION

In this chapter I am interested in ascertaining what Marx says about the future of the communist community—its operational principles and practices, its problems, how to deal with such problems. How clear and helpful—or how absent and confusing—are those principles and practices? Does Marx have an understanding of the problems that will face the established communist community? Does he attempt to build into the communist outlook a theory of continuing prophetic scrutiny of the functioning of the mature communist community, a theory that will aid communists in dealing with future problems? These are, I appreciate, difficult questions, but they serve to illuminate the strengths and weaknesses of Marx's thought.

We have already, of course, adumbrated some of the principles, practices, and problems of the communist community in previous chapters. Chapter 2, "Marx's Guiding Values and the Superior Universal Order," for example, illuminates many of the goals Marx sought to attain in the communist community. And our treatment of the achievement of mature communism, in Chapter 4, "Marx's Theory of Revolutionary Communist Action," highlights some of Marx's relevant communist ideas. Here we build on those earlier chapters and focus more sharply on the future and its problems.

There are considerable difficulties in this endeavor, which we must candidly acknowledge. Although Marx, as early as 1843, criticizes reformers for having "no clear conception of what the future would be," he himself has relatively little to say about the principles, practices, and problems of mature communism. He writes "that we do not attempt dogmatically to prefigure the future, but want to find the new world only through criticism of the old . . . . " He emphasizes that "the designing of the future and the

proclamation of ready-made solutions for all time is not our affair. . . . "[1]
This position Marx repeats again and again throughout his life, as he
criticizes reformers and utopians. He indicates that he is not interested in
idealistic, utopian blueprints and solutions, but in indicating the actual
course of development on the basis of what is, in fact, emerging from the
old bourgeois world.

He does not, however, hesitate to affirm that communism will inevitably emerge from that bourgeois world and make possible freedom, integration, humanity/community, and rich development. He maintains that
the new communist person in the new communist society will overcome
alienation and the various divisions of labor. He argues that cooperative
socialized production will facilitate abundance and the satisfaction of
human needs. He holds that worker control in economics and popular control in politics and society will ensure self-determination and the creative
realization of creative human potentialities.

But how fully does he spell out these principles and practices? And
does he address the problems that might come up in even such an attractive
communist community? Let us, next, attempt to flesh out, as best we can,
Marx's understanding of mature communism and its future. We will explore Marx's views on mature communism in the interrelated domains of
economics, politics, society, and culture.[2]

COMMUNISM AS HUMANKIND'S FUTURE

Communism and Economic Life

Worker control of the means of production and exchange, in and of
itself and as means for achieving rich human development, is perhaps the
central principle of Marx's conception of communist economic life. Only
such control—humane, social, cooperative—would bring about the
aufhebung (the abolition, transcendence, supercession) of dehumanizing
alienation and division of labor. Workers would then be more fully in
charge of their lives. In this "higher phase of communist society," the
"enslaving subordination of the individual to the division of labor" will
vanish. Under communist production "cooperative wealth" will "flow
more abundantly" and human needs will be satisfied generously. In the
communist community workers will "toil with a willing hand, a ready
mind, and a joyous heart."[3]

Worker control will be accompanied by a number of practices crucial
to making work democratic, attractive, creative. Workers will choose (and
be able to recall) their own managers and thus have a significant role in
economic management. The factory will be a self-governing community.

There will presumably be no permanent and irresponsible group of economic managers. The directing authority in the factory and in the economy in general will operate as a democratically chosen orchestra leader. Even management jobs will rotate.[4]

An additional factor making work attractive will be job rotation in the workplace. This will enhance variety, diversity, cooperation, understanding, and relief in the workplace and will be an important way to overcome the stultifying division of labor. The most famous expression of variety in job rotation is, of course, that found in *The German Ideology*: "in communist society, where nobody has one exclusive sphere of activity but each can become accomplished in any branch he wishes, society regulates the general production and thus makes it possible for me to do one thing today and another tomorrow, to hunt in the morning, fish in the afternoon, rear cattle in the evening, criticise after dinner, just as I have a mind, without ever becoming hunter, fisherman, shepherd or critic."[5]

As the idyllic example quoted above suggests, Marx also seeks to transcend the division between vocation and avocation (in Richard N. Hunt's language, between "directly productive labor and pursuits that are associated with leisure time"), and also between mental and manual labor. Such a transcendence will also involve job rotation and will require a richly productive economy, one able to satisfy needs, reduce necessary labor-time, increase leisure time."[6]

These practices, in turn, will make work more creative and fulfilling. They will create the economic foundation for the development and realization of human potentialities. They will enable human beings to live rich human lives. Marx sees the communist community as an "association, in which the free development of each is the condition of the free development of all."[7]

Marx endorses the richly productive capacity of modern industry and technology. Mature communist society is premised on such industry and technology. Communist society will simply put that productive capacity to work for all, especially for the proletariat, who are the overwhelming majority and who have previously been excluded from the benefits of such industry and technology. A high level of productivity will be essential insofar as it makes possible both the satisfaction of basic needs and the time essential for intelligent self-management and rich human development. The communist motto, which Marx had borrowed from Fourier and the French socialists ("From each according to his ability, to each according to his needs!"), depends upon an industrial and technological system able to achieve abundant production.[8]

If, however, worker control is central to Marx's communist vision, and to the operation of the mature communist society, we must emphatically repeat that creative realization of human potentialities—in work or beyond necessary labor—is equally important to his vision and to the operation of mature communism. We have called attention to creative fulfillment, primarily in work, above. Let us now call attention to, and elaborate on what was for Marx "a true realm of freedom" and a "development of human energy" beyond necessary labor. Marx's statement on this realm is found in the third volume of *Capital*, and merits quotation at length.

"In fact, the realm of freedom actually begins only where labour which is determined by necessity and mundane considerations ceases; thus in the very nature of things it lies beyond the sphere of actual material production. Just as the savage must wrestle with Nature to satisfy his wants, to maintain and reproduce life, so must civilized man, and he must do so in all the social formations and under all possible modes of production. With his development this realm of physical necessity expands as a result of his wants; but, at the same time, the forces of production which satisfy these wants also increase. Freedom in this field can only consist in socialized man, the associated producers, rationally regulating their interchange with Nature, bringing it under their common control, instead of being ruled by it as by the blind forces of nature; and achieving this with the least expenditure of energy and under conditions most favourable to, and worthy of, their human nature. But it nonetheless still remains a realm of necessity. Beyond it begins the development of human energy which is an end in itself, the true realm of freedom, which, however, can blossom forth only with the realm of necessity as its basis. The shortening of the working day is its basic prerequisite."[9]

Here Marx links freedom and development. The freedom involved in worker control goes a long way toward overcoming the alienation, oppression, and division of labor of bourgeois capitalism. Communist production is vital to the satisfaction of human needs for all. But the communist community looks beyond the realm of improved and favorable necessary labor to the use of freedom, as self-determined power, to develop and employ its people's creative energies in all domains. This is an exciting vision and clearly influences principles, practices, and problems in the political, social, and cultural domains—domains to which we now turn.

Communism and the Life of the Polity

Here, too, popular control plays a central role. In the communist community the state as a parasitic and/or coercive organ will no longer exist. Here, too, the end of alienation, oppression, and the division of labor means a people free to determine their own destiny in the polity, free to manage their own affairs. Popular control will be exercised through universal suffrage, with adults free both to elect those to handle the affairs and administration of the polity, and to function as such executives, legislators, judges, civic managers. Presumably, the majority principle will operate in reaching decisions in the polity.

Citizens will have overcome the division between individual egoism and the communal interest. Those serving as public officials will be subject to recall to keep them accountable. They will not be isolated, irresponsible, expert bureaucrats. To help such officials stay honest and responsive, they will serve for short terms and be paid workers' wages. Presumably, all citizens—in the tradition of the Greek polis of Pericles—will participate generously in the common affairs of the polity. Citizens will elect representatives, on a short-term and rotating basis, to look after civic affairs. Presumably, differences on issues of public policy will be resolved by caring, socialized, educated citizens. Presumably, differences between a central and many local decision-making communities will be resolved in a comparable way. Presumably, there will be no need for a single vanguard party to lead the communist community. The people, having emancipated themselves, will govern themselves. Parties, understood as parts of the whole, having no function any longer in an integrated, classless society, will cease to exist along with the coercive state and class conflict.

Moreover, Marx sees communism capturing the world—moving out from the advanced capitalist bastions where it has triumphed first to the rest of the world, just as bourgeois capitalism has moved out from its centers of power in Western Europe to encircle and dominate the globe. Consequently, conflicts between communist nations—since all advanced nations would have become communist at approximately the same time—will be unthinkable. And communist nations will be too strong for noncommunist, and less developed, nations to attack. Consequently, domestic and international peace will prevail.[10]

Alhough Marx is silent about the fuller principles of the guiding communist constitution, we may correctly infer from his life-long dedication to such freedoms as genuine freedom of the press, of speech, assembly, and association that these will be operative principles in his communist constitution. Similarly, it is probable that he would have endorsed genuine parliamentary rule, via majority decisions, due process of law, and other key features of a democratic constitution. Presumably, such freedoms and such democratic features will be utilized by all citizens.[11]

Here, as in connection with worker control, Marx recognizes that there might be a price to be paid for participatory as for industrial democracy in a certain amount of inefficiency. But apparently he thinks it is a price well worth paying.[12]

Communism and Social Life

Marx tells us very little about social life in the mature communist community. We do know, however, from his general position about economic
life and the polity, that the same essential (but not crude and dogmatic)
egalitarianism that marks those domains will also characterize social life.[13]
(We recall that equal pay for equal work characterizes only the first phase
of communism. Given differing needs—for example, a bachelor's needs
versus the needs of a married man with a family—incomes will not
necessarily be equal in the higher phase of communism made possible by
abundant production and the ability to satisfy human needs.) We know,
too, Marx sees communism overcoming certain features of the division of
labor between the sexes. All women—and children as well—will be liberated
from the often authoritarian and economic domination of the head of the
family.[14] Presumably, housekeeping and child rearing will cease to be the
exclusive concern of women. Education, too, will be altered to reflect the
new communist system. In *Capital* Marx sees "the germ of the education of
the future" budding, as Robert Owen had shown, from the factory system:
"an education that will in the case of every child over a given age, combine
productive labor with instruction and gymnastics. . . . "[15]

Marx also looks to the transcendence of the division between town and
country, between industry and agriculture, in the mature communist community. This idea, of course, overlaps the economic and social domains. I
include it here because it illuminates Marx's understanding of society. Marx
looks toward, in Richard N. Hunt's words, "a more or less uniform
distribution of communities which combine agriculture and industry."[16] In
brief, society will not be composed of heavily populated cities and sparsely
populated countryside, but by a population more evenly divided across the
nation.

Presumably, unions will continue to exist as a form for worker control
and societal activity. Marx, however, is generally silent on other social
organizations in the communist community—religious, educational, scientific, informational, recreational, and so on. Presumably, if democratic,
they will continue to function as before; if not, they will become democratic
or disappear.[17] Marx does inform us in *The Civil War in France*, as we have
seen, that churches will be disestablished and that education will be free of
interference by either church or state.

It would also appear that serious crime will cease to be a problem in the
mature communist society. The end of oppression and the satisfaction of
needs will apparently make such crime unnecessary.[18]

Marx places great faith in the liberating and reinforcing qualities of his
mature communist community. "Only within the community has each individual the means of cultivating his gifts in all directions; hence personal
freedom becomes possible only in the community."[19]

Communism and Cultural Life

Given Marx's commitment to the "true realm of freedom" and to the realization of human potentiality, it seems reasonably clear that human energy will be expended in the development of the arts and sciences. Unfortunately, Marx never adequately develops his vision of human fulfillment in the cultural domain. It is clear, however, that beyond necessary labor there will be leisure and opportunity to enable people to cultivate their senses and talents widely. Richard N. Hunt writes: "The ultimate and freest form of human activity is that which takes place under no compulsion whatsoever. To expand that realm of freedom, not just for a privileged leisure class but for everyone in equal measure, is the final goal of communism."[20]

What, now, are we to make of Marx's understanding of the principles, practices, and problems of mature communism—and of its future? Here we must return to the three major questions we posed in our introduction. How clear and helpful—or how absent and confusing—are those principles and practices? Does he or does he not have an understanding of the problems that would face the established communist community? Does he attempt to build into the communist outlook a theory of continuing prophetic scrutiny of the functioning of the mature communist community, a theory that will aid communists in dealing with future problems?

CRITIQUE

Marx's suggestive, sometimes dazzling, hints about the principles and practices of mature communism leave us intrigued but dissatisfied. Similarly, we are dissatisfied by his failure to face up to certain problems that are inescapable in human society, even—we conjecture—in the best communist society. Apparently the same realistic Marx who recognizes that important and difficult judgments will be required in preparing for, making, and consolidating the communist revolution, ceases to recognize the comparable judgments that will be required in achieving *and sustaining* mature communism. We are led to this appraisal by Marx's failure to address the tough questions that critics raise about the future of mature communism.[21] These questions speak to the heart of the democratically free, genuinely integrated, humanely social, and richly fulfilling communist society that Marx envisages.

In the economic domain: Will workers really be able to retain control of the means of production and exchange? How? Will democratic choice by workers of rotating, short-term, economic directors and managers really work? Will the costs (in lack of valuable expertise, and in strong, effective leadership, in inefficiency) be worth the gains in democratic control? Who will make the central economic plan and how? Will there be threats to freedom in central economic planning? How will conflicts between central economic planners and decentralized or local economic plans and execution be harmonized? Will communism dispense entirely with the market as a mechanism to establish what workers should produce and at what price products should be sold? Does Marx assume unlimited resources and a cornucopian philosophy of abundance? How will the decision on reducing the hours of necessary labor be made? How productively efficient is the job-rotation that Marx has in mind as a way to overcome the various divisions of labor? Who decides on the trade-offs to be made between productive efficiency *and* diversity, variety, and creative enjoyment in work—and how? Is the rough equation Marx makes between the freedom and interests of the proletariat and the freedom and interests of all humankind accurate? Does Marx overestimate the potential of workers and the impact of the favorable conditions brought about by the communist economic system? Can the communist economic system really overcome oppression, alienation, and the division of labor?

In the domain of the polity: Is the more generous democratic direction and control of the polity realistic? Does a democracy without professional politicians, legislators, executives, administrators, bureaucrats, and judges make sense? Will short terms, worker's wages, and recall of managers really operate to ensure democratic *and* efficient conduct of the civic business of the polity? How will different judgments on policies and about priorities be handled? How will comparably different judgments between a central decision maker and local decision makers be treated? Will noncommunists and anti-communists (assuming that they will not entirely disappear) be entitled to exercise freedom of speech, press, assembly, association, of elections and to seek—legally and peacefully—to rally a majority in order to vote communism out? Will citizens in the communist polity have no need for a single guiding political party or contending political parties? How will the principles and practices of the communist constitution guard against the abuse of power by even well-intentioned communists? Can war between communist nations be ruled out? And war between communist and noncommunist countries? Will all advanced countries come to communism at approximately the same time, and therefore be so strong as to prevent any noncommunist country from attacking them?

In the domain of society: Will the division of labor based on sex disappear in the communist society? Will the authoritarian and patriarchal domination of men end? Will serious crime disappear? Can the classless society be sustained—that is, a society with no class distinctions, a society with no gulf between a privileged and a less privileged class? Will pluralistic freedom prevail—for religions, for the media, in education, and among the other groups that emerge in a free society.?

In the related domain of culture: Will freedom, diversity, variety prevail in the fields of philosophy, art, music, literature, science, social science?

Marx does not seriously address these questions. He apparently does not see them as troublesome problems. He *assumes* freedom, harmony, community, and development with the overthrow of alienating and oppressive capitalism and the advent of democratic communism. Consequently, there is no need to worry about continuing threats to freedom, about continuing conflicts (economic, political, societal, cultural, and international), about persistent human evil and communal divisiveness, about inevitable disputes over alternative ways to achieve development. Hence there is no need to continue to engage in radical criticism of the achieved communist society. There is no need to project scenarios, positive and negative, of life as it might unfold in the communist community—scenarios that might pinpoint difficulties that—if anticipated—might be more easily avoided or overcome. Ongoing prophetic scrutiny is therefore unnecessary.

Marx's failure of prophetic imagination is, I believe, a lamentable failure of intellectual and ethical responsibility. We really do need to continue to ask about the necessary and sufficient conditions of freedom, peace, community, and development. We cannot simply *assume* that these will be achieved in the mature communist society. We need to see whether and how fully they will be achieved under communism. And at what cost? The test of a theory—here, communist theory—is (as Marx himself would agree) the actual practice thereof. Marx, of course, could not really look to the test of ongoing communist practice in his own lifetime. But he could have posed the questions for empirical testing.

For example: When workers are really in control of the means of production and exchange will they really "toil with a willing hand, a ready mind, and a joyous heart"? Is the "enslaving subordination of the individual to the division of labor" really overcome under communism? Can the communist system end not only wage slavery but its associated alienating and oppressive evils? Are there other forms of alienation (in addition to that form rooted in capitalistic exploitation and the division of labor) that we need to look for—for example, alienation springing from man's consciousness that he is a mortal, finite, fallible creature, unsure of his origins or future; or for example, alienation springing from the very character of modern, urban, industrialized life?

For example: Can the social wealth that will supposedly flow from abundant communist production create the basis for satisfying human needs and advancing human freedom? Will the old bourgeois (and the older human) egoism really disappear? Will people in the communist community really overcome the clash between individual self-interest and the communal communist interest? Can harmony and peace prevail not only within each communist country but between communist countries? Should one be on the lookout for abuses of power—economic, political, social, cultural—even in the mature communist society? Will control really remain with people, or will there be a tendency for power to gravitate to a ruling elite? Will a classless society really obtain, or will there be a tendency for new privileged classes to develop in the community? How will dissenters be handled in a communist society? What fuller patterns of cooperation, accommodation, or conflict will emerge?

Marx is silent on most of these important questions. He does not in fact adequately develop the principles and practices of mature communism and he is, for the most part, oblivious of the problems of the communist community—either in the near future of mature communism, or in its more distant future.

Some may contend, of course, that it may be too much to ask that Marx should have done more in exploring the communist future he predicted. On the other hand, grave responsibilities lie on the shoulders of those who would revolutionize the world. We are entitled, I believe, to hold such revolutionaries to exacting standards.

Let me turn next to explore what Marx had to say (if anything) about the distant communist future, and to ascertain whether he makes any effort, via imaginative scenarios, to explore the problems of that distant future.

Here we must avoid a misunderstanding. Those in the prophetic tradition—religious or secular—are *not* characterized by an ability to predict the future. From a biblically religious point of view the imperative to speak God's word is what characterizes the prophet. From a secular point of view the imperative to articulate and to urge people to fulfill prophetic values is central to the prophetic tradition.

Those in the prophetic tradition, religious or secular, are thus inevitably concerned with the future because of their concern for the ongoing life and vitality of prophetic values. That is why they insist that prophetic scrutiny be an ongoing enterprise, vitally concerned with the future, including the long-range future, as well as the past, the present, and the short-range future. Futuristic projection is one way to keep the prophetic vision before humankind. Prediction may enter into the performance of continuous prophetic scrutiny and futuristic projection, but it is not the defining characteristic of the prophetic mode and challenge. What is crucial, I repeat, is concern for the fulfillment of prophetic values.

Does Marx have a vision of the long-range future of communist society—and of its problems? Do we find in Marx any futuristic projections of society in the communist future? And any place for continual prophetic scrutiny in that distant future? How far does his concern for the fulfillment of prophetic values carry him in projecting and addressing the character and ongoing problems of life in the future communist society?

Marx's vision is a vision of workers in a classless and conflictless society in control of the means of production and exchange, working joyfully and cooperatively to produce abundantly, overcoming the divisions that have prevented individual and social harmony, limiting and improving the hours of necessary labor, opening up opportunities for a rich and diverse life, using their democratic power to govern their political and social as well as their economic lives, contributing according to their abilities, and receiving according to their needs, living in peaceful political communites in a peaceful world.

This vision compares favorably with the peaceful "swords into plowshares" vision of Isaiah and Micah. What is lacking, however, in Marx's vision—as compared to that of the biblical prophets—is the covenantal or constitutional framework in which their vision is to be understood. Without that framework biblical prophets (or secular prophets who share it) can be faulted—not for putting before us an inspiring vision of a future, but for living in an unrealistic never-never land.

Although Marx is strong in his analysis of some aspects of bourgeois, capitalistic society—the way, if you will, in which its constitution functions—he is weak in spelling out the economic, political, and social communist constitution, and in insisting on the need for a constitution to guard against the abuse of power.

By way of contrast, the biblical prophets operate within a covenantal framework that limits and regulates the exercise of power, that urges people to fulfill the *mitzvot* (the commandments) and reminds them when they fail to do so. The biblical prophets are continually concerned with oppression by the powerful and protection of the weak. They constantly urge all—kings and people—to repent when they deviate from justice and righteousness and to return to the fulfillment of covenantal commands.

Similarly, secular prophets in the constitutional tradition insist on utilizing the constitution to protect against the abuse of power. Secular constitutions, too, are needed to raise a higher standard of human and political behavior, to guard against the abuse of power, to ensure that human actions operate within the framework of a set of known, regular rules. Neither religious nor secular prophets assume a miraculous transformation of human nature or society in the regular course of human affairs that would make covenant or constitution unnecessary.

Marx apparently does believe that with the advent of communism in the regular course of human affairs a conflictless, classless, harmonious society will come into being. Given the disappearance of serious conflicts in the future, there will be, of course, no danger of the abuse of power, and therefore no clear need for a constitution to guard against such an abuse. Marx's failure here, as I have previously argued, can be seen in his ethical, empirical, and prudential neglect of constitutionalism. Constitutionalism was not a value that Marx explicitly and fully endorsed or scientifically and adequately explored. And, moreover, he does not perceive—and failed to develop—how constitutions could function to enhance wise judgments in the distant communist society.

Marx simply fails to develop a generous and explicit democratic and constitutional theory for his future communist society. Whereas his social scientific analysis of bourgeois capitalism carries him significantly beyond most analysts in the secular prophetic tradition—in getting at the facts and causes of the oppression of workers—he does not bring this same intelligent analysis to the nature and functioning of the communist society. His excuse for not doing so—that such construction of future "blueprints" is utopian, that the communist future has to emerge out of the real struggles in the capitalist present—is not, in my judgment, a convincing argument. His argument, if understandable, is not intellectually responsible. It is, I concede, a common variety of intellectual irresponsibility among all political and social theorists, not only revolutionary ones!

There is good reason at least to clarify fully and develop generously the principles, practices, and anticipated problems of the long-range communist future and its guiding communist constitution, if not to spell out all the details of the future communist society. How will the power of the overwhelming majority of workers be organized and maintained? Under what economic, political, and social rules will the people maintain control? What basic human, political, economic, and social freedoms must the communist constitution protect in the interest of enabling workers to retain and exercise power and control? How can it guard against the actual seizure of power by an elite not responsible to the overwhelming majority of workers, if not to all the people? What will be the relationship between industrial workers and farmers? Among the various segments of any population in a modern, complex society—leaders and led; decision makers and decision executors; governmental bureaucrats; professionals (scientists, doctors, lawyers, architects, teachers); cultural groups (artists, poets, writers); members of the media; religious groups; merchants; and so on?

Marx's failure to develop a communist constitution places in jeopardy the values he desires to advance. His failure to see the need to develop such a constitution is perhaps his most serious failing as a social theorist. One cannot, of course, anticipate all future problems, but it is the case that a proper constitution at least provides a framework that can help one to address those future problems in the most humane and constructive way. Marx, the harsh critic of utopian socialists, ironically opens himself up to criticism by socialists and others that he himself is a naive and unsound utopian socialist for neglecting to articulate a communist constitution!

If Marx neglects to develop a political, constitutional theory (in large part, we suspect, because of his distaste for bourgeois liberal democratic constitutions and the oppression they tolerate or conceal, and because of his naively utopian belief in the end of serious conflict under communism), he also fails to explore the future problems of the communist economy. He neglects, if you will, the economic constitution of communism. How will workers control the means of production and exchange? How will they make the key economic decisions for the economy as a whole as well as for their factories and farms? Who will establish economic priorities and how? And how will conflicts among economic priorities be handled? What will be the relationship of workers to political government? What limits and rules will prevail in the domain of the exercise of economic power, with regard to production, distribution, consumption?

I do not claim that if Marx had devoted himself to these broadly constitutional questions—in the domains of politics and economics—all the problems of communist society would have been solved. I do suggest, however, that if Marx had devoted more of his keen intelligence to these matters some difficulties that have subsequently troubled socialist societies might have been addressed more successfully and with a consequent enhancement of Marx's values of freedom, peace, humanity, and development.

We must also take note of Marx's understanding of the future of capitalism and of liberalism. He believes that communism as an economic and political and social system will replace bourgeois capitalism and liberal democracy. He seems to have missed the adaptability, viability, and staying-power of capitalism and liberalism. His hostility to reforms within liberalism and changes within capitalism make it difficult for him to alter his fundamental conviction that bourgeois capitalism must not be reformed but overthrown, that genuine universal emancipation cannot occur under capitalism. Coexistence as a permanent arrangement is inconceivable. Hence he never entertains the progressive fulfillment of his values in a future world in which reformed liberal democratic capitalistic and democratic socialist and communist communities coexist. Here, theoretically, he cuts himself off from the value of social scientific comparison of these three communities.

Such comparison—on freedom, peace, humanity/community, rich individual and social development—could be very illuminating, and could highlight successes and failures. Because Marx fails to entertain such a future—because he maintains that communism is the only long-range future— he cuts himself off from a vital arena for continuous prophetic scrutiny and futuristic projection. Despite Marx's openness on some issues involving the operation of capitalism, his general position introduces a serious closure to social scientific investigation of capitalism, liberal democracy, and even democratic socialism. This posture adversely affects one's prophetic capability in understanding the future of politics, society, and culture.

Similarly, a freer and more creative openness to a broader range of values, experience, and wise judgment might have enabled Marx to appreciate powerful forces in his day that were highly relevant to his ethical concerns and his social scientific analysis, and that we know have significantly affected the future of socialism and communism. I refer here to such key forces as nationalism, racism, anti-semitism, and sexism.[22] I also call attention to the cornucopian mentality of both liberalism, socialism, and communism. I note further Marx's dismissal of religion as a societal force meriting respect and ongoing investigation in the future. Finally, I call attention to Marx's perhaps understandable inability (despite brilliant anticipatory analysis in *The Eighteenth Brumaire of Louis Bonaparte*) to anticipate that liberalism is not the only serious rival to socialism and communism, that a powerful, authoritarian rightwing movement (which we have called fascism in the twentieth century) and not communism would emerge out of the contradictions and travail of liberalism. All of these forces—cutting across class lines, as they do—raise serious questions about the accuracy and explanatory power of Marx's social scientific analysis, and emphasize again the importance of constitutional protections against the abuse of power.

Marx simply does not adequately address, if he ever really understood, the power of nationalism, racism, anti-semitism, or sexism to shape the present and the future, and to limit the flowering of his preferred values. For Marx these values are not simply his idealistic moral preferences but expressions that history is in the process of fulfilling. He understands, of course, that the battle of some nations to achieve national independence is related to freedom and can be compatible with freedom. But he vastly overrates class solidarity across national lines; he misses the fact that workers would choose nation over class when warfare between nations breaks out.

Although Marx opposed human slavery, and supported the North against the South in the American Civil War, he does not fully appreciate the power of racism as a divisive force—perpetuating enmities between white and black workers (whether in the United States, or Latin America, or between Western Europe and people of color in Asia and Africa).

Although Marx opposes, as a representative of the radical Enlightenment, discrimination against people because of their religious convictions, he argues that battles to give Jews full rights of citizenship should not obscure the most important battle—to give workers control over their destiny. Marx does not see anti-semitism as a virulent force in society—and one militating against his values. For Marx capitalism is the key enemy. Presumably, anti-semitism, like racism, will cease to be a serious matter in the future communist society. In the light of the history of anti-semitism that Marx must have known (and, of course, in the light of our contemporary knowledge of anti-semitism in the Soviet Union and of the Holocaust, to take two modern examples only), Marx's failure to appreciate the dangers of anti-semitism is naive indeed. Marx's insensitivity on the issue of anti-semitism is all the more disturbing in the light of his own Jewish origins (including the suffering of his own father, who converted to Christianity in order not to lose his ability to practice law), and in the light of Marx's perpetuation of certain false Jewish stereotypes in his article on *The Jewish Question*.

Given Marx's concern about *universal* human emancipation, and especially about the plight of the proletariat, it is all the more wonder that he not only fails to grasp fully the plight of people of color, of Jews, and of other ethnic and religious minorities, but also the plight of fifty percent of the human race—women. Marx, of course, was not blind to the plight of women, or of blacks, or of other people of color, but their oppression is clearly not central in his analysis. His understanding of the capitalist present or of the communist future does not reveal a full understanding or exploration of oppressive patriarchy. As he misses the oppression of a nation's minorities by the nation's dominant majority, the oppression of people of color by whites, of Jews by non-Jews, so he misses the full dimensions of the oppression of women by men. Again, Marx's focus on the oppression of the proletariat by capitalism prevents him from appreciating fully other varieties of oppression. This "singular vision" prevents Marx from engaging in continuous prophetic scrutiny on a wider-ranging front. And, given his limited focus, he is unable to undertake the task of futuristic projection and ask about national minorities, people of color, Jews, and other oppressed religious groups, or women, in his future communist society.

Marx's single-minded concentration on liberalism, and his conviction that communism is the wave of the future, does not enable him to ask about other powerful non-liberal oppressive forces that might emerge. Only in the *Eighteenth Brumaire* does he (I think, remarkably) anticipate liberalism's temporary capitulation—its sacrifice of freedom to preserve property, order, and family. But the fuller understanding of authoritarian regimes on the Right, Marx does not possess. Perhaps it is unfair to have expected Marx to anticipate fascism as rightwing authoritarianism. On the other hand, Marx is aware of rightwing, authoritarian regimes, and of terror. And he is aware of how dominant economic forces try to shape the superstructure in their interest. He does not, however, fully appreciate how rightwing regimes might borrow ideas and tactics from the Left, and shape their own non-liberal regimes as alternatives to either liberalism or socialism.

Marx is aware of the capitalistic rape of nature, but he does not challenge the liberal and socialist assumption of limitless abundance, the perpetually overflowing cornucopia. He does not challenge the dominant nineteenth century view that humans can master nature, produce abundantly, and use that abundant production (for Marx, under communist auspices) to achieve prosperity for all. His failure here is important because it crucially affects his conviction that a free and harmonious communist society can be created after workers gain control of the means of production and use them for their own benefit. Conflict is predicated, among other things, on scarcity, and the battle to control resources. Liberals would overcome scarcity under capitalism but at the price of oppression of workers. Marx holds that communism will both overcome scarcity and end oppression—and thus end conflict.

If, however, resources are not limitless, if scarcity is a real problem in any economy—whether capitalist or communist—conflict over scarce resources will be an enduring reality. Marx does not really face up to the danger of ecological malaise—either as ecological scarcity and the need for a steady-state economy, or as exploitation and pollution of the environment. This issue, too, transcends class lines, and again reveals the weakness of singular devotion to class analyis.

We must also again address the question of alienation in the future communist society. Overcoming alienation is an early concern of Marx's and, I believe, a decisive ethical concern of Marx's throughout his life. But will alienation really be overcome in the future communist society? Here we have to fault Marx's affirmative answer, and his neglect of other crucial factors affecting alienation. It is by no means clear that worker control of the means of production and exchange will overcome the varieties of alienation, whether they are rooted in the existential recognition of our being thrust into a world where we are unable to believe in a God as Creator who provides meaning for our existence, or they are rooted in our inability to recover our authentic selves in any society. To call attention to the varieties of alienation is also to suggest the larger dimensions of a free, human, creative life that are left largely unexplored by Marx.

Finally, I should like to suggest that Marx hardly begins to develop a communist theory of international or global relations. How will communist nations interact with each other in the global community? Will there be no conflicts between rich and developed communist countries and poor and developing, or underdeveloped, communist countries? How will the values of freedom, and so on, operate worldwide? Marx remains largely silent on these questions. As he does not develop a democratic and constitutional theory of the national political community, so he does not develop such a theory for the global community.

So it is the case that Marx fails to address important questions of the future of mature communism—of its economic operation, of its democratic and constitutional character, of the global communist community. His future does not take into account the viability of capitalism or liberalism. He simply misses the importance of a number of key factors in shaping the future, which was to be a communist future, but which can hardly be said to be a communist future in which Marx's own values prevail.

CONCLUSION

Marx's vision of the classless communist society—no exploiting and exploited classes, no coercive state—is a powerful and attractive vision. The transcending of alienation and the division of labor is an exciting idea. The view of people in control of their own lives—in economics, in the polity, in society, in the domain of culture—is most appealing. Most freedom-loving people respond favorably to the concept of democracy in the workplace and in public life.

Marx's vision here is powerful, but, as I have argued, not too illuminating. His failure to clarify the principles, practices, and problems of mature communism is a major flaw in his thought. Marx's limitation here seems to stem from several aspects of his intellectual charcter. Despite his revolutionary endorsement of communism, he is unable to address the future and its problems seriously. His hostility to utopian futuristic blueprints makes him unwilling to flesh out the principles and practices of communism or to probe in his usual keen and critical way the problems of communist society. His argument is that the new communist society will emerge from the existing capitalist society and can only be understood in the light of conditions at the time of the communist revolution to overthrow capitalism and in the light of the conditions brought about subsequently by communist revolutionaries. Yet, even if this is substantially true, it does not excuse the failure to probe those conditions, to extrapolate as best as one can, and also to take seriously the continuing problems suggested by a critical knowledge of history, economics, and political theory.

Marx's failure to engage in continuous prophetic scrutiny of the communist future seriously jeopardizes the claim that he is squarely in even the secular tradition of prophetic politics.

NOTES

1. *For a Ruthless Criticism of Everything Existing* (letter, 1843), in Robert C. Tucker (ed.), *The Marx-Engels Reader,* 2nd ed. (New York: Norton, 1978), p. 14.

2. In exploring Marx and his vision of the future I have found particularly helpful Chapter 9, "The Classless Society as a Polity," in Richard N. Hunt's *The Political Ideas of Marx and Engels: II: Classical Marxism 1850–1895* (Pittsburgh, PA: Univ. Pittsburgh Press, 1984), pp. 212–265. However, despite the help I have derived from Hunt's study, I do not agree that "it is possible to reconstruct a reasonably complete picture of what Marx and Engels expected and desired the future society to be like." We differ, I suppose, in our different understanding of what a "complete picture" is.

3. See *Critique of the Gotha Program*, in Tucker, p. 531; and *Inaugural Address of the Working Men's International Association*, in Tucker, p. 518.

4. See Hunt, Vol. II, esp. pp. 249–50 and 257–58. Although I will be critical of Marx's position, I should point out that many (but not all) key features of Marx's communist society—worker control, a democratic polity, job rotation, for example—can actually be seen in operation in the Israeli kibbutz.

5. *The Germany Ideology*: Part I, in Tucker, p. 160.

6. Hunt, Vol. II, pp. 221 and 224.

7. *Manifesto of the Communist Party*, in Tucker, p. 491.

8. See the *Manifesto* and *Capital*. The communist motto is found in *Critique of the Gotha Program*, p. 531.

9. *Capital,* Vol. III, in Tucker, p. 441.

10. See especially *The Civil War in France*, in Tucker. For the ultimate communist triumph in the world, see, for example, *The German Ideology*, in Tucker, pp. 161–62, and also *Manifesto of the Communist Party*. See also Hunt, Vol. II, esp. pp. 223, 231, 233, 239, 247, 248, 251, 252, 258.

11. See Hunt, Vol. II.

12. Ibid., p. 262.

13. Ibid., p. 263.

14. Ibid., pp. 219–21.

15. *Capital*, Vol. I, in Tucker, p. 412.

16. See Hunt, Vol. II, p. 218.

17. One could argue, however, that unions—which Marx sees as important in the struggle against capitalism in bourgeois society—will no longer have a mission once communism is achieved. However it seems more likely that, since workers will need some kind of organization to exercise their control in a communist society, they will continue to use their unions. Here is another example of a problem that Marx does not adequately explore.

18. I say "appear" because I don't find a clear and adequate treatment of crime in Marx. Hunt writes: "No doubt they left many questions unanswered, or only barely answered. Did they, for example, imagine *all* antisocial acts would cease, even crimes of passion or youthful vandalistic pranks, for example; and if not, how would such acts be dealt with, particularly in the absence of any coercive apparatus?" Hunt, Vol. II, p. 252.

19. *The German Ideology*, in Tucker, p. 197.

20. See Hunt, Vol. II, p. 226.

21. Not all of these critics are anti-Marxists. Many are themselves Marxists. Many Marxists have attempted to address these tough questions. For a sample see the articles and bibliography in Tom Bottomore, et al. (eds.), *A Dictionary of Marxist Thought* (Cambridge, MA: Harvard Univ. Press, 1983).

22. It is the case that a number of Marxist scholars— inspired by Marx's values, social science, and revolutionary theory—have addressed themselves to these issues, sometimes

with illuminating results. Their complete success in incorporating these factors within a Marxist framework is, however, open to question. Again, for an introduction, see the relevant articles (e.g., on nationalism, race, feminism, Judaism) and the helpful bibliography in Bottomore, et al., *A Dictionary of Marxist Thought*. For an illustration of discontent among feminists with the Marxist perspective, see Lydia Sargent (ed.), *Women and Revolution: A Discussion of the Unhappy Marriage of Marxism and Feminism* (Boston: South End Press, 1981).

Clearly, a different reading of Marx—and a different appraisal—will be found in the writings of a number of Marxists scholars. The following brief sample is illustrative: Louis Althusser, *For Marx* (London: Allen Lane, 1965); *Essays in Self-Criticism* (Atlantic Highlands, NJ: Humanities Press, 1976); Louis Althusser and Etienne Balibar, *Reading 'Capital'* (New York: Pantheon, 1971); Hal Draper, *Karl Marx's Theory of Revolution*, 2 vols. (New York and London: Monthly Review Press, 1977); Ben Fine, *Marx's 'Capital'* (London: Macmillan, 1975); Ernest Mandel, *Introduction to Karl Marx*, Capital I (London: Penguin, 1976); Nicos Poulantzas, *State, Power, Socialism* (London: New Left Press, 1978).

6
Conclusion

And so we return to our original questions: Does Marx illustrate the prophetic mode and challenge? Can we place him within the tradition of prophetic politics? Is he a true or a false prophet? By now I hope that I have convinced the reader that it is sensible to use the model of prophetic politics—and its commitments to prophetic values, to fearless criticism, to creative constitutional action, to continuous scrutiny, and to futuristic projection—to analyze and appraise Marx.

Marx emerges—I believe—as a powerful, often illuminating, fearless, but still limited and seriously flawed secular prophet. He reveals both the strengths and weaknesses of the secularization of the prophetic tradition. Concentration on these strengths and weaknesses helps us to understand both Marx's thought and the prophetic mode and challenge.

THE STRENGTHS AND WEAKNESSES OF MARX'S THOUGHT

It should now be clear that Marx is a powerful political theorist in large part because—in the tradition of prophetic politics—he links ethical concerns, social scientific analysis, a call for bold action, and a vision of the future in his theory. His values engage us; they appeal to our own strong ethical sense of universal liberation and fulfillment.

Marx's social scientific diagnosis of our condition under bourgeois capitalism and liberal democracy constitutes an effort to understand some vital matters about our existential condition: the plight of working people as the least free, the most oppressed; the "secret" of exploitation and the key to overcoming alienation; the alleged need to unmask all illusions that prevent us from seeing the truth of our human condition; our history in

147

terms of a movement toward human fulfillment; the forces and conditions of social change; the key role of economics (broadly understood) in shaping our economic, political, social, and cultural lives; the crucial role of classes and class conflict in human history; how social scientific knowledge clarifies the connection between values that are coming to be in history, the shaping economic and social forces of human life, and revolutionary action to bring a brave, new communist world into existence.

His theory of revolutionary action demonstrates for many the fruitful tie between theory and practice. Action to achieve the communist society is guided by a philosophy of history that seemingly ensures success in making the revolution, in consolidating the revolution, and in achieving the higher phase of communist society.

For some the power of this theory is not seriously affected by its crucial limitations and flaws—limitations and flaws affecting its values, its social science, its theory of action, and its vision of the future. However, any fair appraisal of Marx calls upon us to appreciate both his strengths and weaknesses.

Marx is partially in the tradition of a secular prophetic politics. In some respects he has deepened our understanding of such prophetic values as freedom, peace, humanity/community, and rich individual and social development—and thus of the good political life. Yet his failure to do justice to the value of constitutionalism and to other important prophetic values—such as love, compassion, repentance—suggests serious trouble ahead for a theory unable to appreciate that key values can only be sustained in a genuinely constitutional society, one acutely aware of the dangers of the abuse of power, one keenly suspicious of those who claim a monopoly of truth, a vigilant society in which deep caring about human rights unites people in common respect for human integrity. We must search beyond Marx (although incorporating some of Marx's ethical insights) to arrive at a deeper, fuller, and more satisfactory understanding of the good political life.

Marx is also partially in the prophetic tradition in his commitment to fearless criticism of the existing order in the light of his ethical values. His is a social scientific criticism clearly motivated, I believe, by his values and dedicated to demonstrating both the gap between ethical aspirations and existential reality *and* the reasons for this gap. He is partly successful in highlighting the ways in which economic systems—especially capitalism—can alienate and enslave, divide and weaken, degrade and narrow, retard and stunt human beings in the work place, in political life, and in society. He makes a valuable, if sometimes overemphasized, contribution to our empirical understanding of the role of classes and class conflict in human history. He certainly calls attention to the difficulties—

contradictions—of capitalism as an economic system. He highlights the enormous influence of economic forces in history in shaping politics, law, education, and other aspects of society.

Yet Marx's social science—committed to fearless criticism—is badly flawed in key respects. His empirical analysis of the operation of capitalism is simply not correct in a number of instances. The fated self-destruction of capitalism as a result of contradictions and severe crisis, and as a result of the growing power of the proletariat in advanced capitalistic countries, has not occurred, nor does Marx's social scientific logic, the operation of his social scientific laws, persuade us that the destruction of capitalism is inevitable. The growing misery of workers as a result of the irrepressible urge of capitalists to enhance profits at the expense of workers is not to be found, at least not in the Western world. Capitalism, despite severe economic crises, and despite the continued exploitation and alienation of workers, has demonstrated a resilience and staying power, and a willingness to live with reforms (some radical, some quite modest), some of which have paradoxically reduced its power but probably enhanced its life. Liberal democracies have demonstrated that they are not simply and solely puppets of the dominant capitalist ruling class. They have modestly, if not adequately, responded to popular, and worker, cries for key economic and social reforms. Similarly, democratic socialist governments have been able, peacefully, to achieve governmental power and to enact modest socialist programs. Marx especially misses the importance and value of the democratic constitution as the safest vehicle for advancing the interests of workers and others oppressed in or left out of the economic, political, and social system.

Marx, moreover, misses a great deal in his analysis. Because of his concentration on the proletariat and capitalism, he misses the oppression of other groups and other oppressive forces. He misses—or, at least, does not adequately appreciate—racism, anti-semitism, sexism, and the oppressive rule and role of whites, anti-semites, and patriarchy. He misses the ways in which nationalism (as an idolatrous secular religion) functions as a more powerful force than class in obtaining the allegiance of all peoples, including workers. He does not adequately stress the ways in which minorities within nations are often oppressed by dominant majorities, regardless of class. And he does not fully appreciate how conflicts between nations can destroy the brotherhood and sisterhood of workers and inflict dreadful damage on human freedom, peace, humanity/community, and rich human development. Marx also fails to see other important causes of malaise—-whether ecological imbalance or forms of human alienation unrelated to the workers' lack of control over their primary work activity.

Marx's social science, in brief, leaves a great deal to be desired. We have to search more fully and deeply (again incorporating some parts of Marx's social science) for a social science that more universally explores the gaps between prophetic values and existential reality.

It is difficult to reach the judgment that Marx's theory of revolutionary action is a wise theory. His extravagant early judgment, which I do not believe he ever abandons, that communism is a solution to the riddle of history cannot be easily sustained. It is by no means clear that a majority of the population in advanced capitalist countries, even a majority of workers in such countries, are communists and endorse the desirability or wisdom of a communist revolution. Marx's theory of revolutionary action is seriously flawed by a failure to address the difficult but necessary problem of the calculus of costs. Marx does not satisfactorily address the question of how the costs of the loss of life and freedom in making the revolution, the costs of despotic actions during the period of the dictatorship of the proletariat, or the continuing costs for workers and noncommunists under mature communism, will be balanced by the presumed benefits of mature communism. Marx does not articulate a safisfactory theory of the just revolution, certainly not of the prophetically just revolution. And he fails to commit himself unmistakably—clearly, explicitly, fully, generously—to a democratic constitution for his communist society. The absence of a democratic and constitutional framework for his theory of revolutionary and communist action puts his theory at grave risk. If we have doubts about key aspects of Marx's ethical and social scientific breakthroughs, we have even greater doubts about Marx's theory of revolutionary action.

Marx's short- and long-range vision of the future of economics, politics, society, and culture in his mature communist community—its principles, practices, problems—is defective because he does not clearly establish the logical or empirical link between his inspiring goals of freedom, peace, humanity, community, and development—clearly in the prophetic tradition—and the actual fulfillment of those goals in a communist world by fallible humans. The vagueness of Marx's picture of the future, mature communist community, the absence of a more fully developed democratic and constitutional framework within which communism can go forward, Marx's failure to analyze and criticize the probability of a classless, conflictless, harmonious society—these considerations force us to conclude that Marx himself, despite his own adverse criticism of utopian socialists, is himself a utopian socialist. In some key respects Marx is not as creative or imaginative as some of the socialists he excoriates. Continuing prophetic scrutiny of the achievement of the necessary and sufficient conditions of freedom and development is apparently not required in Marx's communist society, or—if required—could be left to an intelligent and vigilant people. We pay dearly for Marx's noble faith in the people unsupported by a prophetically interpreted democratic constitution. Similarly, the need to project futuristic scenarios in order to identify future problems of that communist society is a task badly neglected by Marx. Marx's failure here leaves a dangerous vacuum that can be filled by those who are, unlike Marx, totalitarian. Marx's neglect also means that he would not do justice to other important problems—whether racism, anti-semitism, sexism, war, nationalism, ecological malaise—and that he would not develop a more comprehensive theory of political health. Such a comprehensive and integrating political theory awaits a new generation of scholars able to build on Marx's work as a powerful but flawed prophet, scholars able to profit from both Marx's notable strengths and his serious weaknesses.

CONCLUSION

Our central conclusions will perhaps seem contradictory, unnecessarily complex, and therefore somewhat baffling to those who prefer to see the battle lines drawn neatly between the children of light and the children of darkness. Marx is not a true secular prophet. But, on the other hand, he is not a completely false secular prophet! Marx illustrates the prophetic mode and challenge in important respects, but fails to do so in other crucial matters. He illustrates key aspects but not all the cardinal features of the tradition of prophetic politics.

The twenty-first century, faced by the promise of universal freedom and development or by the peril of universal degradation and destruction, may draw upon some of Marx's contributions, but still awaits the work of a more genuinely and completely prophetic generation. Those in this generation will need to explore the deeper meaning of the good political life (and thus of prophetic values); the deeper meaning of empirical/scientific reality (past, present, and future) as it sustains or threatens those prophetic values; the deeper meaning of wise judgment on those public policies that can enhance the necessary and sufficient conditions of the good life, healthy growth, and creative development; and the deeper meaning of continual prophetic scrutiny and futuristic projection.

Those in this generation, as they undertake these authentically prophetic tasks, will profit from Marx's insights and from his failures. Consequently, they will more seriously and fully explicate prophetic values. They will in their social scientific analysis and criticism more ably attend to key threats to prophetic values. They will more carefully work out a calculus of costs that will enhance genuinely prudent judgment in politics. They will more insistently demand a genuinely prophetic theory of the just revolution. They will more urgently undertake the never-ending task of continuous prophetic scrutiny and futuristic projection. Pursuing these tasks, those in a more genuinely prophetic generation can yet—more responsibly, creatively, and scientifically—address, if not Marx's riddle of human history, at least the necessary and sufficient conditions for the fulfillment of prophetic values in the twenty-first century.

Select Bibliography

Althusser, Louis. *For Marx*. London: Allen Lane, 1965.

———. *Essays in Self-Criticism*. Atlantic Highlands, NJ: Humanities Press, 1976.

——— and Balibar, Etienne. *Reading 'Capital'*. New York: Pantheon, 1971.

Aptheker, Herbert (ed.). *Marxism and Christianity*. New York: Humanities Press, 1968.

Avineri, Shlomo. *The Social and Political Thought of Karl Marx*. Cambridge, U.K.: Cambridge University Press, 1968.

Berlin, Isaiah. *Karl Marx: His Life and Environment* (4th ed.) Oxford: Oxford University Press, 1978. (With Guide to Further Reading by Terrell Carver.)

———. *Against the Current: Essays in the History of Ideas*. New York: Penguin Books, 1982. (Especially the essays, "The Life and Opinions of Moses Hess," and "Benjamin Disraeli, Karl Marx and the Search for Identity.")

Blenkensopp, Joseph. *A History of Prophecy in Israel*. London: SPCK, 1984.

Bottomore, Tom (ed.). *A Dictionary of Marxist Thought*. Cambridge, MA: Harvard University Press, 1983.

Bowle, John. *Politics and Opinion in the 19th Century*. London: Jonathan Cape, 1963.

Brinton, Crane. "Utopia and Democracy." In Frank Manuel (ed.), *Utopias and Utopian Thought* (Boston: Beacon Press, 1967), pp. 50–68.

Brueggemann, Walter. *The Prophetic Imagination*. Philadelphia, PA: Fortress Press, 1978.

Buber, Martin. *Paths in Utopia* (1949). Boston: Beacon Press, 1958.

———. *The Prophetic Faith* (1949). New York: Harper Torchbook, 1960.

Carlebach, Julius. *Karl Marx and the Radical Critique of Judaism*. London: Routledge & Kegan Paul, 1978.

Carver, Terrell. *Marx's Social Theory*. Oxford: Oxford University Press, 1982.

Cohen, Gerald A. *Karl Marx's Theory of History*. Princeton, NJ: Princeton University Press, 1978.

Cohn, Norman. *The Pursuit of the Millennium: Revolutionary Millenarians and Mystical Anarchists of the Middle Ages*. London: Secker and Warburg, 1957; Rev. ed., Oxford University Press, 1970.

Draper, Hal. *Karl Marx's Theory of Revolution* (2 vols.). New York and London: Monthly Review Press, 1977.

Dunn, John. *Rethinking Modern Political Theory*. Cambridge, U.K.: Cambridge University Press, 1985.

Dupre, Louis. *Marx's Social Critique of Culture*. New Haven, CT: Yale University Press, 1983.

Elster, Jon. *Making Sense of Marx*. Cambridge, U.K.: Cambridge University Press, 1985.

Fine, Ben. *'Capital'*. London: Macmillan, 1975.

Freeman, Gordon. *The Heavenly Kingdom: Aspects of Political Thought in the Talmud and Midrash*. Lanham, MD: University Press of America/Center for Jewish Community Studies, 1986.

Fromm, Erich. *Marx's Concept of Man*. New York: Ungar, 1961.

——— (ed). *Socialist Humanism: An International Symposium*. Garden City, NY: Doubleday, 1965.

Gay, Peter. *The Enlightenment: An Interpretation*. New York: Knopf, 1966.

Hanson, Paul. *The Dawn of the Apocalyptic*. Philadelphia, PA: Fortress Press, 1975.

_____ . *The Diversity of Scripture: A Theological Interpretation*. Philadelphia, PA: Fortress Press, 1982.

_____ . *The People Called: The Growth of Community in the Bible*. New York: Harper & Row, 1986.

Heller, Agnes. *The Theory of Need in Marx*. New York: St. Martin's Press, 1974.

Heschel, Abraham J. *The Prophets*. New York: Harper & Row, 1962; Torchbook Edition (2 vols.), 1969–1971.

Hook, Sidney. *Marx and the Marxists: The Ambiguous Legacy*. Princeton, NJ: Van Nostrand/Anvil Books, 1955.

Howard, M.C. and King, J.E. *The Political Economy of Marx*. New York: Longman, 1975.

Hunt, Richard N. *The Political Ideas of Marx and Engels: I: Marxism and Totalitarian Democracy, 1818–1850*. Pittsburgh, PA: University of Pittsburgh Press, 1974.

_____ . *The Political Ideas of Marx and Engels: II: Classical Marxism, 1850–1895*. Pittsburgh, PA: University of Pittsburgh Press, 1984.

Pope John Paul XXIII. *Pacem in Terris*. Glen Rock, NJ: Paulist Press, 1963.

Kalin, Martin G. *The Utopian Flight from Unhappiness: Freud against Marx on Social Progress*. Totowa, NJ: Littlefield, Adams & Co., 1975.

Kamenka, Eugene. *The Ethical Foundations of Marxism*. New York: Praeger, 1962.

Kateb, George. *Utopia and Its Enemies*. New York: Free Press, 1963.

King, Martin Luther, Jr. *Stride Toward Freedom*. New York: Harper, 1958.

_____ . *Why We Can't Wait*. New York: Harper & Row, 1964.

_____ . *Where Do We Go From Here: Chaos or Community*. New York: Harper & Row, 1967.

Kolakowski, Leszek. *Main Currents of Marxism: Its Origins, Growth, and Dissolution* (3 vols.) (1978). Oxford: Oxford University Press, 1981.

Lichtheim, George. *Marxism: An Historical and Critical Study*. New York: Praeger, 1961.

McLellan, David. *Karl Marx: His Life and Thought*. New York: Harper & Row, 1973.

_____ (ed.). *Karl Marx: Selected Writings*. Oxford: Oxford University Press, 1977.

_____ . *Marxism After Marx*. Boston: Houghton Mifflin, 1979.

McMurtry, John M. *The Structure of Marx's World-View*. Princeton, NJ: Princeton University Press, 1978.

Mandel, Ernest. *Introduction to Karl Marx, Capital I*. London: Penguin, 1976.

Manuel, Frank E. *The Prophets of Paris*. Cambridge, MA: Harvard University Press, 1962.

_____ (ed.). *Utopias and Utopian Thought*. Boston: Beacon Press, 1967.

_____ and Manuel, Fritzie P. *Utopian Thought in the Western World*. Cambridge, MA: The Belknap Press of Harvard University Press, 1979.

Marx, Karl. *The Economic and Philosophic Manuscripts of 1844*. Edited, with an Introduction by Dirk J. Struik. Translated by Martin Milligan. New York: International Publishers, 1964.

_____ and Engels, Friedrich. *Collected Works* (Vols. 1–19, 1975–1984; Vols. 39–40, 1983). New York: International Publishers.

Mazlish, Bruce. *The Meaning of Karl Marx*. New York: Oxford University Press, 1984.

Miliband, Ralph. *Marxism and Politics*. Oxford: Oxford University Press, 1977.

Miller, Richard W. *Analyzing Marx: Morality, Power and History*. Princeton, NJ: Princeton University Press, 1984.

Niebuhr, Reinhold. *The Nature and Destiny of Man* (2 Vols.) (1941). New York: Scribner's, 1944.

Nisbet, Robert. *History of the Idea of Progress*. New York: Basic Books, 1980.

Ollman, Bertell. *Alienation: Marx's Conception of Man in Capitalist Society*. Cambridge, U.K.: Cambridge University Press, 1971.

Ophuls, William. *Energy and the Politics of Scarcity*. San Francisco: Freeman, 1977.

Parsons, Howard L. "The Prophetic Mission of Karl Marx." In Herbert Aptheker (ed.), *Marxism and Christianity* (New York: Humanities Press, 1968), pp. 143–62.

Pennock, J. Roland, and Chapman, John W. (eds.). *Marxism*. New York: New York University Press, 1983.

Plamenatz, John. *German Marxism and Russian Communism*. London: Longmans, 1954.

Pollak, Fred L. *The Image of the Future* (2 vols.). New York: Oceana, 1961.

Popper, Karl R. *The Open Society and Its Enemies*. Princeton, NJ: Princeton University Press, 1950.

Poulantzas, Nicos. *State, Power, and Socialism*. London: New Left Press, 1978.

Rader, Melvin. *Marx's Interpretation of History*. New York: Oxford University Press, 1979.

Riemer, Neal. *The Revival of Democratic Theory*. New York: Appleton-Century-Crofts, 1962.

_____ . *The Democratic Experiment*. Princeton, NJ: Van Nostrand, 1967.

_____ . *Political Science: An Introduction to Politics*. New York: Harcourt Brace Jovanovich, 1983.

_____ . *The Future of the Democratic Revolution: Toward a More Prophetic Politics*. New York: Praeger, 1984.

_____ (Guest Editor). "The Prophetic Mode and Challenge in Religion, Politics, and Society." *The Drew Gateway*, 55, Nos. 2 & 3 (Winter 1984/Spring 1985).

_____ . *James Madison* (1968, 1970). Wash. D.C.: Congressional Quarterly Press, 1986.

Rubel, Maximilien, and Managle, Margaret. *Marx Without Myth*. New York: Harper Torchbooks, 1976.

Ruether, Rosemary Radford. *The Radical Kingdom: The Western Experience of Messianic Hope*. New York: Harper & Row, 1970.

_____ . *Liberation Theology: Human Hope Confronts Christian History and American Power*. New York: Paulist/Newman, 1972.

_____ . *The New Woman/New Earth: Sexist Ideologies and Human Liberation*. New York: Paulist Press, 1975.

_____ . "Prophetic Tradition and the Liberation of Women." In "The Prophetic Mode and Challenge in Religion, Politics, and Society," *The Drew Gateway* (Neal Riemer, Guest Editor), 55, Nos. 2 & 3 (Winter 1984/Spring 1985), pp. 114–24.

Sargent, Lydia (ed.). *Women and Revolution: A Discussion of the Unhappy Marriage of Marxism and Feminism.* Boston: South End Press, 1981.

Sassoon, Anne Showsack. "Civil Society." In Tom Bottomore (ed.), *A Dictionary of Marxist Thought* (Cambridge, MA: Harvard University Press, 1983), pp. 72–74.

Springborg, Patricia. *The Problem of Human Needs and the Critique of Civilisation.* London: George Allen & Unwin, 1981. (Especially Chapter 6, "Marx on Human and Inhuman Needs.")

Talmon, A. J. *The Origins of Totalitarian Democracy.* London: Secker and Warburg, 1952.

———. *Political Messianism: The Romantic Phase.* London: Secker and Warburg, 1960.

Tucker, Robert C. *Philosophy and Myth in Karl Marx.* Cambridge, U.K.: Cambridge University Press, 1961.

———. *The Marxian Revolutionary Idea.* New York: Norton, 1970.

——— (ed.). *The Marx–Engels Reader* (2nd ed.). New York: Norton, 1978.

U.S. Catholic Bishops. *Pastoral Letter on Nuclear Weapons.* [Preliminary Draft 1983].

———. *Pastoral Letter on Catholic Social Teachings and the Economy.* [Preliminary Draft 1984].

Vardys, V. Stanley (ed.). *Karl Marx: Scientist? Revolutionary? Humanist?* Lexington, MA: D.C. Heath, 1971.

Von Rad, Gerhard. *The Message of the Prophets.* New York: Harper and Row, 1967.

Walker, Angus. *Marx: His Theory and Its Contents.* New York: Longman, 1978.

Walzer, Michael. *The Revolution of the Saints: A Study in the Origins of Radical Politics* (1965). New York: Atheneum, 1968.

———. *Just and Unjust Wars.* New York: Basic Books, 1977.

———. *Radical Principles.* New York: Basic Books, 1980.

———. *Exodus and Revolution.* New York: Basic Books, 1985.

———. "Prophecy and Social Criticism." In "The Prophetic Mode and Challenge in Religion, Politics, and Society," *The Drew Gateway* (Neal Riemer, Guest Editor), 55, Nos. 2 & 3 (Winter 1984/Spring 1985), pp. 13–27.

Waskow, Arthur. *The Rainbow Sign: The Shape of Hope.* New York: Schocken, 1985.

———. "The Future of Prophesy and the Future (or Fate) of the Earth: Addressing the Danger of Nuclear Holocaust from a Prophetic Perspective." In "The Prophetic Mode and Challenge in Religion, Politics, and Society," *The Drew Gateway* (Neal Riemer, Guest Editor), 55, Nos. 2 & 3 (Winter 1984/Spring 1985), pp. 55–68.

West, Cornel. *Prophecy Deliverance! An Afro-American Revolutionary Christianity.* Philadelphia, PA: Westminster Press, 1982.

———. "The Prophetic Tradition in Afro-America." In "The Prophetic Mode and Challenge in Religion, Politics, and Society," *The Drew Gateway* (Neal Riemer, Guest Editor), 55, Nos. 2 & 3 (Winter 1984/Spring 1985), pp. 97–108.

Wolfe, Bertram D. *Marxism: One Hundred Years in the Life of a Doctrine.* New York: Dial, 1965.

Wolff, Robert Paul. *Understanding Marx: A Reconstruction and Critique of Capital.* Princeton, NJ: Princeton University Press, 1984.

Wolfson, Murray. *Marx: Economist, Philosopher, Jew: Steps in the Development of a Doctrine.* New York: St. Martin's Press, 1982.

Index

alienation, 27, 28, 29–30, 31, 32, 33
  36, 38, 39, 41–42n, 43, 44–45, 57,
  58, 59, 70, 82, 142 (*see also* exploitation; integration)
Althusser, Louis, 145n
Amos, 20n, 21n
anarchists, 82, 112, 118, 121n
anti-semitism, 72, 140, 149
Aptheker, Herbert, 22n
art, 48n, 138
authoritarianism, rightwing, 140, 141

Balibar, Etienne, 145
Bebel, August, 101
Beer, Max, 13
blacks, 5, 34, 72, 140
Blenkensopp, Joseph, 20n
Bonaparte, Louis, 65–66
Bottomore, Tom, 40n, 74n, 144n, 145n
bourgeois society, 31, 47, 61–62, 71
  (*see also* bourgeoisie; civil society),
bourgeoisie: and freedom, 26–27,;
  and Marx's critique of bourgeois
  reformers, 66–70, 85; and Marx's
  critique of bourgeois state, 65–66;
  and Marx's critique of ideas, 62–63,
  64–66;   and Marx's critique of
  superstructure, 63–70
Brinton, Crane, 18, 22
Brueggemann, Walter, 20n, 21n
Buber, Martin, 13, 22n

calculus of costs and benefits, 109, 112
Calvin, John, 10, 11, 21
capitalism: and exploitation, 56–60;
  Marx's criticism of economic foundation, 53–63; and Marx's values,
  25–33; overcoming, 60–63; positive

contributions, 63; viability, 139;
  weaknesses of, 60–63; and working
  class, 53–56
Carlebach, Joseph, 15
Carlebach, Julius, 1–2, 12–15, 20n, 22n
change, 44, 49, 112–13 (*see also*
  revolution)
children, 132
Christianity, prophetic, 11–12, 21n
civil society, 27, 47, 49, 51 (*see also*
  bourgeois society)
class struggle, 30, 33, 50–51, 62–63, 64,
  83, 147–48
Cohen, Gerald A., 74n
Cohn, Norman, 22n
communism: and cultural life, 133; and
  economic life, 128–30; as an end,
  81–82; final goal, 133; first phase,
  106–07; future, 144n; higher phase
  of, 32, 105–06, 107; and integration;
  30, 73; and Marx's theory of revolutionary communist action, 79–120;
  and Marx's values, 25–33; mature,
  105–08; motto, 106; and the polity,
  130–31; and questions about
  culture, 135; and questions about
  economic future, 133–34, 135; and
  questions about polity, 134, 135;
  and questions about society, 134,
  135; and social life, 131–32
community, 28–29, 30–31, 34, 35, 39,
  73, 110, 111
constitutionalism, 7, 8–9, 38–39, 72,
  103, 104, 109, 111, 115, 117,
  137–39, 148; and communist constitution, 108, 111, 115, 116, 117,
  131, 137, 138; and democratic constitution, 111, 131; and freedom, 72
criticism, Marx's concept of, 43–46
Cromwell, Oliver, 13

democracy, 41n, 85, 87; and democratic revolution, 86, 87, 94–95; and Marx's democratic commitments, 89–90, 93, 103–04, 108, 115
determinism, 48, 74n
development, individual and social, 31–32, 34–35, 38, 39, 73, 110, 111
dialectic method, 45, 52
dictatorship of proletariat, 90, 97, 98–105, 116–17
division of labor, 30, 82, 106, 110, 128–30, 132, 134
Draper, Hal, 145n
Dunn, John, 23

ecological malaise, 142
education, 132
Elster, Jon, 22n
emancipation, 31, 33, 35, 39, 42n, 44–46, 72, 73, 141 (see also freedom)
Engels, Friedrich, 41, 74, 89, 90, 93–94, 96, 121n, 122n, 123n, 125n, 241n
Enlightenment, 11, 18, 21n, 26, 140
estrangement, 29–30, 53, 54, 59, 60, (see also alienation; integration)
ethics, 40n, 48
exploitation, 34, 43, 52, 53–60, 147 (see also alienation)

family, 41n, 64, 65, 66
feudalism, 49, 50, 57
Feuerbach, Ludwig, 5–6, 16–17, 74n
Fine, Ben, 145n
foundation, economic, 47–48, 53–64, 71
Fourier, Charles, 129
freedom, 26–29, 33–34, 35–36, 37, 38, 70, 72, 73, 110; true realm of, 28, 130
Freeman, Gordon, 20n
Fromm, Erich, 15, 22n

Gay, Peter, 21n

Hanson, Paul D., 20n
happiness, 32–33, 44
Hegel, Georg, 40n, 43, 74n

Heschel, Abraham J., 20n, 22n
history, 43, 83, 147–48 (see also materialist conception of history)
Hook, Sydney, 121n
Howard, M. C., 58, 74n, 75n
human being, 30–31, 34, 41n (see also species-being)
humanism, 30
Hunt, Richard N., 23n, 86–87, 89–91, 93, 94, 95, 98, 121n, 122n, 123n, 124n, 125n, 129, 133, 144n
Hyndman, Henry Mayers, 122n

ideology, 48
imperialism, 58
insurrectionists, 82, 89, 92, 112, 118, 121n
integration, 29–30, 34, 36, 39, 110
international relations, theory of, 142
Isaiah, 21n, 137

Jefferson, Thomas, 21n, 122n
Jeremiah, 13
Jesus, 10, 17
Jews, 12, 16–17, 140–41 (see also anti-semitism; Judaism)
John XXIII (Pope), 11–12, 22n
Jonah, 20n
Judaism, 11
judgment: on agrarian revolution, 95–97; on alliance of workers, peasants, and progressive bourgeoisie, 88–91; on communism as an end, 81–82; and communist cultural life, 133; and communist economic life, 128–30; and communist polity, 130–31; and communist social life, 331–32; on consolidating the revolution, 97–105; in four stages, 81; and the future, 127–43; on legal, peaceful revolution, 91–95; on making the revolution, 85–97; on mature communism, 105–08, 119; on preparatory means, 82–85; and problems, 133–43; on proletarian majority revolution, 86–88; on universal suffrage, 83
Kamenka, Eugene, 40n, 41n

Kant, Immanuel, 43
Kateb, George, 18, 22n
Kaufmann, Yehezkel, 13
Kautsky, Karl, 98
King, J. E., 58, 74n, 75n
King, Martin Luther, Jr., 12, 22n
Knox, John, 10, 21n
Kolakowski, Leszek, 18, 21n, 22n, 40n, 74n
Kunzli, Arnold, 15

law, 41n
Lenin, V. I., 85, 98
liberal democracy, 71, 120, 138–139
liberal democratic politics, 4, 5
Liberation Theology, 12
Lichtheim, George, 121n
Liebknecht, Wilhelm, 101
Locke, John, 122n

Machiavellian politics, 4, 5
McLellan, David, 17, 22n, 40n, 44, 74n, 122n, 123n
Madison, James, 21n
Mandel, Ernest, 145n
Manuel, Frank, 11, 18, 21n, 22n
Manuel, Fritzie, 18, 21n, 22n
Marx, Eleanor, 13
Marx, Karl: and achieving mature communism, 105–08; agrarian revolution, 95–97; and alienation, 28, 29–30; and alliance of workers, peasants, and progressive bourgeoisie, 88–91; and anarchists, 82; apocalyptic strain in, 18; on bourgeois ideas, 64–65; on bourgeois state, 65–66; and capitalist exploitation, 56–60; on communist cultural life, 133; on communist economic life, 128–30; on communist polity, 130–31; on communist social life, 131–32; and community, 30–31; concept of criticism, 44–46; and condition of working class, 53–56; and consolidating the revolution, 97–105; and critique of bourgeois superstructure, 63–70; and critique of capitalism, 53–63; and development, 31–32; and dictatorship of proletariat, 98–105; and faith in the masses, 91; and fear of counter-revolution, 92, 94, 95; and freedom, 26–29; and the future, 127–52; guiding values, 25–39, 147; and happiness, 32–33; and human being, 29–31; and insurrectionists, 82; integration, 29–30; and intellectual responsibility, 135–36; and making the revolution, 85–97; and materialist conception of history, 46–52; and model of prophetic politics, 18–19; on noncommunist alternatives, 66–70; and overcoming capitalism, 60–63; and peaceful revolution, 91–95; and political Messianism, 18; preparing for revolution, 81–85; and proletariat majority revolution, 86–88; and reformers, 66–70, 95, 101; and social science, 70, 73, 147–48, 149–50; and social scientific criticism, 43–73; strengths, 33, 35–37, 70, 73, 118, 147–48; and theory of revolutionary action, 79–120, 150; and totalitarian democracy, 18, 23n, 89; as tough-minded democrat, 94, 95, 118; and tradition of prophetic politics, 1–19, 72–73, 115–20, 147–49, 151–52; and truth, 32–33; as utopian, 18, 37, 150; weaknesses, 35, 71–73, 117–20, 143, 149–51
Massiczek, Albert, 1, 15
material forces of production, 46–47, 49, 50, 51, 63
materialism, 33, 43, 48, 49 (see also materialist conception of history)
materialist conception of history, 46–52, 74n
Mayer, Gustav, 15
Mazlish, Bruce, 17, 18, 22n, 40n
Mazzini, Giuseppe, 122n
Micah, 21n, 137
morality, 41n, 48
Morse, J. Mitchell, 20n

Moses, 15, 70–71

Nader, Ralph, 12
nationalism, 72, 140, 149
naturalism, 18, 30
necessary working time, 58, 76n, 130
necessity, realm of, 28, 130
Niebuhr, Reinhold, 11–12, 22n

obshchina (commune), 96–97
Ollman, Bertell, 40n
Owen, Robert, 132

Paris Commune, 102–04, 123n
Parsons, Howard L., 17, 22n
party, 131; open mass, 90;
    vanguard, 90, 131
peasants, 72, 114 (*see also obshchina*)
Pericles, 131
philosophy, and prophetic politics, 7
Polak, Fred L., 21n
politics, 48, 82–83, 87–88, 103, 105,
    121n; and alliance of workers,
    peasants, and progressive
    bourgeoisie, 88–91
Poulantzas, Nicos, 145n
private property, 41n, 64, 66
proletariat: and alliance with peasants
    and progressive bourgeoisie, 86–91;
    condition of, 53–56; dictatorship of,
    98–105; and legal, peaceful revolu-
    tion, 91–95; and majority revolu-
    tion, 86–88; and universal eman-
    cipation, 26, 44, 45; as universal
    suffering class, 45
prophetic: and apocalyptic, 1, 2; and
    predicting, 1, 2; and utopian, 1, 2–3
prophetic politics: characteristics, 3–6;
    controversy about Marx and the
    prophetic, 12–18; as a model, 3;
    roots, 6–12 (*see also* Protestant
    Reformation)
prophets, Hebrew, 1–2, 6–7, 9–10; and
    Marx, 12–18; Walzer's views on,
    20–21n
Protestant Reformation, 10–11
Proudhon, Pierre-Joseph, 74n

racism, 72, 140, 149
Rader, Melvin, 74n
realization, 31, 39, 133 (*see also*
    development)
relations of production, 46, 47, 48, 49,
    51, 63
religion, 31, 32–33, 41n, 48, 64,
    68, 72; and prophetic politics, 6–9
revolution: agrarian, 95–97, 114; and
    alliance of workers, peasants, and
    progressive bourgeoisie, 88–91, 114;
    consolidating, 97–105; and dictator-
    ship of proletariat, 86–88, 98–105;
    just, 88, 109–19, 122n; making,
    85–97; Marx's theory of, 79–120;
    and mature communism, 105–08;
    peaceful, 91–95, 112–13, 119; "per-
    manent," 90, 121n; preparing for,
    81–85; and proletarian majority,
    86–88, 113–14
Riemer, Neal, 20n, 21–22n
Rotstein, Abraham, 17
Ruether, Rosemary Radford, 20n,
    21–22n
ruling class, 48; proletariat as, 87–88

Sargent, Lydia, 145n
Sassoon, Anne Showstack, 74n
Sassoulitch, Vera, 96
science, 41n, 45; and prophetic
    politics, 7
service workers, 72
sexism, 72, 140, 149
Silberner, Edmund, 17
slavery, human, 58, 140; wage, 58–60,
    112, 113
socialists, wrong-headed, 66–70
species-being, 27, 29, 37–38 (*see also*
    human being)
Stalin, Joseph, 85
state, 37, 41n, 46, 48, 64, 65–66,
    102–03, 104, 108; and withering
    away, 82, 104
suffrage, universal, 83, 91, 110, 112,
    113, 115
superstructure, 47, 48, 64; bourgeois,
    63–70, 71

surplus value, 55–56, 57, 58, 59, 61; absolute, 75n; rate of, 59; relative, 75n

Talmon, A. J., 18, 23n
terror, revolutionary, 90
Tillich, Paul, 18
totalitarian democracy, 18, 23n; and Marx, 118
truth, 32–33, 44–45, 147–48
Tucker, Robert C., 40n, 41n, 42n, 74n, 75n, 76n, 121n, 122n, 123n, 124n, 144n

unions, 56, 83, 132, 144n
U.S. Catholic Bishops, 12, 22n
utopian politics, 4, 5

violence, 73, 86, 87, 90, 91, 92, 93, 94–95, 98–99, 101, 102, 103–104, 109, 112, 113, 114–15, 119, 122n, 123n, 125n

Von Rad, Gerhard, 20n

Walker, Angus, 75n
Walzer, Michael, 20n, 21n, 122n
war, 108, 131
Waskow, Arthur, 20n, 21n
Weber, Max, 13
West, Cornel, 20n, 21n
Willich, August, 90
Wolfe, Bertram D., 121n
Wofson, Murray, 15–16, 22n
women, 34, 72–73, 132, 141 (*see also* sexism)
worker control, 70, 73, 107, 108, 110, 115–16, 128–130, 133
working class, condition of, 53–56, 147–48, 149

About the Author

Neal Riemer is Andrew V. Stout Professor of Political Philosophy at Drew University. He has previously taught in the Department of Political Science at The Pennsylvania State University and at the University of Wisconsin-Milwaukee, where he also served a term as Associate Dean of the Social Sciences in the College of Letters and Sciences. He received his B.A. (1943) in History and International Relations from Clark University, and—after three years of military service in World War II—his M.A. (1947) and Ph.D. (1949) in Government from Harvard University. He is a member of Phi Beta Kappa. In 1968 he received the "Outstanding Professor Award" at the University of Wisconsin-Milwaukee, and in 1985 he received the "Distinguished Professor" award from the graduate students at Drew University. He has pioneered an approach to political science that stresses the importance of integrating its ethical, empirical, and prudential concerns. His books—illuminating this approach—include *James Madison: Creating the American Constitution* (Washington, D.C.: Congressional Quarterly Press, 1986, first published in 1968 by Washington Square Press); *The Future of the Democratic Revolution: Toward a More Prophetic Politics* (New York: Praeger, 1984); *Political Science: An Introduction to Politics* (New York: Harcourt Brace Jovanovich, 1983); *The Democratic Experiment* (Princeton, N.J.: Van Nostrand, 1967, *The Representative: Trustee? Delegate? Partisan? Politico?* (Lexington, Mass.: D. C. Heath, 1967; editor); *The Revival of Democratic Theory* (New York: Appleton-Century-Crofts, 1962); *World Affairs: Problems and Prospects* (New York: Appleton-Century-Crofts, 1957; co-author); *Problems of American Government* (New York: McGraw-Hill, 1952; editor). He is also the guest editor of, and a contributing author to, a volume entitled *The Prophetic Mode and Challenge in Religion, Politics, and Society* (1985), a double issue of *The Drew Gateway*, a publication of Theological School at Drew University (Volume 55, Numbers 2 & 3, Winter 1984/Spring 1985). Dr. Riemer's main teaching and research interests lie in the area of political theory, especially American and modern democratic theory. He is currently at work on the theme of "Creative Breakthroughs in Politics."